GOD STAYS NEAR

Faith and Flight

B. Dwayne Bell

Copyright © 2025 by B. Dwayne Bell

Unless otherwise noted, all Scripture quotations are taken from the NEW AMERICAN STANDARD BIBLE®, copyright© 1960, 1962, 1963, 1968, 1971, 1972, 1973, 1975, 1977, 1995 by The Lockman Foundation. Used by permission. Scripture quotations marked AMP are taken from the AMPLIFIED® BIBLE, Copyright © 1954, 1958, 1962, 1964, 1965, 1987 by the Lockman Foundation Used by Permission (www. Lockman.org). Scripture quotations marked NLT are taken from the HOLY BIBLE, NEW LIVING TRANSLATION, Copyright© 1996, 2004, 2007 by Tyndale House Foundation. Used by permission of Tyndale House Publishers, Inc., Carol Stream, Illinois 60188. All rights reserved. Scripture quotations marked NIV are taken from the NEW INTERNATIONAL VERSION®. Copyright© 1973, 1978, 1984, 2011 by Biblica, Inc.TM. Used by permission of Zondervan. Scripture quotations marked ESV are taken from the HOLY BIBLE, ENGLISH STANDARD VERSION® Copyright© 2001 by Crossway, a publishing ministry of Good News Publishers. Used by permission. Scripture quotations marked KJV are taken from the KING JAMES VERSION, public domain. Scripture quotations marked NKJV taken from the New King James Version®. Copyright © 1982 by Thomas Nelson. Used by permission. All rights reserved.

Bolding text in Scripture quotations reflect the author's added emphasis.

All rights reserved. No part of this book may be used or reproduced by any means, graphic, electronic, or mechanical, including photocopying, recording, taping, or by an information storage retrieval system without the written permission of the publisher or the author except in the case of brief quotations embodied in critical articles and reviews.

ISBN: 979-8-9875826-3-3 (Paperback)
      979-8-9875826-4-0 (Hardback)
      979-8-9875826-5-7 (eBook)

Published in the United States of America.

Interior design by Booknook.biz

ACKNOWLEDGMENT AND DEDICATION

THANK YOU, JOE CARRUTH, FOR encouraging me to write and for the many thoughtful hours devoted to editing this book. You have added much value by your well-rounded worldview, keen intellect, education, and grasp of the Bible. Beyond that, I treasure our decades of friendship and travel adventures to Europe, Africa, Asia, and Israel. You inspire by the way you encourage people in their faith and kingdom living—loving them and honoring the King.

THIS BOOK IS DEDICATED TO JESUS OF NAZARETH, King of the Jews, the Lord of Heaven and Earth.

Photo Credits
Cover- Design by S.M. Savoy
Cover- Photo and chapter photos by Dwayne Bell
Cover- Art by Ralph Irwin "Portal to Portal" (Used by permission.)
Cover- Author photo by Jacob Crouthamel

TABLE OF CONTENTS

An Introduction vii

Chapter 1   Let's Define the Soul 1
Chapter 2   Don't Lose Your Mind 9
Chapter 3   The Human Spirit 25
Chapter 4   The Present Flying Chapter 37
Chapter 5   Flying Adventures—Alaska 43
Chapter 6   Flying Adventures—Idaho 77
Chapter 7   Flying Adventures—Honduras 91
Chapter 8   Flying Adventures—Aircraft Delivery 127
Chapter 9   Growing Older—Grey Eagles 149
Chapter 10 Prepare For War 171
Chapter 11 Israel—A Time for War 199
Chapter 12 Avenues of Soul Care 215
Chapter 13 Community and Soul Care 239
Chapter 14 Self Control 245
Chapter 15 Vignettes of Flight and Faith 251
Chapter 16 The Unfinished Story 319

Appendices: Quotes and Thoughts for Meditation 331
                     History and Meditation 351

Introduction

In a sense, this book continues my memoir and spiritual journey chronicled in *God Came Near*. The stories included here contain personal and family miracles and circumstances demonstrating that God stays near. In a broader sense, it continues the story related in my previous three books: *A Friend of the King*, *God Came Near*, and *Puzzling 2020*. Each was packed with Biblical perspectives on truth for living interspersed with personal stories and Bible stories about how those play out in history and life.

I am now past seventy years old and in the last chapters of my life. Hopefully, with some wisdom and insights gained, I will pass on the most salient and essential truths and practices I've discovered for living life under the sun. For brevity and emphasis, I'll label it **soul care**. I may emphasize it in bold when it's discussed or mentioned.

Soul care is about experiencing God, knowing him, being known by him, and hearing his still, small voice—the one He uses with His sons, daughters, and forever family.

Soul care is about getting and keeping the proper perspective to live an enjoyable and rewarding life during your sojourn. But it's more than that. It's the adventure of living, moving, and being while proving this paradigm works. It's a satisfying, relational adventure with God, your Creator, Father, and Friend, as you seek to know Him better and the truth about your life and destiny.

Soul care is intimacy, peace, and rest. It's a portal into a deeper and lasting relationship with the Lover of your soul. It's an awareness of knowing Him better daily, weekly, and monthly as you journey. And it's a growing awareness that He knows you, loves you, and cares for you even in your imperfection and great need. That's usually where we feel His love the most.

We live in a time of war. That will also be a theme of our time together, especially regarding soul care. **Soul care** is the best way to live in times of relative peace or times of war, which we see breaking out all around us.

Even though I've completed the seventh decade of my sojourn, I feel as much wind in my sails and beneath my wings as ever. And because I've learned the value and practice of **soul care**, I'm on a more joyful, intentional, and meaningful flight path than ever before.

Along the journey, I've come to see that God's plans for me are better than my plans for me. So it's easier to "Let go and let God." He's a good Father who knows how to give good gifts to His children. Soul care is a discovery and exploration of the phenomenon called grace. It's a guide to experiencing rest and peace—something every soul craves.

Thanks for taking this journey with me into **soul care**, stories of faith and flight, and God's goodness in the land of the living.

****

> *"I will be your God throughout your lifetime—*
> *until your hair is white with age.*
> *I made you, and I will care for you.*
> *I will carry you along and save you."*
> (Isaiah 46:4 NLT)

> *"Yet I am confident I will see the Lord's goodness*
> *while I am here in the land of the living."*
> (Psalm 27:13)

> *"And He will be the stability of your times,*
> *a wealth of salvation, wisdom and knowledge;*
> *the fear of the Lord is his treasure."*
> (Isaiah 33:6)

CHAPTER ONE
Let's Define the Soul

"And the Lord God formed man of the dust of the ground, and breathed into his nostrils the breath of life; and man became a living soul."
(Genesis 2:7 KJV)

"I praise you, for I am fearfully and wonderfully made. Wonderful are your works; my soul knows it very well."
(Psalm 139:14 ESV)

It would be insightful to ask some friends to define the soul. I'm sure you would get some interesting answers, but the most common would probably be, "I don't know." Yet whether we have a cognitive understanding of our soul or an intuitive understanding, we all have a soul. We've observed the facets and activities of our souls and the souls of friends and family. Still, it's hard to wrap your mind around something incorporeal, complex, and familiar, like the soul.

It's essential to your health and happiness, so trying to understand it and practicing soul care is important. The soul is not easily defined but easy to appreciate if you pause to ponder how it interacts with your spirit and body.

Understanding the soul's composition and how its parts are woven together to function and make us who we are is helpful. Our souls help us find our way, reach our destiny, and live joyfully during the journey.

The most significant discovery when looking at the composition and functioning of the soul is that our destiny and the joy we experience in our journey through life are not fixed. They are not hardwired but plastic, and within specific design parameters, the soul's two primary functions are (1) to sense and make sense of the world around us and (2) to determine to some significant degree our level of joy and success in pursuing destiny in this world.

More evidence supports this than the most common alternative view that the brain or mind (which are not the same thing) is hardwired and that our destiny is predetermined. Thus, nothing is more important than caring for your soul. Let's ponder what the soul is, how it works, and how its parts interact. It's beautiful in its design and creation and is the vehicle to your happiness and destiny.

Start Here — Three Parts

You're already wondering how deep are we going to go with this. There is a lot of incredible engineering and design in high-performance jet aircraft, like fighters. After getting a college degree, as we USAF student pilots progressed through the intense two years of academic and practical training to fly airplanes to the edges of their abilities, a prevalent sentiment was felt and often expressed: "Just tell me how it works—not how to build it."

We had to know a little about the design and construction to understand how it worked and how to fly it. But it was complex enough just to know all the facts, procedures, rules, and limits of flying the plane. There weren't enough brain cells to go into all the technical elements of its design.

So we're only going to define the major parts of the plane or soul, "the systems" we call them in aviation. We will discuss some ways these individual parts and systems work together. Then, you can figure out what's valuable as you fly the thing.

I just returned from Oshkosh, the biggest airshow in the world, with the largest collection of airplanes, for a one-week duration. There, you can walk near fighter aircraft like the F-16, the F-18, the F-35, and the F-22. They look impressive but also cold and lifeless, sitting on the ramp. Then, with a few hundred thousand friends, you stand at the edge of the runway, while they come screaming over your head at 50 feet and more than 500 miles per hour before twisting, turning, spinning, and diving loudly with long afterburner streaks of flame extending from their tails. You then have a different opinion than seeing them on the ramp. Even the pilots who fly them are in awe, as are the spectators and the army of engineers and technicians who built them. Everyone has a different perspective of what they witnessed because of their knowledge and experience.

Our souls are a bit like that fighter jet, only more powerful, with the capability for enormous good or destruction, sitting on the ramp of our bodies. We all have a soul! We must learn to fly it, with its exhilarating dashes into the heavenlies while avoiding crashing into the earth.

Let's start our engines. But let's start with a Cessna-172 or something simpler and slower. Let's learn to crawl, walk, and then run. That's the rhythm of an earth life. But eventually, we all fly, with our souls, alone and with others. Let's learn how to do it properly and how the systems work, at least well enough to operate them safely and effectively. And let's learn how to take care of the plane and pilot—you. We will call it soul care.

By the revelation of the Holy Spirit, the apostle Paul tells us that we have three parts functioning together. They are the spirit, soul, and body in that order. "Now may the God of peace Himself sanctify you entirely; and may your **spirit and soul and body** be preserved complete, without blame at the coming of our Lord Jesus Christ" (1 Thessalonians 5:23).

The spirit is incorporeal (not made of matter) and even more mysterious than the soul. We'll get to that part of us later. The body is familiar to all of us and self-evident. It houses our soul and spirit, gets us around, and possesses the five senses we use to explore, catalog, and sense the world around us. Our souls sit between our spirits and bodies and decide how we act, grow, and go. It's a God-given faculty and gift just for that purpose. Let's explore and ponder the soul to see how it works and how to best care for it—because it's responsible for caring for you.

The Soul — Three Parts

It's often said and thought that **the soul comprises three parts: the mind, the will, and the emotions.** Those are fairly good descriptors and a good starting place, a way to think about the soul, but they are incomplete. This soul is more complex than that and harder to pin down. Even if we could catalog all the parts, how they function together is a beautiful mystery and perhaps meant to stay that way—something to be enjoyed more than understood, like art and beauty.

The best we can do is look at the different words in the Bible that describe the soul, getting below the surface a bit but not so far as to lose track of our purpose.

No language is cast in concrete, and the meanings of certain words can change over time. However, Hebrew and Greek, the languages the Holy Spirit chose for the Old and New Testaments of the Bible, are more concrete than most languages. In addition, the Bible's claim of divine authorship and its age, which covers many epochs and cultures, as well as its descriptors and discussion of the human soul, make it the most insightful and authoritative source available. Let's see what it says.

The first use of the word "soul" in the Old Testament is: "And the Lord God formed man of the dust of the ground, and breathed into his nostrils the breath of life; and **man became a living soul**" (Genesis 2:7 KJV). The Hebrew word for soul used here is *nephesh*.

The Brown, Driver, and Briggs Hebrew/English Lexicon has this to say about the word: נפש Transliteration: nephesh Pronunciation: neh'-fesh Part of Speech: **Noun Feminine** 1. **soul, self,** life, creature, **person**, appetite, **mind**, living being,

desire, emotion, passion ... the inner being of man, the man himself, seat of the appetites, seat of emotions and passions, the activity of mind, the activity of the will, the **activity of the character** [emphasis added]. The word occurs in the Bible 753 times and in the KJV it's translated soul (475x), life (117x), person (29x), mind (15x), heart (15x).

The first use of the word "soul" in the New Testament is: "Do not be afraid of those who kill the body but cannot kill the **soul.** Rather, be afraid of the One who can destroy both **soul** and body in hell" (Matthew 10:28 NIV). The Greek word for soul used here is *psuchē.*

The Thayer Greek/English Lexicon has this to say about the word: ψυχή psuchē Pronunciation: psoo-khay' Part of Speech: Noun Feminine 1. breath a. the breath of life 1. **the vital force which animates the body** and **shows itself in breathing** a. of animals b. of men b. life c. that in which there is life 1. **a living being**, a living soul 2. the soul a. **the seat of the feelings, desires, affections, aversions (our heart, soul etc.)** b. the (human) **soul in so far as it is constituted that by the right use of the aids offered it by God it can attain its highest end and secure eternal blessedness**, the soul **regarded as a moral being designed for everlasting life** c. the soul as **an essence which differs from the body and is not dissolved by death** (distinguished from other parts of the body)[emphasis added]. This Greek word occurs in the Bible 105 times, and in the KJV, it's translated as soul (58x), life (40x), mind (3x), and heart (1x). Strong's Definition adds, "Exactly corresponds to the Hebrew *nephesh.*"

If you read the definitions above, or just the bolded words and phrases, you see the soul comprises our "mind, will, and emotions," plus "desires, affections, aversions, passions, and appetites." This is breathed into us by God—into a part of us not composed by matter. It's akin to the life force within us—mysterious, beautiful, observable. It's a joy to experience and behold in ourselves and others.

To confuse things a bit more, or perhaps to illuminate things, the word "soul" is often used interchangeably with a couple of its components—the "heart" and "mind" and even the "spirit." We'll explore that as we go.

I asked my pastor, Ben Wilson, a former Professor of Greek at Moody Bible Institute in Chicago, for a quick definition of the "soul" while visiting his office last week. He pondered momentarily and said, "The soul is our **thoughts, will, emotions, and affections** [emphasis added]. There are distinctions, but these overlap. We tend to divorce or draw a line between the mind and the soul, but you never find that in the Bible." That's simple and well said.

Why do I want us to see these facets of the soul and have some cognitive idea of how they might affect each other or work together? So you can fly the thing (your soul) without crashing and to new heights and vistas—for joy.

Who do you trust to know how this works? Yourself? Family? Friends? Educators? God? Who do you trust to help you? If something is broken, the person who made it probably knows how to fix it.

So, as you reflect on the soul care ideas and suggestions listed on these pages and the stories that demonstrate many of them, feel free to glance back at these definitions and word pictures of the soul. You'll be reminded of its composition and its function. As you meditate, internalize, and make this study personal, the Holy Spirit will give you the understanding you need and the help you desire to live free and live a life above the fray. You can "mount up on wings like eagles" (Isaiah 40:28-31).

****

*"As the deer pants for streams of water,
so my soul pants for you, my God."*
(Psalm 42:1 NIV)

*"Take my yoke upon you and learn from me,
for I am gentle and humble in heart,
and you will find rest for your souls."*
(Matthew 11:29)

*"For what shall it profit a man,
if he shall gain the whole world,
and lose his own soul?"*
(Mark 8:36 KJV)

*"Now may the God of peace Himself sanctify you entirely; and **may your spirit and soul and body be preserved complete**, without blame at the coming of our Lord Jesus Christ."*
(1 Thessalonians 5:23)

CHAPTER TWO

Don't Lose Your Mind

Have we lost our minds? As a nation, culture, and church? I think the honest answer is "yes."

One piece of evidence that recently came my way was a Barna survey of the Christian worldview in America. He used his craft of scientific statistics and analysis to determine how many Americans had a Biblical perspective on life or a Christian worldview as defined by the Bible and 2000 years of Christian history.

Here are some of his findings:

Everyone has a worldview, but relatively few people have a biblical worldview.
Only 9% of born-again Christians have such a perspective on life.
Among Protestants 7%.
Protestants who attend mainland protestant churches 2%.
Catholics 1%.
Nondenominational protestant churches 13%.
Pentecostal churches 10%.
Baptist churches 8%.

Here are some of the questions he used to determine those findings:

Does absolute moral truth exist?
Is truth defined by the Bible?
Did Jesus Christ live a sinless life?
Is God the all-powerful and all-knowing creator of the universe?
Does He still rule today?
Is salvation a gift from God and cannot be earned?
Is Satan real?
Do Christians have a responsibility to share their faith in Christ with other people?
Is the Bible accurate in all of its teachings?

If you're familiar with the Bible and have studied church history, you'll find these questions resonate with the core truths of our faith. These principles guide our lives, shape our futures, and determine our destinies.

I was born seven years after the end of World War II. My parents were part of what's been called "the Greatest Generation." This was in part or in whole because they were willing to hold to that truth, fight for the truth, sacrifice for the truth, and lay down their lives for the truth, their family, and their friends. The words of Jesus come to mind: "No greater love has any man than this, that a man lay down his life for his friends" (John 15:13). Jesus would demonstrate this with His life and set a very high bar for all of us to enjoy and to aspire to.

So, I grew up, was parented, and was mentored by the Greatest Generation. I am certain more than 90% of the people I knew had a Christian worldview. They would have quickly said "yes" to all those questions. The vast majority would have agreed that those facts were true. A solid majority would have said they have a personal, experiential relationship with the Truth, Jesus Christ, by faith and the perceived presence of the Holy Spirit in their lives. What happened? In one or two generations, no less! And what's happening in the church and culture today? Look around, and please tell me.

This book is not a treatise on worldview, history, or a prognosis of the future unless we change our ways. It is a book on setting your mind in the proper direction—and keeping it there, because where you set your mind is where you'll go and end up. The mind is the gatekeeper and direction setter of the soul—that immaterial, complex entity that is who you are.

Your soul is the amalgamation of your personality, passions, feelings, memories, mind, will, and emotions. It's who you are, have become, and are becoming—the real you, different from all others yet similar. God breathed it into you as a gift. It's yours to keep, program, and enjoy—with or without God—to your destiny. But those are two very different destinies. And that is the focus of this book. How do we care for our souls and end up with the most joyful journey to our best destiny?

Spoiler alert—the short answer is: "Go with God." Spend time with Him. Get to know Him and allow yourself to be known by Him. Dwell in His presence often and much. You will benefit from His counsel. And you will mysteriously become more like Him.

Back to the soul for a moment. I looked up the definition of "immaterial" on a whim and found it humorous and telling. Ask Siri to define it for you or look it up on dictionary.com. A modern lexicon produced by some of the intelligentsia of our Western civilization, the product of 2000 years of blessings and success, says these two things in the same breath about "immaterial": [1] "Unimportant under the circumstances and irrelevant" [2] "We have immaterial souls." Of course, these definitions are not wrong, but taken together, they point to a coincidental, perhaps unintentional, sad truth: We don't think our souls are important. That truth is borne out by the lack of attention and care we give to our souls.

We attach so little importance to what we don't understand. We blow it off as unimportant because we don't know how it works or what it actually is. Doesn't that belie blinding pride and hubris? We essentially say, "I am the center of my universe, and all that matters is what I see, hear, taste, feel, experience, and think."

Again, we hear Jesus say, "For **what does it profit a man to gain the whole world and forfeit his soul? For what will a man give in exchange for his soul?**" (Matthew 8:36-37).

It seems like the soul has great worth to Jesus and to those who know Him. And not so much to those who don't—even if their soul is who they are, a precious life of infinite worth. What kind of deception or false programming must be at play here?

It's almost as if God's plan, or permissive will, is to let wheat (enlightened ones) and tares (deceived ones) grow together to enjoy their lives and pursue their chosen destinies until the end. Then, He will send His holy angels to separate them and reveal their true identities. The soul made in the image and likeness of God is a gift of infinite worth given for us to enjoy like a son or daughter of God. The angels gasp at the magnanimity of this gift, and we would too, if we saw it for what it is. With proper soul care, you can. Without soul care practices, you can't and won't.

Some of the greatest minds or intellects on record had a Biblical or Christian worldview. Sir Isaac Newton, Pascal, Kepler, Pasteur, Bach, Handel, Blackstone, Augustine, Aquinas, Anselm, Chesterton, Eliot, and C.S. Lewis come to mind. But many great minds didn't. So evidently, it's not a matter of the mind or the facts we come to believe. There's something else involved. It's a revelation. It's light revealed in a dark place or on a darkened heart from the Creator. The light ignites faith, which grows as we respond to the Word of God and the whispers of His Spirit. And that is the essence of soul care. Stay in that quiet, still posture; stay attentive to that leading.

I find it interesting what some great minds who only wanted to use their minds, not revelation, thought about the soul and spiritual matters. The philosopher René Descartes comes to mind. He struggled with a problem called "the problem of knowing." He thought the brain was easy to fool, but the only way a person experiences reality is by sensory inputs to his or her brain.

He wondered how you could trust your perceptions of reality, that they "were not the illusions of a demon." That is an interesting and telling position. It drove him to ponder how people know they exist. That's where trust in yourself, reason, and denial of the more influential spiritual realm can lead you—to consider if you exist.

His conclusion, famous in philosophy and Western civilization, was, "I think, therefore I am." To him, thinking could not be faked. It was the way individuals knew that they existed.

At least his conclusion was good, if elementary, to creatures who know God by looking at creation and by revelation. They know they exist, are loved, and are created in God's image for their good and His purposes. In that reality, they live like joyful, innocent children and adults. Descartes at least narrowed in on the importance of our minds in interacting with the spiritual realm and its connection to our destiny and existence. A summary of his thoughts on the matter may be more accurately phrased, "Whenever I'm thinking, I exist." And that is certainly applicable and descriptive of the mind's function in soul care.

As a side note, Descartes is considered a father of rationalism, a Western philosophical view that regards reason as the chief source and test of knowledge. "The rationalists' confidence in reason and proof tends, therefore, to detract from their respect for other ways of knowing" (britannica.com). In reality, however, the soul is wired to know the spiritual realm and truth by other means, given its proper care.

I suppose my point is this. You can have a Biblical worldview, paradigm, or Christian perspective on what's real and what's true. Or you can have a secular one, a progressive one, or an agnostic one. You choose. You get to choose. You have that privilege. The mechanism you will use to make that decision is your mind.

That makes me want to say the mind is the soul's most important part or function. It is the gatekeeper of the soul. It adjudicates or decides between all the inputs to the soul and from the soul which ones will be considered true, valuable, and internalized into the soul's memory. The mind is instrumental in deciding who you are and how you function. By itself, it does not program your soul. But it determines what does and does not. Therefore, mind control, in the healthiest sense of the word—you controlling your own mind—is a tenet and most important activity in soul care.

But is it the mind that always decides? Or is it the will that decides? Or sometimes the emotions? Do you see the quandary? Something that is not material or made of matter defines us. It also works in a highly convoluted, sometimes chaotic, and always mysterious fashion in the process of living, being, and finding our way. The mind sets the stage and our course most of the time for all our lives.

Reclaim Your Mind

Let's continue in that vein while talking about improving our minds' function and availability to serve us, improve our relationships, and propel us toward happiness and our best destiny.

First, <u>the mind is not the brain</u>. Intuition and our language tell us that. In a fascinating scripture about the King of Kings, we read: "**Have this mind among yourselves, which is yours in Christ Jesus**, who, though he was in the form of God, did not count equality with God a thing to be grasped, but emptied himself, by taking the form of a servant, being born in the likeness of men. And being found in human form, he humbled himself by becoming obedient to the point of death, even death on a cross. Therefore God has highly exalted him and bestowed on him the name that is above every name" (Philippians 2: 5-9 ESV). We're told to have the mind of Jesus. That's not the brain of Jesus. I suppose you might say the brain is the physical mechanism the mind uses to process information, but it's not the driver. The British are good about calling things what they are with the simple, colorful, artful use of language. If you've spent any time in London using the underground, you've heard over the loudspeaker at the stations, "Mind the gap!" They are not saying "Brain the gap." They are saying, "Pay attention or focus on the fact that there is a space between the train car and the platform, a gap, where you could trip, fall, or get your apparel or luggage entangled.

Scripture tells us that our minds must be renewed for them to work properly. The text above from Philippians is the most profound statement about humility in the Bible. And it's connected to the mind. Could humility be a portal for the mind to do its best and highest work? To get, keep, and process the best information accurately and reject harmful data or patterns of thinking?

There appears to be a gap between how humanity tends to see itself, if left alone, that's quite different from how God sees us. The human tendency and our modern culture [especially] projects pride, hubris, and self-exaltation. It's the norm.

The only Being in the universe who could rightly have those traits and attitudes about Himself doesn't. That's what makes Him and the quality of humility so beautiful and unusual. Wisdom is seeing things like God sees them because that's how they really are. There is a significant gap between how our church in the West, religion, and culture see pride and how Jesus sees pride. We should mind this gap.

It doesn't matter how fast you're going if you're on the wrong track. Humility is one track or characteristic that a properly functioning mind should have at its foundation. There are others, but this is one of the most fundamental and perhaps the most important. If you're a follower of Jesus, you want to emulate and become like your Master. You do this by spending time with Him in solitude, silence, meditation, reading His Word, praying, and hanging out with other followers. The mind that holds humility high and as a filter will not be led astray to the hurt of itself and others. Instead, it will become highly functioning—leading the heart and will in healthy directions and paths.

"**The fear of the Lord** is instruction in **wisdom**, and **humility** comes before **honor**" (Proverbs 15:33 ESV). "The **reward for humility and fear of the Lord** is **riches and honor and life**" (Proverbs 22:4).

Interestingly and consistently, the first use of the word **mind** in the Philippians passage above **is a** Greek **verb**. Thayer's Lexicon defines it like this: "1. to have understanding, be wise 2. to feel, to think a. to have an opinion of one's self, think of one's self, to be modest, not let one's opinion (though just) of himself exceed the bounds of modesty.

The same meaning and nuances are expressed in Strong's Definitions: "to **exercise the mind**, that is, entertain or have a sentiment or opinion; by implication to be (mentally) disposed (more or less earnestly in a certain direction); intensively to **interest oneself in** (**with concern or obedience**): - set the affection on.**"** It's interesting to see the connection between humility and obedience.

Dallas Willard said, "We don't believe something by merely saying we believe it, or even when we believe that we believe it. We believe something when we act as if it were true." James, the half-brother of Jesus said it this way: "For if anyone is a hearer of the word and not a doer, he is like a man who looks at his natural face in a mirror; for once he has looked at himself and gone away, he has immediately forgotten what kind of person he was. But **one who looks intently at the perfect law**, the law **of liberty**, and **abides by it**, not having become a forgetful hearer but **an effectual doer, this man will be blessed** in what he does" (James 1:23-25).

Spiritual habits, disciplines, and rhythms are to be practiced, not just memorized, learned about, and cataloged. A good picture of what this looks like can be found in Brother Lawrence's short book, *Practicing the Presence of God*. Beware of short books!

Back to being mindful, or focusing the mind as a necessary practice for being whole and healthy, especially spiritually, which is often the missing ingredient, consider this quote:

> *"The first and most basic thing we can and must do is to keep God before our minds... to direct and redirect our minds constantly to Him. In the early time of our practicing, we may well be challenged by our burdensome*

habits of dwelling on things less than God. But these are habits – not the law of gravity – and can be broken. A new grace-filled habit [can be developed]... If God is the great longing of our souls, He will become the polestar of our inward beings."

—Dallas Willard

Plastic Minds

By plastic minds, I don't mean something that is imitation, cheap, or unimportant, but in the same sense as plastic surgery. One definition of plastic is "easily shaped or molded." That's the main science, discovery, and topic of the medical researcher and author Caroline Leaf, M.D., in her best-selling book, *Switch on Your Brain: The Key to Peak Happiness, Thinking, and Health*. I recommend it highly for the reasons above and the reasons that follow. You will get the flavor and main message of it from a few quotes:

> *"Our mind is designed to control the body, of which the brain is a part, not the other way around. Matter does not control us; we control matter through our thinking and choosing. We cannot control the events and circumstances of life but we can control our reactions."*
>
> *"What your mind creates only your mind can take away."*
>
> *"Main Scripture: We destroy arguments and every lofty opinion raised against the knowledge of God, and take every thought captive to obey Christ. 2 Corinthians 10:5 ESV Linked Science Concept: When you objectively observe your own thinking with the view to capturing*

> *rogue thoughts, you in effect direct your attention to stop the negative impact and rewire healthy new circuits into your brain."*
>
> *"Research shows that 75 to 98 percent of mental, physical, and behavioral illness comes from one's thought life."*
>
> *"Daytime thinking is a building process, whereas nighttime thinking is a sorting process."*
>
> —Caroline Leaf, M.D.

> *"How we think not only affects our own spirit, soul, and body but also people around us."*
>
> —Dallas Willard Reflects on the Mind

Our minds have the ability to program themselves, our hearts, our wills, and who knows what else. The observations and science are telling, along with theology, philosophy, and history. How do we constructively enter into that arena? Time with God, in silence, solitude, meditation, Bible reading, praying—the spiritual disciplines, habits, and rhythms. Let's note things Dallas Willard has written about this:

> *"We live in a culture that has, for centuries now, cultivated the idea that the skeptical person is always smarter than the one who believes. You can be almost as stupid as a cabbage, as long as you doubt. The fashion of the age has identified mental sharpness with a pose, not with genuine intellectual method and character."*
>
> *"What is thinking? It is the activity of searching out what must be true, or cannot be true, in the light of the given facts or assumptions."*

> *"If we allow everything access to our mind, we are simply asking to be kept in a state of mental turmoil or bondage. For nothing enters the mind without having an effect for good or evil."*
>
> *"Why doesn't God just force us to do the things he knows to be right? It is because that would lose precisely that which he has intended in our creation: freely chosen character."*
>
> *"The ultimate freedom we have as human beings is the power to select what we will allow or require our minds to dwell upon."*
>
> *"History has brought us to the point where the Christian message is thought to be essentially concerned only with how to deal with sin: with wrongdoing or wrong-being and its effects. Life, our actual existence, is not included in what is now presented as the heart of the Christian message, or it is included only marginally."*
>
> *"In solitude and silence you're learning to stop doing, stop producing, stop pleasing people, stop entertaining yourself, stop obsessing — stop doing anything except to simply be your naked self before God and be found by him."*

Make a quality decision to begin today. Focus your mind today on soul care! Take time to think, reason, and be alone with your thoughts. Meditate on those thoughts presented in the Word of God. Breathe deeply. Take a long walk.

Charles Simpson, an influential spiritual mentor, describes the mind's function as follows: "The mind is like the driver of an automobile full of people going down the highway, all trying to grab the steering wheel." Charles went to his reward this year at the age of 87. Two of his last sermons were "Touching the Eternal" and "Don't Lose Your Mind." There seems to be a connection.

This chapter is not so much about your worldview or paradigm for living as it is about how you got there. And more so, how do you go on from here? Where you set your mind and how you keep it will be the major factor in where you end up.

Remember what Martin Luther said: "Even if I knew the world would go to pieces tomorrow, I would still plant my apple tree." Someone else said, "The best time to plant a tree was forty years ago; the next best time is today." So focus your mind on soul care today!

****

> *"And do not be conformed to this world, but be transformed by the renewing of your mind, so that you may prove what the will of God is, that which is good and acceptable and perfect."*
> (Romans 12:2)

> *"For as he [man] thinketh in his heart, so is he."*
> (Proverbs 23:7 KJV)

> *"He [God] jealously desires the Spirit which He has made to dwell in us"? But He gives a greater grace. Therefore it says, 'God is opposed to the proud, but gives grace to the humble.'"*
> (James 4: 5b-6)

*"Set your mind on the things above,
not on the things that are on earth."*
(Colossians 3:2)

*"You will keep him in perfect peace,
whose mind is stayed on You."*
(Isaiah 26:3a NKJV)

CHAPTER THREE

THE HUMAN SPIRIT

"Now may the God of peace Himself sanctify you entirely; and may your spirit and soul and body be preserved complete, without blame at the coming of our Lord Jesus Christ."
(1 Thessalonians 5:23)

The Spirit and the Soul

One morning, as I was returning to the house from the Nehemiah group, I opened the door to find our young friend Taylor in the kitchen, talking to Elizabeth. Elizabeth had to go to work, so she left Taylor and me to visit for a few minutes before Taylor had to be off on her day. "What did you study in your men's group this morning?" Taylor asked. I told her we were looking at the verse above and studying the soul. She replied, "Aren't the spirit and soul the same thing?"

I told her they were not, and we talked about some of the differences, but the real distinctions were not clear enough to me to explain them to her. That's one reason I've put off writing about the human spirit. I've been awaiting more revelation and peering into the matter in Scripture while meditating and journaling. But today, it's as clear to me as it's ever been, and I'm going to give it a shot. Remember this caveat, my intention and passion is to help you fly the thing—I've never known how to build it. Only God can and did. But He's given us hints in His Word, and we should study them if we want insight and to know more about Him. He's evident in His creation, and we're made in His image.

We can start with the obvious. God is a three-part being: Father, Son, and Holy Spirit. We are three-part beings: spirit, soul, and body. But let me get to the point about the differences between the soul and the spirit. That's been the most perplexing distinction for me to understand. Part of the problem is language. Language is a gift and gives us so much understanding about everything around us, but it has limits.

Consider this foundational verse: "Then the Lord God formed man of dust from the ground, and breathed into his nostrils the breath of life; and man became a living being" (Genesis 2:7 NASB). "And the Lord God formed man of the dust of the ground, and breathed into his nostrils the breath of life; and man became a living soul" (Genesis 2:7 KJV).

In Hebrew, the word for soul is *nephesh*. It's found 753 times in the Bible, and the King James translators chose to translate it "soul" 475 times or 63% of those times, and they never translated as "spirit." There is a different Hebrew word for spirit (*ruach*), which puzzled me.

Could it be that what God breathed into man was too big for one Hebrew word? Or any word? Could He breathe both the spirit and the soul into mankind simultaneously? The human spirit is the life force that starts and keeps man breathing. The soul, triune like its Creator, is an organism not composed of matter, like the spirit, that allows man the incredible opportunity to live and move and have a being with God or apart from God. The soul is allowed much free rein to choose its destiny, affections, and path in its life journey on the planet. The soul comprises our mind, will, emotions, passions, desires, character, conscience, and more. We are given it as a gift to enjoy and program. But how about the spirit?

The human spirit is the center of our being, with the capacity of being eternal if not destroyed. Do you recall this verse: "**But of the tree of the knowledge of good and evil, thou shalt not eat of it: for in the day that thou eatest thereof thou shalt surely die**" (Genesis 2:17)? I'm sure you do, and you also recall they did eat of it, and their spirits became dysfunctional. Long after that, their bodies died, according to the word of the Lord. Since Adam, mankind has been born with the human spirit dead and dysfunctional. And the soul and body are left to make their way alone.

But, "Thanks be to God for His indescribable gift!" (2 Corinthians 9:15). Our human spirits can be made alive and able to abide or commune with His Holy Spirt anew as we place our faith in Jesus, receiving His gift of rebirth and eternal life. Then we have much help in life available to us. We still make choices but everything changes. As I told a brother in the Nehemiah group this morning, "We can now live on 220 volts instead of the AA batteries many use to grope along." That's the nature and function of the human spirit—its ability to personally hear and know God, the Holy Spirit, and to access His spiritual power.

Rick Renner, an excellent Greek scholar, says there are definite articles in front of "spirit, soul, and body," indicating we are three-part beings. We are a spirit, have a soul, and live in a body. God intends that all three parts of us function in sync. When we are born again, as Jesus told the Teacher of Israel in John 3, we instantly have a brand new spirit that's not subject to wear, tear, and age. Best of all, this spirit functions with the Holy Spirit to make us back into the image of God. It's still a learning and practicing process and a choice of our will to a great extent, in a mystical dance, but the power and promise are there!

Remember what Jesus told the Pharisees: "**You blind Pharisee, first clean the inside of the cup and of the dish, so that the outside of it may become clean also**" (Matthew 23:26). And recall what Paul by the Spirit told the church of all time: "But **we have this treasure in earthen vessels, so that the surpassing greatness of the power will be of God and not from ourselves**" (2 Corinthians 4:7).

Andrew Wommack presents an insightful YouTube series, *Spirit, Soul & Body*, in which he clarifies most of these points.

He especially points out that our spirit is the life-giving part of our triune makeup: "For just as **the body without the spirit is dead**, so also faith without works is dead" (James 2:26).

That's such great news! Our soul (mind, will, and emotions) and body are completed with a revived spirit as we enjoy God's power and presence, along with His leading and protection. As we practice spiritual rhythms, we can soar with Him in the Spirit in this life!

If you want to investigate this further, I recommend the book, *There's More To You Than Meets The Eye*, by Rick Renner or the video series available on YouTube under the same name. This teaching helps put it together in your mind. Speaking of the mind, let's explore how this works in the process.

Romans 12

Romans 12 is impressive! Throughout Scripture, I see so much of the mystery of living under the unseen hand of God. It's exciting that He shares these insights and revelations and that we can see them while living them and learning about them.

It must feel like my college graduate friend Wilkins's joy and wonder, having started on a journey and dream of becoming an airline pilot and then experiencing the flying we've done in the last five days. He's flown five hours on five flights with me in the last week, preparing him in a relaxed atmosphere to begin training and a career change. I have wanted to know and experience spiritual things and look into the unseen realm to understand how they work. Now, the

Spirit is letting me do so through reading, living, meditating, and spending quiet time of reflection with Him.

I must fight for alone time with God, even in retirement. But the habits of solitude and silence continue to expand, making the revelation and relationship with the Almighty's Spirit tangible, satisfying, and exciting. His name be praised for Who He is, what He does, and for His humility to hear our prayers and hearts and bend low to be with us as Immanuel.

These insights flow from such times. Journaling can be cumbersome because I see so much sometimes, and writing slows me down. Yet noting it causes me to meditate and chew on it, which facilitates more insights and aids in remembering. So it's a quandary, a beautiful one that I embrace. I enjoy and flow with it, sometimes noting what I see and sometimes just pausing to smile, reflect, and enjoy what I see.

Romans 12:1-2 is so profound as to be life-changing and directional! The Spirit gave Paul two distilled packets of truth for the church in Rome and the church of all times. "And **do not be conformed to this world**, but **be transformed by the renewing of your mind**, so that you may prove what the will of God is, that which is good and acceptable and perfect" (Romans 12:2a).

When the human spirit is made alive, being born of the Spirit from above (John 3), by faith in Jesus, it can commune with God's Holy Spirit and access the power of the Spirit to be transformed into a new image and being—like from a cocoon to a butterfly. This transformation is a process that takes time, but the power is now present and available. Yet the soul, with its gatekeeper, the mind, is still calling the shots or deciding how much change it will accept, what is to be trusted, and what it wants.

Your spirit is new and perfect and given access to the Holy Spirit. He abides with you now. But your mind is still the same and needs to be renewed. It exists between your spirit and your flesh. It will likely let your flesh call the shots if it's not renewed. It now hears from your spirit, the Holy Spirit, and your flesh. It's the gatekeeper of the soul. Here's the Thayer's Lexicon definition of the Greek word transliterated "mind":

"Thayer Lexicon: 1. the mind, comprising alike the faculties of perceiving and understanding and those of feeling, judging, determining a. the intellectual faculty, the understanding b. reason in the narrower sense, as the capacity for spiritual truth, the higher powers of the soul, the faculty of perceiving divine things, of recognizing goodness and of hating evil c. the power of considering and judging soberly, calmly, and impartially 2. a particular mode of thinking and judging, i.e thoughts, feelings, purposes, desires."

Other places in the Bible tell us to renew our mind: "And that you be renewed in the spirit of your mind" (Ephesians 4:23a). The abiding part of the equation lets the mind and soul rest, trust, and bathe in God's truth and life, dissolving walls of fear, hurts, and objections. So, the choice is whether to abide in His presence with the practices of soul care or not—whether to habitually practice T-I-M-E with God or distractedly or willfully go your way, ignoring such a great salvation.

The verbs "conformed" and "transformed" in Greek are in the present perfect tense. This means that the process is ongoing with or without action on your part. You only get to direct which way it goes. You choose to be conformed by doing very little and deciding you want to conform to what surrounds you. Or you choose to be transformed into something different by spending time with God via spiritual habits—renewing your mind!

How It Works — Motivation for Transformation

"Therefore **I urge you,** brethren, by the mercies of God, to present your bodies a living and holy sacrifice, acceptable to God, which is your spiritual service of worship. And **do not be conformed to this world, but be transformed by the renewing of your mind**, so that you may prove what the will of God is, that which is good and acceptable and perfect" (Romans 12:1-2).

How does it work? By God's mercies. He will start to do the heavy lifting if you desire it and show it by staying in His presence daily, habitually. He has the big part to do, and we can't do His part, but we have a small part, and He won't do our part.

What is to be our motivation? A spiritual act of worship, demonstrating we acknowledge He is worthy of our worship and praise. And we want to bring Him something—our obedience and cooperation. We bow in the presence of One so good and mighty with our lives.

What is the obedience? Don't conform to the world. Choose transformation by the renewing of your mind. He will help you. This is your spiritual service of worship. And your ticket to a life like His, recreated gradually into His image, soaring in the Spirit and moving like the wind.

Do not be conformed to the world or age. Come out of her and be different, live differently: "**I heard another voice from heaven, saying, 'Come out of her, my people,**

so that you will not participate in her sins and receive of her plagues'" (Revelation 18:4). You will come to know and live out the will of God—to experience things good, acceptable, and perfect.

He's certainly worthy of your worship and obedience. He says you are worthy of His love, created in His image and redeemed by His blood. He desires to spend time with you. He wants to help you along your journey and enjoy it with you. *Pilgrims' Progress* comes to mind. After Pilgrim comes to a knowledge of the truth by revelation, he embarks on a spiritual journey to know the source of truth and seek help for his family and friends in a world where he must contend with evil, dark spirits.

His battle is the same as ours and is fought and won with soul care, in abiding (John 15:5), over time—habitual, consistent time—in solitude and silence, listening while reading, praying, meditating, and practicing the presence of God. These are the tools of soul care and they invite the presence and power of the Holy Spirit to work through your spirit to help transform your soul to look more like Him for your good and His glory.

You have already received his mercy if you can hear this and propose to practice these things. And by practice, you will receive more and more of His grace and power for living differently. You will live a life energized by the Holy Spirit, winsome, compelling, and joyful for yourself and others. Godspeed as you journey practicing these habits and rhythms to know Him, and fly in His Spirit like the wind.

****

"You, however, are not in the realm of the flesh but are in the realm of the Spirit, if indeed the Spirit of God lives in you. And if anyone does not have the Spirit of Christ, they do not belong to Christ."
(Romans 8:9 NIV)

"But it is a spirit in man, and the breath of the Almighty gives them understanding."
(Job 32:8)

"The Spirit of God has made me, and the breath of the Almighty gives me life."
(Job 33:4)

"Thus says God the Lord, Who created the heavens and stretched them out, Who spread out the earth and its offspring, Who gives breath to the people on it and spirit to those who walk in it."
(Isaiah 42:5)

"And when He had said this, He breathed on them and said to them, 'Receive the Holy Spirit.'"
(John 20:22)

"And have put on the new self who is being renewed to a true knowledge according to the image of the One who created him."
(Colossians 3:10)

"The Lord will protect you from all evil;
He will keep your soul.
The Lord will guard your going out and your coming
in from this time forth and forever."
(Psalm 121:7-8)

CHAPTER FOUR

THE PRESENT FLYING CHAPTER

*"Delight yourself in the Lord; and
He will give you the desires of your heart."*
(Psalm 37:4)

You might wonder how this present backcountry flying chapter of my life came about. When people ask about that, I normally answer, "The Lord gave me this airplane. That's my story, and I'm sticking to it!" I don't elaborate more than that because people smile and smirk, "Yeah, right?" But since this

God Stays Near

is a story about God staying near, I'll share the details with you, and you can decide for yourself.

Background

After I retired from the USAF and Air National Guard, where I flew fighters for twenty years, and from American Airlines, where I flew commercially for twenty-five years, I thought my flying days were over. I was content with that. Only a few people have the opportunity to do those kinds of things.

Also, even though I knew how to fly, owning a small aircraft is known to be a bit expensive. Pilots are known to be a bit cheap—we like to say frugal. There's an old joke in the flying business that copper wire was invented by two airline captains fighting over a penny. It's considered among pilots that if you're going to fly small airplanes, it's wiser to rent one rather than own one.

So, a couple of years after I retired from the airline, I was resistant when a friend approached me and wanted to sell me his Cessna 172. I smiled at Ivan and said, "Thank you very much, but I do not need an airplane. I'll try to help you sell yours by telling people and posting an ad on the pilot bulletin board at the Dallas-Fort Worth airport."

But Ivan insisted he needed to sell it and wanted me to have it. Finally, I began to consider the idea. His mechanic was doing the annual inspection at a nearby airport, and Ivan invited me to come and watch the process. I could ask the mechanic questions about that particular airplane and the expense of owning an aircraft. What harm could that do? I liked hanging out with Ivan and would enjoy learning about this facet of general aviation again.

The Present Flying Chapter

The mechanic, Tim, was friendly, funny, honest, and matter-of-fact. He told me that this was the most mass-produced airplane in history, that parts were reasonably priced and plentiful, and that this particular airplane was a good one. He also quoted me the typical yearly maintenance cost, which he said was less than most airplanes. Hmmm, I thought.

Wisdom and Three Counselors

I had already decided that if the mechanic interview went well and I liked what I saw, I would seek the counsel of three people and decide based on their counsel. Verses in the Bible say a wise man will seek the counsel of many (Proverbs 15:22, 12:15, and others). So, this has been my practice. I wanted to hear the Lord's voice on this matter for my family's highest good.

First, I felt led to ask Bob, who owned the airport where I was standing and had owned many airplanes. He was older, a Christian, and had made his fortune doing construction in California. He wasn't retired but was seeking a quieter life near family in Arkansas. And he was a bit of a character, I would find out.

He stopped by to chat with the mechanic and Ivan and then started walking away. I chased him down. "Bob, Bob, hey, can I ask you for your wisdom about something?" A bit gruffly, he retorted, "Wisdom?! I don't know if I have any wisdom. What do you want?"

"Well, I'm thinking about buying Ivan's airplane over there, and I'm so practical…." Bob interrupted, "Whoa, you can't use 'practical' and 'airplane' in the same sentence. Besides, if everything had to be practical, a guy would probably never get married, would he?" I meekly replied, "Thanks, I see what you mean, I guess." He turned and walked away. That was my first bit of counsel.

Secondly, I asked one of my best friends, Scott, a bank president and a bit of a Dave Ramsey enthusiast. I knew without a doubt he would say, "No." But in the interest of wanting an honest answer from the Lord, I determined to ask him. We met at the International House of Pancakes early one morning before he went to his office. I respected his candor, honesty, wisdom, and love for the Bible and Jesus. He was a straight shooter.

I began, "Scott, I want to ask for your wisdom about something. I'm considering buying Ivan's airplane, and I wondered what you might say?" I was just about to follow up with the facts and specifics of the purchase, but he didn't give me a chance. Instead, he quickly replied, "I think it's a great idea for you! You already know how to fly. And you will share it with others. You should buy it." Well, I'm not prone to fainting, but it crossed my mind. That was the second bit of counsel I received.

Thirdly, I often flew to Europe or Japan as a Boeing-777 pilot with a funny, bright pilot named Mark. Mark and his father, who had been the Air National Guard unit commander in Birmingham, Alabama, had a small airplane sales business on the side. They bought and sold airplanes routinely, and he would tell me about some of these situations on our long flights across the ocean. I respected his wisdom, honesty, and experience, so I decided to give him a call.

The conversation went exactly like this: "Mark, this is Dwayne, and I'm thinking about buying an airplane up here, a Cessna-172." Mark quickly interrupted me, "You told me they had a good flying club up there in Fort Smith. How much do they charge to rent a Cessna-172?" "$95 per hour, wet," I replied. "That's cheap! You should just rent one." "Okay, thanks for your time and counsel." "You're welcome. How much does he want for his 172?" I told him the amount, and he quickly said, "Buy it! You can fly it for a few years, sell it, and not lose a penny."

So, I took that as a yes vote, bought the airplane, and flew it joyfully for a couple of years. I flew mainly back and forth to visit my aging father. I also flew it around the five-state area on short trips and regularly took up friends who wanted the experience of viewing things from above. And I rediscovered the joy of flying, with its link to solitude, beauty, and creation—in the sky, at a peaceful pace, near the earth.

After a couple of years, I sold this airplane to a friend. I then bought a backcountry plane with another friend, bringing a similar but different set of joys and relationships. I will continue to recount some of those to you. Clearly, God was staying near to me and leading me in this chapter of my life. I often think we don't really know the desires of our hearts, but He does. We must learn to seek Him and listen—via soul care.

****

> *"Trust in the Lord with all your heart,*
> *and lean not on your own understanding;*
> *in all your ways acknowledge Him,*
> *and He shall direct your paths."*
> (Proverbs 3:5-6 NKJV)

*"The mind of man plans his way,
but the Lord directs his steps."*
(Proverbs 16:9)

*"Delight yourself in the Lord; and
He will give you the desires of your heart."*
(Psalm 37:4)

CHAPTER FIVE

Flying Adventures — Alaska

"Have you entered the storehouses of the snow, or have you seen the storehouses of the hail? From whose womb has come the ice? And the frost of heaven, who has given it birth? Water becomes hard like stone, and the surface of the deep is imprisoned."
(Job 38: 22, 29–30)

Flight & Faith

One of my good friends, Tommy Park, recently invited me to speak at a hunters' banquet. He thought I would be perfect for it since I was raised by a game warden and spent much time in the woods as a youth hunting and fishing.

I agreed to it and told them one story about wildlife. When I was twelve years old, my dad rescued a kidnapped black bear cub. He took me in a patrol car about seventy miles, sitting in the backseat with the young bear to keep it occupied before releasing it back into the forest, hopefully, to be reunited with its mother and sibling, but big enough to make it on its own if they didn't find each other.

Then I told the group of hunters, about 150 mixed men and women, that I was pretty sure they were better hunters than me and had better stories. Therefore, I would tell them stories about Flight and Faith because those are the paths in which the Lord led me in the intervening years.

On the flying side, I told them stories about flying fighters, flying for the airlines, and flying my bush plane in the backcountry—something I never saw coming. Alaska stands out as the coup de grace among all those stories, so I will relate it to you first among stories of flight.

Alaska 2017

Two airplanes and four USAF pilot friends for almost forty years teamed up for an epic friendship, flying adventure to spend a month together flight-seeing in Canada and Alaska, enjoying creation's majesty and each other's company.

It sounds like a dream, and it was, with more than two

years in the planning. I made the following post on our Alaska blog (http://flytoalaska.blogspot.com/), where we shared and updated information during our preparation and journey: "Well, the day has come. Our comrade is well. We met for lunch yesterday with our wives for fun and additional witnesses to confirm Ken wasn't rushing it. Everyone feels good about a dawn launch. So, in about twelve hours, we'll be off on our adventure."

We're Off!

After meeting at the hangar at 5:45 AM and spending a few minutes with media and camera crews (our fighter pilot friend, Sam, and my wife, Elizabeth), the Maules broke ground at 0630L. We headed to SF, Kansas to pick up our fourth member, Doug, spending a few minutes in his kitchen with family (and homemade cookies, coffee, fruit, and yogurt).

The Maules then turned NW to the Boulder, Colorado, area, where we enjoyed dinner, a night's rest, and wonderful hospitality from Ken's sister Jill and husband Walt. It was a great day of flying, even if hot and bumpy at times, and we had a tailwind all the way. The airplanes were flying well.

Wyoming and Montana

We departed early to take advantage of the cooler temperatures and headed north along the front range of the Rockies over Cheyenne, Wyoming, stopping for lunch and gas in Gillette, Wyoming. Later, we made an airborne decision to spend the night in Lewistown, Montana. Along our route were lots of beautiful and varied terrain and man-made features, including the largest mines we'd ever seen and maybe on the planet, the source of most of America's coal. Central Montana was a big surprise for its beauty, friendly people, and wonderful summertime climate.

After a hardy breakfast on the old-west main street, we headed to the airport and flew straight to Lethbridge, Alberta. There, we cleared customs without problem or delay, fueled, and got on our way toward the Alaska Highway and points further north. The air was cool and still, and the scenery was pleasing and beautiful. We'd come a long way in three days, flying about six hours daily. Some say the most scenic part of the journey is about to begin.

Canada

Memorable were the views of passing overhead Calgary and landing with a flight of nine RV-7s just finishing airshow practice at Rocky Mountain House, Alberta.

The flight from there to Grand Prairie, Alberta, where we spent the night, was long and sparsely populated. But it was well populated with spruce trees, lakes, oil and gas wells, and its own beautiful array of colors—sky, clouds, forest, lakes, streams, and an occasional farm, ranch, or town.

The joy of flying formation again, not experienced since flying fighters together twenty years ago, added its own special joy and dimension to this leg of the journey...north to Alaska.

We all thank God, feeling grateful, humbled, and blessed for this amazing opportunity. Sometimes, when you experience God's grace, you feel overwhelmed in a good way but have no words. Only humility and silent gratefulness seem appropriate.

On day four of our adventure, we flew fifty miles to Dawson Creek, the beginning point of the Alaskan Highway. Then we took wing up the highway over Fort St. John to Fort Nelson, where we spent the night. We had an excellent meal followed by what soon would become a staple of the trip—an A&W Root Beer!

Besides enjoying the beauty of British Columbia and the Yukon, most of us were learning the history of the ALCAN as we traveled it. Fascinating!

The Alaska Highway was constructed during World War II to connect the lower United States to Alaska across Canada. It begins at Dawson Creek, British Columbia, and runs to Delta Junction, Alaska, via Whitehorse, Yukon. It was completed in 1942 at approximately 1,700 miles and opened to the public in 1948. Legendary over many decades for being a rough, challenging drive, the highway is now paved over its entire length.

The vastness of this beautiful and rugged wilderness has started to settle in as we've flown for several hundred miles and three days over British Columbia and the Yukon. From White Horse, we'll have about 250 miles to go before reaching the US border and the wilderness of Alaska.

Of the three or four routes commonly flown by aircraft to Alaska, we were told this was the safest, having the highway nearby for emergency landings should the need arise, and the most beautiful.

Yukon and Whitehorse

We flew from Watson Lake to Whitehorse, from where we hoped to fly into Alaska at the first opportunity. I say opportunity because tomorrow's weather looks iffy, and we may need to wait here until it clears and the forecast improves.

The vast splendor and beauty of the Yukon were jaw-dropping on the leg into White Horse, making us joyfully anticipate what might lie ahead. The Yukon is a special, beautiful wilderness, and White Horse is a delightful town with a pleasant atmosphere and a colorful history. We all took walks around town and along the Yukon River during the day and separately as desired. The peace, rest, and fresh mountain air were rejuvenating.

Alaska

Alaska! At last! Today, day seven, we entered the "Last Frontier" of the USA and the goal of our adventure. Not to take anything away from the beauty, wonder, and camaraderie of our dream trip to this point! To our great surprise, the beauty and majesty level were about to take a notch up!

We arrived in Alaska after a flight from White Horse to McCarthy along the ALCAN. We passed Haynes Junction, Destruction Bay, and Beaver Creek to arrive in the USA and clear customs at Northway, AK. From here, we proceeded to Tok for lunch and fuel. Then, we flew to Gulkana for another fuel top-off before continuing SE to the amazing Wrangell Mountains-St Elias National Park. What a day of enjoyable flying and beautiful scenery!

McCarthy and Kennicott

On day one in Alaska, we flew down the beautiful Copper River and then up the Chitina River toward McCarthy, the only town of any size in the area. We spotted the runway and were heading that way when we looked NE and were overcome with the other-worldly beauty in front of us and near. We instinctively forgot about landing and headed toward the amazing sight. Almost immediately, we were over the gargantuan feet of two glaciers, which looked like a moonscape that had ragged, deep crevasses that could swallow large buildings or trains. Then we were over the ice and snow fields of the same glaciers just a thousand feet above them, giant mountains and beautiful clouds surrounding the entire scene.

After landing, we found out that these were the Kennicott and Root Glaciers and that our lodge for the night was at a famous old mine we had just flown over perched on the side of a mountain at the edge of the glacier.

Peacefully, we settled into our rooms, walked about the mine and grounds, had dinner, and basked in the indescribable beauty and pleasant temperature. What an arrival! What a first day—north in Alaska!

Gentle rain is falling as I sit on the long deck of our lodge early the next morning and look out on umpteen zillion acres of lakes, rivers, forests, and the Wrangle Mountains of SE Alaska. Real and surreal—words fail me. Healing, feeling, peaceful, pleasant to the soul.

A few other lodge residents are starting to stir and come to the deck, coffee in hand, to peer into this humbling, quiet expanse as they await breakfast inside. Few words are being uttered.

Yesterday was an excellent flying day in the local area. When I say the local area, I remind myself that Wrangle-St. Elias National Park is five times as big as Yellowstone and larger than Switzerland! It's easy to get alone here, to feel small and awed.

Of course, walking on a nearby glacier or wandering around the massive old Kennicott copper mine is the normal way and has its own "up close" appeal. Still, flying and flightseeing is what we came to do and our modus operandi, for which we are joyful and grateful. One feels small and humble as we fly between towering mountains like the legs of colossal giants unlike any the earth has seen, with streams, granite, forest, and glacier quietly peering back at us.

Those are my musings and reflections as I sit on the deck this morning in a gentle rain, coffee in hand, and quietly thank God for what we saw yesterday and apparently will continue to see as we journey.

Before beginning our adventure while gearing up, I asked a young man at our local outdoor store, who travels extensively, where he'd been lately. He mentioned Yellowstone and Glacier National Parks and Patagonia. I then asked where was the most beautiful place he'd ever been. He spouted out "Wrangell Mountains-St Elias National Park in SE Alaska" without hesitation. He said, "The towering mountains, 14,000' plus, many rising from near sea level, glaciers, ice fields, lakes, streams, and forests are amazing." From that report I knew I wanted to give it a look if weather and circumstances allowed when we were within striking distance. Little did I know this would be the day!

During our stay at Kennicott Glacier Lodge, we met a beautiful young couple from Anchorage with backcountry aviation experience. In fact, Hans and Bee were on their yearly visit to the Wrangell Mountains in their Husky.

They opened their hearts to us, and we became friends.

After breakfast, Hans said, "Break out your map, and we'll make some suggestions for today's flying!" That was music to our ears; no coincidence, we were certain! They proceeded to map out a few routes that were their favorites. Bee especially liked the Bagley Ice Field. And we'd soon see why!

But all their suggestions sounded excellent, being offered by a knowledgeable pilot with extensive Alaskan aviation experience.

While I was going through the images from the Wrangell-St. Elias Mountains, I later discovered I had omitted some images. Some very important and deserving ones, I might add. That happens occasionally when manipulating and organizing large numbers of images. But what was I to do?

I'm choosing to pause, consider those photos slowly, and reflect on what we experienced there—something up close and personal that's not ordinary or common to human experience—glaciers!

Here are some interesting facts about glaciers that I learned after seeing them.

[1] Ten percent of the land area on Earth is covered with glacial ice.
[2] Glacierized areas cover over 5.8 million square miles.
[3] Glaciers store about 75 percent of the world's fresh water.
[4] If all land ice melted, the sea level would rise approximately 230 feet worldwide.
[5] In the United States, glaciers cover over 30,000 square miles, with most of the glaciers located in Alaska.

When we rounded a mountain near McCarthy, Alaska, on July 29th, 2017, two of these glaciers surprised and astounded us greatly. Our friendship flight of two Maule MX7s was drawn like a magnet to fly right up to the glaciers and then over them instead of landing immediately as we had planned.

The sight was awe-inspiring, and the sense of immensity and otherworldliness has not waned. It couldn't be processed at the time or since. Being close to such a sight and phenomenon seemed so special and mystical that there wasn't a feeling that it could be or should be understood, just experienced and appreciated…a new reality previously outside our experience. Majesty. Mystery. Marvel.

At first glance, it appears the large foot of the glacier is all stones of undetermined size, type, and origin—with very little ice. As it turns out exactly the opposite is true. Landslides on the mountains provide the stone covering as the glacier slowly passes through, and stone is scooped up from the valley floor as it passes with enormous force and embedded within. But that stone covering varies from only a few inches to about 15 feet. The main component is below what you see and, in the case of the Root Glacier, is ice 1300- 4000 feet thick! That's right, what appears as rocks is actually a thin covering of the densest ice imaginable, which is 1/4 to 3/4 miles deep!

Viewing photos from that portion of the flight, I was very impressed with the image quality of my Sony Alpha 55. However, it must be noted that the human eye is an amazing sensor that deals much better with the wild variations of light present in such an environment. Still, I'm grateful to have the images for memory and reflection.

Our wonder from this day wasn't facts in our heads but

awe in our hearts—the majesty and beauty we had seen, felt, and experienced from the cockpits or our Maule MX7s with friends!

It was a day of breathtaking beauty, solitude, and grandeur-imparting peace. It was a day and experience where words failed. It was also a day where words seemed small and unnecessary. All that was mixed with the joy of camaraderie and friendship, having experienced something so special with close friends by your side!

Valdez and Anchorage

The clear skies, good weather, and smooth sailing we had experienced so far changed slightly. We departed the beautiful Kennicott Glacier Lodge and the extraordinary Wrangle Mountains-St. Elias Park and headed south for Cordova, keeping in mind our fuel state and options for refueling, weather, and other pilot-type considerations.

We intended to fly down the Copper River to its mouth at the Gulf of Alaska and Prince William Sound, landing at Cordova on the coast. But as we continued down the Copper River, the terrain became more rugged, and the weather was deteriorating, so we made an inflight decision to turn around and fly instead to Valdez.

The terrain was rugged and remote, and the weather deteriorated even further, but we were able to get to the Thompson Pass and, from there, at least had the highway to Valdez beneath us. Not for landing—it's much too steep and twisting—but for the rescue effort, I suppose.

At any rate, we soon swooped beneath the low scud and into the surreal Prince William Sound at Valdez. It was beautiful, still, and peaceful beyond description. The watercolor was amazing, with glacier-perforated mountains surrounding us. It seemed like we had landed on another planet as we glided between towering mountains and patchy clouds into the most peaceful, still, surreal, other-worldly coastal village I've ever seen—Valdez.

Prince William Sound is on the Gulf of Alaska on Alaska's south coast. It is located on the east side of the Kenai Peninsula. Its largest port is Valdez, at the southern end of the Alaska Pipeline. The sound contains 150 glaciers, including 17 tidewater glaciers, known for dramatically calving huge ice chunks into the sea. It's a very deep water port, very protected from the sea by mountain ranges, and boasts an abundance of sea and land wildlife.

You will know it by its reputation as the port that filled the giant oil tanker Exxon Valdez, which ran aground nearby and spoiled the pristine Prince William Sound and the port of Valdez in 1989. Or perhaps, if you're a backcountry pilot, you will know it as the site of the world competition for STOL (short takeoff and landing) airplanes.

Ironically, we paid more for AVGAS here than anywhere else in Alaska, $7 per gallon—right at the end of the Alaska pipeline! But the distances are so vast, and fuel stops are so infrequent that we decided before we began our journey that we would gladly pay whatever the price of fuel and say not another word about it.

We enjoyed being there and experiencing its peaceful, hushed beauty. Its serene, beautiful harbor is home to 4000 residents. We took a cab into the harbor for a seafood lunch and a walkabout, then returned to fly down the sound to the Gulf of Alaska. We then did a one-eighty and flew back through the Thompson Pass to Gulkana for fuel. We intended to head for Talkeetna, but that's when things suddenly changed.

At our fueling stop in Gulkana, I noticed that my prop had been damaged after picking up a rock or gravel, probably in McCarthy. This damage is a known hazard for gravel or dirt strips, yet it isn't that common. But there it was, the worst nick any of us had ever seen, so Doug went to look for a mechanic.

The threat is that the nick will lead to a crack inflight with part of the prop breaking off, followed by violent shaking, quickly shutting down the engine, and a forced landing—nothing we wanted to chance without seeking a professional opinion. Thankfully, a kind flight instructor called an off-duty aircraft mechanic who came and evaluated the situation for us. The decision was made to fly straight to Anchorage, a two-hour flight, where we could get the damage further evaluated and properly repaired.

This necessary diversion seemed to add to the adventure. We were counting on a safe flight and hoping for a quick resolution to our newfound maintenance issue.

The flight down the Glenn Highway to Anchorage and Merrill Field was unexpectedly beautiful and dramatic. It's reportedly one of Alaska's most dramatic drives with river valleys, glaciers, mountains, and alpine country.

The fight was beautiful beyond description as we followed the highway to Palmer and descended toward the Cook Inlet and Merrill Field. I can't say the four of us weren't a bit anxious while at the same time trusting our sturdy steed. The beauty around us was a pleasant distraction, as was studying charts. That made the flight a little less stressful. With the

Cook Inlet and Anchorage in sight, we let down between majestic mountains, transitioning from some of the most sparsely occupied airspace in the world to some of the most congested, but we experienced a very peaceful approach and landing.

One humorous thing happened at Merrill Field. We had reported we were a formation "flight of two," but apparently, the controller didn't get the word. After clearing us to land, he said, "Hey, did you know there is an airplane right behind you?" I wished I had the presence of mind to say, "Yes, he's been following us for days! Can you call the authorities?"

Shep, our lodging procurement officer, found us a hotel for the night. They came and picked us up, and we had a nice dinner recounting the day's flying delights. The following day, one good lead led to another, and friendly Alaskans helped us get the prop evaluated and repaired. What could have been a week or month delay turned into one peaceful, fun, relaxing day. And Anchorage has become a memorable anchorage for two Maules and four friends.

"I will lift up my eyes to the mountains; from where shall my help come? My help comes from the Lord, Who made heaven and earth. He will not allow your foot to slip; He who keeps you will not slumber...The Lord will guard your going out and your coming in from this time forth and forever" (Psalm 121).

Reflection on Overcoming and Dreams

Our day of rest in Anchorage was also a day of reflection. Peaceful, quiet reflection.

While trusting and resting in the conviction the right

people would appear and get our plane ready to fly again, I received a text from a good friend named Roger Morris, who had just completed an Ironman event in Canada!

That led me to reflect on "dreams" and "overcoming." They seem to go together, do they not? You must dream and walk in the direction of those dreams, or you will never experience life above the fray. You will not accomplish what you were destined to do or experience what you could experience.

The old cliche comes to mind, "If you aim at nothing, you are sure to hit it!" So dreaming is a big part of doing or experiencing something big and meaningful—perhaps experiencing the life you've been given to the fullest or at least more of its fullness.

But once you dream and walk in the direction of those dreams, everyone knows there will be obstacles to overcome. It seems to go with the territory and an earth life, right?

But if the dream is worth doing, it's worth doing well. It's also worth doing poorly. It's worth doing, period! So expect some obstacles and never give up or quit walking in the direction of those dreams. Overcome. You can. If you never give up.

My heart is full as we are in Alaska, celebrating friendship, creation, and the gift of flight. It seems like a dream. Yet it started with some friends talking and getting the vision that it might be possible. Then, a date was put on a calendar. Some preparations began to be made…and we're here!

Did we have some obstacles? Even today? Yes! But we overcame because we believed in the dream and kept walking toward it. Hearing about Roger completing his Ironman competition in Whistler today was interesting and reflective. I know something of his preparation, sacrifice, and training because I went canoeing with him this spring. I know he overcame many obstacles and wouldn't give up.

For those of you who do not know exactly what an Ironman race is, one must swim 2.4 miles, bicycle 112 miles, and immediately run a marathon of 26.2 miles. All this must be done in under 17 hours, one event right after the other, without a break. Are you kidding me?!

That inspired me today, and it inspires me still. I'm proud of Roger. He's inspiring. I'm also proud of my friends in flight, who've overcome many obstacles to make this trip and day possible.

Let's encourage all we know to aim high and never give up! Godspeed on your journey.

Anchorage and Rest

Today was a day to rest, get my prop inspected and repaired, and explore Anchorage. After a delicious, leisurely breakfast, I started making phone calls, procured a rental car, and drove to the airport to meet a mechanic. Doug had his office set up and was taking care of business. Jim and Ken met up with Jim's son Thad, a new FedEx captain on an Anchorage layover, and walked around downtown before having lunch.

After the prop issue was promptly addressed and repaired—a miracle—the afternoon was spent touring and enjoying Lake Hood, the world's largest seaplane base, boasting about 200 daily operations. With Alaska's vast spaces, its many lakes and streams make ideal landing strips. Floatplanes are wildly popular. We noticed by their numbers that C-185s and Super Cubs were the backcountry airplanes of choice. Many of these are rigged for floats, tundra tires, or skis, depending on the season or the need. What a Mecca for back-country flying!

It's a fun fact worth noting that this massive seaplane base is a stone's throw from the Anchorage International Airport. It's also the home of the Alaska Airman organization, of which we became members; and we visited their headquarters while strolling the docks and admiring airplanes.

Rested up and refreshed from a day of little activity, we had a nice dinner and retired for the evening. The next day would be "South in Alaska" as we explored the Kenai Peninsula.

Kenai

Light showers were moving in and out of the area when we arrived first at Kenai and rented a car for the next couple of days. From there, we made the short flight to Soldotna while Shep drove the car to meet us. We fueled the airplanes, tied them down for the night, visited with the friendly staff at Marc Air, who would change our oil two days later, made a grocery run, and drove about twenty minutes to Sunset Cabins, our home for the night.

Doug taught us a new card game that would become our nightly entertainment most evenings for the rest of the trip. We decided to take Bee's advice on Seldovia for the following night, so Shep called and reserved us a room.

Doug and I walked to the beach and observed the dramatic tide fluctuation firsthand. Ken got a head start on resting for the night, and after some lively card games, we all hit the hay.

Seldovia

We were on our way again, flying down the beautiful peninsula above lakes, streams, and coastline, with distant, snow-covered mountains on both sides of us. We had a nice view of Homer—the city, airport, spit, and harbor—as we flew over the end of the peninsula, across the bay, and SE to Seldovia.

Seldovia's population was 255 at the 2010 census. It is located along Kachemak Bay, southwest of Homer. There is no road system connecting the town to other communities, so all travel to Seldovia is by airplane or boat.

We arrived during a rain shower that quickly moved off. We unloaded our bags for the night and were talking about how we were going to get them to the hotel when a nice couple from upstate New York who spent their summers in Seldovia and Alaska approached us and offered to give us a ride to the hotel. They were super friendly and gave us a driving tour of the village before dropping us at the hotel. They also showed us an iPhone video of a black bear that had charged them while they were on the deck of their nearby cabin the previous day! This did more than confirm the stories we had heard from locals that the black bears were unusually aggressive this year and not their typical, shy selves.

We strolled around the town's elevated boardwalks and the harbor together before enjoying a tasty lunch at the water's edge. The rest of the day was filled with individual walks, naps, relaxing, and exploring.

We had dinner at the local pub as it was the only place open at that time of the evening. The hot soup and beverage really hit the spot as the temperatures had begun to plunge. A beautiful, young, blonde-curly-haired woman was playing the guitar and singing Irish folk music in the restaurant, adding to the ambiance of the journey and evening. Then, it was a short walk one last time down the main street to our hotel for the obligatory card games and sleep.

"Seldovia is to Alaska what Alaska is to the USA." That's what they say on their brochure and what we've heard several Alaskans say. That's why we decided to overfly Homer and spend the night there.

Kachemak Bay is a 40-mile-long arm of the Cook Inlet, located on the southwest side of the Kenai Peninsula. The communities of Homer, Halibut Cove, Seldovia, and a few others dot the bay and enjoy its beauty, serenity, and abundant sea life.

The next morning, we flew back across it. It was Ken's turn to lead the flight back to Soldatna for our oil change, so I took advantage of the relaxed flying and smooth air to practice close formation flying, which is a joy unto itself—especially for aviators with fighters in their flying DNA. Actually, we had smooth air for the majority of our time in Alaska.

We dropped off our planes and were informed that the maintenance would only take a few hours. So we stopped at the visitors center in Soldotna for a look inside and a scenic stroll down the newly constructed boardwalk along the Kenai River. The silver salmon were still running, albeit a bit slower than peak, and we talked to a few anglers who had nice stringers of the tasty fish.

Back in the air, and having experienced so much beauty already, I don't think we were ready for the beauty we were about to experience flying into our destination for the night, Seward, Alaska, at the head of Resurrection Bay.

Seward

Plans change. This trip was designed that way. We met at the beginning of this dream trip and decided to go without a plan!

We knew we wanted to fly to Alaska with two airplanes and four long-time friends. We knew it would take about a week to get here and a week to get home, and we wanted to spend about two weeks exploring and flight-seeing. And we knew a few places we might like to see. That's about all the plans we had. With fast-changing weather possibly affecting our route and timing, we didn't want the stress of reserving rooms and having to be somewhere on a certain day and time. So the decision was made to take the chance we'd find places to stay or camp and fly by the seat of our pants, so to speak.

With this mindset, we flew into Seward from Soldotna and loved it! The approach and landing were knock-dead beautiful. We called for a taxi into town, which was just a couple of miles away. They arrived by the time we finished tying our planes down for the night and unloading our overnight bags onto the ramp.

We checked into our rooms right on the harbor. We walked the docks and were enthralled by the pristine, beautiful boats. There was also a giant cruise ship in the harbor. We had a nice dinner at the water's edge. We took longer walks around the outside of the harbor for the mountain and sea views. We stayed out, experiencing the clean, fresh air and beautiful views in all directions until dark. Our plan was to fly out the following day.

So it wasn't a big surprise when our plan changed. We

were to fly north to Kenai again midway to our next destination when Doug piped up and said, "Why don't we just stay here another day?" We looked at each other as if to say, "Why didn't we think of that?!" It's beautiful, relaxing, charming, and we feel like we just got here. The place is begging us to stay longer.

That's how it went down. We reconvened for dinner that night at a splendid local restaurant downtown and then walked back. Reading historical plaques as we walked from dinner, we learned that Seward is the birthplace of Alaska's state flag and the start of the famed 1049-mile dog-sled race, the Iditarod, from Seward to Nome, in the 49th state.

The following day, Ken and Jim enjoyed a flight to Homer, lunch, and observing harbor activities. Doug enjoyed a day of relative rest and solitude and some needed business attention via phone and laptop. I enjoyed the wildlife and glacier tour by boat in Resurrection Bay and the Gulf of Alaska. It was a day all of us treasured and will not soon forget!

I met some interesting folks and had nice conservations here and there. I took every piece of warm clothing I had in my backpack and used it all at one time or another. I saw lots of wildlife and sea life. The seas were smooth, the coffee from the galley was hot, and life was good.

To be a little more specific, we saw sea lions, eagles, puffins, whales, otters, and many other sea creatures of the north. When we arrived at the glacier destination for calving, we almost immediately saw a huge mass of ice fall from the glacier, crashing into the sea below with a monster splash. We were reasonably close, but the boat was still running and slowing to a stop to drift, so I didn't hear it. Then we drifted for about 30-40 minutes more with no other calving observed. It was very pleasant and awesome to just be there. And the sunny day we had with unlimited visibility could not be taken for granted. When I looked around, I saw a major waterfall gushing out from beneath the glacier, maybe ten feet above sea level. It was probably a hundred feet across with a flow of many thousands of gallons per minute, maybe per second, and I'm sure, very, very cold.

In fact, there were waterfalls all around, running down cliff faces from glaciers. The sea was emerald green, with big chunks of white ice floating all around and out to sea. It was certainly something you don't see every day, and I couldn't even imagine properly without being there.

On the voyage out of Resurrection Bay to the Gulf of Alaska, we passed the ship *Wizard* of *Deadliest Catch* TV fame. At the end of the day, we took a taxi downtown to a halibut and steak restaurant and, after dinner, walked back to the harbor and our hotel for the night. Over the delicious dinner everyone shared about their day, and life certainly was good...north in Alaska.

Talkeetna

Soon, we were airborne and flying north toward Anchorage and beyond to our destination for the next couple of days, Talkeetna. We decided on a slightly different route than our ingress to Seward to see some new territory. But the scenery was just as beautiful and dramatic as we flew over Six Mile Creek and Hope, Alaska, before heading toward Anchorage.

We talked to Anchorage ATC, but they scarcely paid us any attention as we flew up against the mountains at low altitudes and stayed east of their busy airline and military airspace. Once clear of the Anchorage area, we turned our steady steeds NNW toward Talkeetna.

We flew over the town before landing at the state-owned strip but took note of the grass Village Airstrip that Don Sheldon and others used in the past. Once settled in, we walked to the airport to arrange a glacier landing and a Denali flightseeing trip the next day. Then, we walked into town via a wooded path to explore and have dinner.

Talkeetna is charming, colorful, small, and vintage Alaska. Besides browsing the shops and looking over the restaurant possibilities, we visited the National Park Headquarters a few minutes before it closed. Then we wandered back to the Village Airstrip to look it over from the ground, planning to land our Maules on it the following day. It was something we all wanted to do to connect more with the rich aviation history that was birthed and lived out in Talkeetna, sort of a bush pilot rite of passage. It looked fine to us, and we decided it would be our first stop the next day.

With our nightly card games in the history books, we nodded off to sleep, reflecting on the wonderful trip, the wonderful weather, and the wonderful times we had experienced to this juncture. And with keen anticipation, we reflected on what our next day in Talkeetna might hold, with its Denali discovery flight and a glacier landing on the mountain! Also landing on the Village Airstrip and flying our own airplanes around Mt. Denali and the area?

Talkeetna is a small village about an hour's flight, or a hundred miles north of Anchorage. It's special for several reasons. It's probably best known for its location just south of Mt. McKinley, also known as Denali, "The Great One," by the First Nations people. This mountain, at 20,320 feet, is the highest in North America and attracts climbers from all over the globe.

Secondly, it's well known in Alaska for its rich aviation heritage. Some of Alaska's most famous bush pilots hail from Talkeetna, where they earned their reputation for courage, piloting skills, and being the mountain climbers' and hunters' best friends for perilous rescues.

Ever since reading *Wager with the Wind*, the story of the famous bush pilot Don Sheldon, a guy my father's age, Ken and I have wanted to come here, get to know the town, its history, and what it would feel like to fly around these hallowed places where so much of Alaskan bush pilot history was written.

But Denali and the other giant peaks in its neighborhood are so massive and tall that they often create their own weather…clouds, winds, and storms. In fact, we were told that visitors see the summit less than twenty percent of the time due to clouds.

But this morning, Wow! Oh Wow! We took our Maules to the sky to scout the cloud situation around Denali and looked over our shoulders as we climbed above the trees. It was looming gargantuan, beautiful, and cloud-free fifty miles to the north. Our excitement and anticipation of our afternoon Denali flight with a glacier landing shot through the roofs of our cockpits.

But there was little time to enjoy the view at the moment because Ken, who was leading this morning's flight, had made a quick turn to the north, put his flaps down, and called "short final for the Village Airstrip." I quickly reacted by doing an S-turn to get a little spacing and followed him in a close trail to a formation landing on the pristine, short grass strip.

Mainly due to Ken's prop wash, perhaps exacerbated by the Susitna River, light winds, and the tightly tree-lined strip, we had the most impressive wake turbulence event I have ever experienced at about 50 feet above the ground! But with some quick reaction and abrupt control inputs, we righted ourselves and touched down with a burst of power.

Seconds later, we shut down and climbed out. Doug surprised me by calling an impromptu aviator meeting and awarding me the "Maule Flying Cross" for the landing. After a short round of applause and handshakes, we forgot all about that and reveled in the amazement of landing and standing on the very field Don Sheldon had departed and landed on his many, many rescue flights of Mt. McKinley climbers needing help and Alaskan bush hunters or outdoorsman in need of rescue.

Don Sheldon's story, *Wager With The Wind*, is a must-read if you're an outdoorsman, aviator, or adventurer. We enjoyed several minutes there, just letting it sink in. Quietly chatting and looking around at the strip, the river, and the town—all in the shadow of Mt. Denali, "The Great One."

Speaking of Denali, it was time to climb back in and fly toward the mountain. The idea was for us to change lead a few times, and each crew would photograph the other plane in front of the giant mountain, the tallest on the North American continent. It was a delight to see the monolith on a clear day, and having photos of our planes in front of it was special indeed.

In fact, we kept making circuits in front of it, admiring it and taking pictures, until someone remarked on the radio, "We're borderline late for our glacier flight!" Quickly, we turned our flight of two and sped toward the airport, landed, fueled, tied down, and walked fast or jogged to K2 Aviation, and the appointed time of our chartered flight-seeing adventure to Mt. Denali, complete with a glacier landing on skis. Something similar to what Don Sheldon did hundreds of times on many different glaciers, often in less-than-optimum weather, and flying underpowered WWII vintage airplanes.

The smiling girl at the counter remarked, "You're just in time." We were handed our ice boots and directed to the briefing area where the pilot of our turbo Otter was starting his roll call and briefing. Soon, we were airborne, climbing out in a beautiful red airplane perfectly matched for its mission with lots of power for the altitude and lift for the landing. Also, the speed to cover the distance from Talkeetna to the mountain quickly before slowing to make many turns with awe-filled splendor no matter where you looked, and then the beautiful glacier landing.

We touched down, deplaned, and spent about thirty minutes in the rare air and rare beauty of Mt. Denali, now surrounding us and still towering close above us. Far above us. It was quiet, peaceful, surreal. It would seem a dream if you didn't see the others in your party milling around, gazing, quietly chatting about it, and two other bright red planes from the same fleet which, by coincidence, were there at the same time. Even so, it seemed like a dream to be there. Remote, on ice, towering granite all around, with friends, on a clear day. Amazing.

We had ample time to soak in the moment and the grandeur. At the same time, we were airborne again too soon, as we all felt we could have spent hours there. Leaving the flanks of Mt. McKinley, we soared down glaciers through passes to the flat but rugged river valley below and back to Talkeetna with a smile on our lips and in our hearts from having experienced something so unique, majestic, and special.

We enjoyed a late lunch or early supper, walked around the village some more, and returned to our lodging for the now-customary card games, recounting the special day's activities and a good night's sleep…north in Alaska.

Denali National Park

It was tough leaving Talkeetna. We had a good time there, with good weather and great adventures. But alas, we could say that of all our Alaska destinations! So, with great joy in our hearts from this last successful adventure, we started to fly north again.

Past the great Denali, which was as clearly in view this day as the previous—at least in the morning. Then, the mountain started to make its own weather. Our destination for the evening was Fairbanks. But along the way, we would fly past the entrance to Denali National Park, which has its own gravel backcountry strip! So, of course, we decided to land and take a look, eat lunch, and enjoy a mid-day break. It was beautiful and unique.

After landing, we walked across the tracks of the Alaska Railway, which also serves the park, and just a few yards more to the park's entrance and headquarters. It's very well done and a fitting introduction to the massive park of over six million acres, almost 10,000 square miles. It has only one road, ninety-two miles long. Big, big, and wild is perhaps the best description.

As we've mentioned, the centerpiece is the tallest peak in North America, Denali, at 20,320 feet above sea level. Talkeetna to the south and Fairbanks to the north (and perhaps all within many miles) claim it as their own. When you're near, you want to call it your own. And indeed, it does feel like your own. It's very special!

Beautiful and amazing. Where can you do something like that in the lower forty-eight? To top it off, the train came by for our enjoyable viewing just as we finished securing our planes. Did I mention that the train up here between Talkeetna and Denali is a flag service? That is, if you need a ride, you make your way somewhere along the tracks and wave a flag at the approaching train. The conductor will see you, stop the train for you to board, and continue the route. What a state! What a country!

Fairbanks

Well, we made it to the top of the world! Or at least as far north as our budget of time and money allowed on this adventure.

Fairbanks, Alaska (64.82 N) is far north, less than 120 miles from the Arctic Circle. It's the largest city in the interior of Alaska (population 32,469 with 100,605 within the metro area) and second only to Anchorage.

Shep found us a hotel. Doug found us a dinner place, but not just any place. It was a genuine Alaskan Salmon Bake, with fresh fish and fixings prepared right in front of us, served outdoors on picnic tables under a grove of aspen trees. Are you kidding me? Well, it was as good as it sounds and plentiful. We caught the same bus back to our hotel and began the obligatory card games. This was followed by a good night's sleep and the realization that the Alaskan part of our trip was almost over. Tomorrow, we would fly SE, join the ALCAN, and cross into Canada at Beaver Creek, beginning the long, beautiful road home. But tonight, we're sleeping and dreaming north…in Alaska.

Fairbanks continued to impress us as the hotel van drove us to the general aviation side of the airport the following morning. It just had a good Alaskan feel to it that's hard to explain. It's a nice place to live and fly out of, with many services and social opportunities. And it offers unlimited outdoor recreational opportunities year-round—not the least of these is backcountry flying.

After looking over the many long rows of beautiful backcountry airplanes on big tires and floats, we walked out to ours, and after the customary loading and pre-flighting, we were climbing out on a perfect day, looking over the city and airport from the air, heading SE and home. We'd join the ALCAN at Delta Junction, its northernmost point, and follow it back across the Yukon and British Columbia to its starting point at Dawson Creek, where it more or less dumps us out onto the plains of Alberta in western Canada. On my blog, I noted, "It's time to sign off. Tomorrow is a big travel day. I'll report back from Canada as we begin the 2,500-mile journey back to our homes and families."

When the day came for us to leave Alaska, cross into Canada, clear customs, and plan and contemplate the long journey home, it was funny to us that, typically, none of us knew what day it was, how long we had been in Alaska, or how long we had been on our journey to this special part of the world.

Obviously, as my good friend Charles Saulsbery used to say, we'd slowed to "the speed of life." Beaver Creek, Yukon

Territory, Canada, Mile Post 1202, would do nothing to speed us up. It's small, quaint, charming, rustic, restful, and friendly. Due to the intriguing name, we tried to get a room at Buckshot Betty's. For some reason, Doug seemed fixated on it. But they were full up, so we got a humble room a hundred yards down the road and ate a fine dinner at Buckshot Betty's before turning in for the night and making our way homeward. Beaver Creek afforded more good memories of gravel landing strips, friends, food, adventure, and fun. The nightly card games were suspended due to cramped quarters, exhausted participants, and a planned early departure. The next games should resume at Watson Lake...Mile Post 635.

Watson Lake

I tried to report our travels and adventures to family, friends, and those who enjoy seeing and hearing about them. But I also try to live by the mantra, "It's better to live life than to record it." So the GoPro went into the bag a few days ago not to resurface, and photo taking has slowed to a trickle, although in the interest of honesty, the collection is sizable. Dealing with all that will have to wait as we "sip the moments," and concentrate on the present.

Watson Lake, at Mile Marker 635 on the ALCAN, was our home for the night. It's a beautiful airfield with WWII beginnings and lots of history. It saw many thousands of service men and women and airplanes being delivered to Russia, then our ally in Europe. Now, it's sleepy, picturesque, and typically Canadian.

The beauty and peace of this place and these flights make a fitting way to transition slowly back into a more normal environment than the wild, rugged, expansive beauty we've experienced for over two weeks.

Home

It was good to arrive in the USA on August 12th, the 21st day of our journey, where one of our members proved you don't really need a passport in your possession to reenter the US. We had a BBQ dinner on the banks of the Missouri River near where Lewis and Clark would have passed in their boats, exploring the western U.S. just a little more than two centuries earlier.

The next morning early, we were on our way across the plains and home via Miles City, MT, Hot Springs, SD, with a fly-by Mt. Rushmore, then North Platte, NE, where we spent the night in Kit Carson Country, Concordia, KS, Beaumont, KS, Benedict, KS, and then Fort Smith, AR. This U.S. part of our journey took two days and encompassed 1270 miles.

On the final day, our flight of two Maules took to the skies again and arrived in Fort Smith at about 5 PM, in cool, still, fresh air as storms had moved through the area. It all seemed surreal, just as did the whole Alaska experience when we looked back on it! We looked with joy in our hearts, smiles on our lips, and deep, deep gratitude for what we were able to do and experience together. Amazing!

Words fail, and thankful hearts seem small, but they are the only appropriate response to what we experienced together. A tremendous "Blessing of the Lord in the land of the living."

"For the Lord is good; His lovingkindness is everlasting and His faithfulness to all generations" (Psalm 100:5).

Those who followed our Garmin inReach tracking devices know we arrived home on August 14 at 4:41 P.M. Once we left Watson Lake, we intentionally put our heads down and flew longer legs and days while still enjoying the journey and musing about what we experienced individually and together each night.

Aside from a few ball caps and T-shirts, we all brought back thousands of internal images and memories of what we saw and experienced. Collecting my thoughts and meditating on them, I realized that we flew the same number of miles as if we'd flown to Frankfurt, Germany, then back to Boston, MA. I knew it was far, but that put a different perspective on the magnitude of the journey we dreamed of and completed.

As I sorted through the 10,000-plus photo and video images I collected during the journey over the following days, I continued to blog (flytoalaska.blogspot.com) with some reflections, thoughts, and links to the best images for the participants and those interested.

One summary of our epic journey might read like this: Our inReach tracking device sent its first position from the ramp in front of our hangars in Fort Smith, AR (35.33N 94.36W) on July 23rd at 6:05 AM, and the last position was sent from the exact location upon our arrival on August 14th at 4:41 PM.

So our journey encompassed 23 days, 22 nights, 8205 miles, 83 hours in the air, and 646 gallons of fuel for each of our two aircraft. That's one summary.

Another summary might go like this:

Great Weather
 Great Fellowship
  Great Flying
   Great Adventure
    Great New Friends
     A spiritual experience, really, on many levels...
    Great Worship
     Great Peace

All this seems to cry out for a response.... But the only appropriate response seems to be... Deep inner gratitude and silence...

...Worship and thanksgiving to Him, Who made all we've seen and invited us to experience it.

> *"The heavens are telling of the glory of God;*
> *and their expanse is declaring the work of*
> *His hands. Day to day pours forth speech,*
> *and night to night reveals knowledge.*
> *There is no speech, nor are there words;*
> *their voice is not heard. Their line has*
> *gone out through all the earth,*
> *and their utterances to the end*
> *of the world...."*
> (Psalm 19:1–4)

CHAPTER SIX
FLYING ADVENTURES — IDAHO

*"He makes the clouds his chariot;
He rides on the wings of the wind."*
(Psalm 104:3b ESV)

Backcountry Flying Takes a Notch Up

By 2019 I had enjoyed flying the Maule for five years. I flew mainly with my friend Ken Duncan, who also had a Maule, and a growing group of friends in Northwest Arkansas who enjoyed backcountry flying. In the Ozark and Ouachita mountains, we had plenty of mountain-top and river-bank strips to test our skills and enjoy our airplanes in the outdoors. We often took our sleeping bags and minimal camping equipment to spend the night in nature.

Backcountry flying is somewhat like flying fighters and airliners but is also totally different. Like your early flying lessons, you're back to flying much slower and closer to the ground. You can feel the light wind currents and enjoy the clouds and nature peacefully. You see the earth's surface from 500 or 1000 feet much of the time instead of miles high. The exciting part is that you land these airplanes in places you never expected airplanes to operate.

I flew my plane to Oshkosh with friends in 2016 and on the epic trip to Alaska in 2017. I was flying about 100 hours a year, so I had amassed 500 hours and was confident in the airplane and my backcountry flying skills. Best of all, I was enjoying the experience with college and Air Force friends in the beautiful part of the country where I grew up, the Ozark Mountains near Jasper, AR, on the Buffalo River.

I couldn't imagine much more fun or adventure. It was already as if I was living a dream. Still, I got very excited when a pilot from my Air Force flight training days called me and asked me to fly to Idaho with him and a few Bentonville friends.

"Billy Bell, Craig Gorely here. Hey, I've moved to Northwest Arkansas and bought a Cessna-185 backcountry airplane. Some friends here are planning a trip to the Rockies and Johnson Creek, Idaho. I was wondering if you'd like to come along, renew our friendship, and teach me how to fly this thing in the backcountry."

A giant grin came to my lips and in my heart. I liked Craig, and we had each been the leader of the two sections of our pilot training class. We also went to fighter lead-in training together in Alamogordo, NM, after we finished flying T-38s at Vance AFB in Enid, OK. But then we went our separate ways and hadn't heard much from each other in the intervening years. Once at DFW, he stuck his head in the cockpit of the Boeing-777 I was about to fly to Frankfurt, Germany, and surprised me. I learned he had been promoted to General Officer and was flying to Europe on USAF business. He had also been in the USAF aggressor squadron, where some of our best pilots flew against our fighter pilots using enemy tactics and airplanes. He was a reserve F-16 squadron commander and was a Delta Airlines pilot. He has a distinguished flying resume, yet he is one of the most humble guys I know.

Of course, I would like to hang out with him and get reacquainted! We were close friends then, and I felt sure that part hadn't changed. And Johnson Creek, Idaho, to boot! That airstrip is considered by most to be the Mecca of backcountry flying in the US. It would be a dream to fly there and experience it—with friends, no less!

I did have one concern, but I knew that could be addressed in some fashion. I had promised myself long ago that if I ever flew in the Rockies, I would stop at the front range, Colorado Springs, Pueblo, or someplace like that and hire an instructor to give me 5 to 10 hours of mountain flying instruction. Why?

Before being selected for flight school, I was a USAF air traffic controller at Tyndall Air Force Base in Panama City Beach, Florida. They have an aero club there, and since I had my private pilot's license from AFROTC, I got checked out in their Mooney-M20E, a fast, powerful four-place airplane. It was the first airplane to fly 200 miles per hour with a 200-HP engine. My brother Gene, his best friend Bert, and our cousin Steve, who was more like a brother than a cousin, talked me into renting the airplane and flying the four of us to Utah on a low-budget skiing trip, staying with one of my best friends from college, Ron Oholendt, who flew F-4s at Hill Air Force Base.

I told them I would do it but was reluctant because I had no experience flying in the mountains. Therefore, I would plan the trip, but if there were a single cloud between Florida and Utah the day we were to fly, I would call the trip off. They all agreed. I had read too many accident reports about good pilots having accidents while flying in mountainous terrain simply because there are considerations for flying there you don't experience at lower altitudes in the rest of the country.

What are the chances? There wasn't a single cloud between Florida and Utah the day we were to fly. So off we went. I first flew to Harrison, Arkansas, and picked up the guys. The flight overall went very well, with lots of anticipation, joyful experiences, and camaraderie. But I never forgot Laramie, Wyoming. We stopped for gas, and my weight and balance computation said we could fill up. So we did. I knew it was a high-altitude airport, so I checked my computations three times, ensuring that the airplane, with its powerful 200-HP engine, could fly with the weight of passengers, luggage, and fuel. We took off and rolled to the very end of the runway before slowly lumbering off in ground effect, an area of more dense air near the ground measuring up to the distance of the airplane's wingspan or about 40 feet. We cleared fence posts and fences for about two miles, which seemed like fifty miles, before we slowly climbed due to cooler air and burning off some weight in fuel. The airplane, which seemed like a sea-level rocket, seemed like a slug at this altitude. I never forgot the experience. It left a mark on me.

I asked Craig, "Who's going?" "Some guys you know that say they've flown with you, Chip, Dave, and Harper. There is also Greg, a student pilot in the flying club, Presley Melton from North Little Rock, who has been out west many times and is leading the trip, and a friend of his from Mississippi—eight airplanes counting you." "When are you leaving?" "September 20th, and probably be gone a week or ten days." "Okay, I'm in and looking forward to it!"

I talked to Elizabeth to ensure our calendar was clear, and she had no objections. She wanted to know why I couldn't fly with someone and split the gas to save money. It's a reasonable question for a wife and any human. It's also like asking a motorcycle rider why he doesn't wear a helmet. If you have to ask the question, you won't understand the answer. We all wanted the experience of flying our own airplanes in the wild, beautiful, safe, but unforgiving environment of the Rocky Mountains.

As for my concerns about getting some flight instruction before flying in the Rockies, flight instructors with mountain flying experience were going with us. Chip was a flight instructor. Dave was an airplane mechanic. Harper was an airline captain I'd flown with at American Airlines and in the backcountry. Craig was an airline and military pilot with thousands of hours of flight time, like me. Presley and Dave had made the trip out west many times. This turned out to be a beautiful arrangement with lots of flying insights and experiences shared.

We departed Bentonville a day early due to the weather, with a very windy landing our first afternoon in Garden City, Kansas. The winds were 25 gusting to 35 knots, with at least half of it a crosswind. We were all flying tailwheel airplanes, and they are known for their propensity to ground loop (drag a wing tip) in these conditions. We all felt like kissing the ground after landing and taxiing to the ramp. We chocked our airplanes quickly to keep them from being blown around. Then we watched as our most junior member, Greg, the student pilot flying a Husky, made his approach and landing. It was touch and go for a minute as it looked like it might get away from him as he fought the winds touching down. We were all cheering for him and, simultaneously, gritting our teeth, praying, knowing what kind of challenge this was for a pilot without much experience. He did it! This was the most adverse flying weather we encountered during the whole trip.

The next day we crossed the front range of the Rockies at Pueblo, CO, then flew directly over the Arkansas River and the Royal Gorge bridge. We continued on to Salida, and then turned north to beautiful Buena Vista where most of the guys spent the night. After a meal with the guys, and looking over the classy hotel on the banks of the Arkansas River, Craig and I opted to fly back to Salida for less expensive rooms and to catch up on old times. We flew a nice, tight, low-altitude formation flyby around the hotel as we departed Buena Vista for the benefit of our flight mates. The next day, we joined the formation as they flew overhead Salida.

Our third night was spent camping at a pristine grass

strip near Marble, Colorado. We had two very pleasant days, punctuated by a cold night, experiencing the joy, adventure, and serenity of the backcountry. A kind local couple picked us up and took us to a local BBQ restaurant for a nice dinner.

The aspens were turning yellow, and September in the Rockies at 8000 feet elevation made for a cold night of camping. I had a nice down sleeping bag. I often used it for winter canoeing and camping on the Buffalo River, so I was very comfortable. Not everyone in our crew reported the same results. Our airplanes were covered with dense frost the next morning and we repositioned them so the sun coming over the mountains could melt it off. Then we were on our way NW to Rangely, CO, where we took a flight planning and rest break before flying through the spectacular Dinosaur National Park at a relatively low altitude. Then we flew across Wyoming into Bear Lake County, Idaho, where the Idaho portion of our backcountry flying adventure began!

As we continued northwest to Challis for fuel, the scenery became more beautiful and spectacular. A sign at the airport read, "Welcome to Challis, Gateway to the Wilderness." We enjoyed stretching our legs, full fuel tanks, and the growing anticipation of backcountry strips and vistas near fabled Johnson Creek, Idaho.

We made the short flight to Stanley, ID, elevation 6253 feet, to spend the night. The hotel van picked us up, and we walked to an excellent dinner and a beautiful time of camaraderie, recounting the day's flying and scenery. There was also time to hear each other's stories and learn about flying experiences and lives. Clearly, this group of eight aviators were very compatible and would bond into some close friendships.

The subject of tactical call signs came up, like CB Radio handles for truckers. The fighter pilots mentioned they had names they used on the radio to identify each other and bark out time-critical instructions in aerial combat. The decision was made that we all should have individual call signs. Craig's was "Gore Dog," which makes sense. Mine was "Zadok." "What's that?" they all chimed in on the question. "He was a warrior priest under David, king of Israel, in the Bible." One of the guys piped up, "That's too hard. We're going to call you Prophet." And so it went. Harper was christened "Crispy," indicating how he liked his bacon. And Greg was given the name "Magellan." We're not saying he got lost a couple of times; he was finding his way.

The first full day of flying in the Johnson Creek area began with breakfast at the fly-in Sulphur Creek Ranch. Amazing! The whole place was decorated like the Wild West, with stuffed animals and saddles for bar stools. The chef wore a six-shooter on his hip as he made our delicious breakfast. We parked our airplanes beside the grass strip and walked a few steps into the lodge.

Later, at Indian Creek, our eight airplanes made a big impression on the forest ranger, closing up for the winter. We also visited with a Salmon River rafting group near the end of the runway. They were surprised by airplanes appearing in the remote wilderness and wanted to look at our planes and ask questions.

The canyons in the area were getting narrower and steeper. It was unwieldy to fly our eight-ship formation through them safely, keeping the terrain and all the other airplanes in sight, so we split up into four flights of two and put a half-mile space between our flights. This made for more relaxed flight-seeing. Craig and Dwayne were the first flight to land at Big Creek Lodge, where we all enjoyed a tasty lunch in gorgeous surroundings that resembled a Ralph Lauren designed log home.

Johnson Creek

A few more backcountry stops, a beautiful day of flying, and we arrived at our base of operations, Johnson Creek—3U2, N44-54.2 W115-29.1, elevation 4933 feet—the Mecca of Idaho's backcountry flying. Presley had arranged for us to borrow an old pickup truck from the lodge where we stayed in Yellow Pine. We loaded up and headed to our rustic rooms, which would be home for the next few days. With our gear put away, we drove into the small town and had dinner at the restaurant, followed by some pool games at the bar next door. But there were few games due to the lack of talent on display and because we anticipated more knock-dead-beautiful scenery the following day and wanted to rest before starting early. We had arrived, and it was as charming and awe-inspiring as we had imagined.

McCall, ID, was the nearest fuel stop in the region, so we all topped off there the next morning. It was a picturesque ten-minute flight from Johnson Creek, with an alpine feel and a glacial lake on the north end of town large enough for a dock and sailboats. Half the guys spent the day fishing on drift boats on the Salmon River. But Presley, David, Craig, and I struck out to enjoy more mountain flying and backcountry strips.

Presley told us about a short strip into the side of a mountain in rugged terrain, so we headed there first. The notes for

Soldier Bar, Idaho, read, "Recommended for emergency use only" and "Steep canyon walls in all directions." That was an accurate description, and it was a blast! We lingered there for some time, gazing at several thousand feet of granite above and below us.

The next day, the whole group flew together again, as per normal. After fueling at McCall, we climbed and crossed the Snake River, landing at a high-altitude grass strip called Memaloose, Oregon, elevation 6708 feet. It's on a precipice high on the west bank of the Snake River Hells Canyon National Recreation Area. The depth of the canyon below and the commanding view in all directions are surreal. We didn't want to leave this sight, but more vistas were calling us. We plunged off into the Snake River canyon and headed north, flying about 2000 feet above the river and 2000 feet below the rim of the canyon above, under some massive highline wires.

Presley, David, Craig, and I landed on a grass strip on the west bank of the Snake River, sat by the beautiful, dark, clear water, and enjoyed our sandwich lunches. We were amid Nez Perce National Historical Park, Oregon, and enjoyed reading informational plaques about the area's native American history at a boat-launching ramp near the water's edge.

We took off and headed north again, following the Snake River. When we got to the Salmon River, Presley and David turned to follow it and headed home to Johnson Creek and Yellow Pine. Craig and I decided to continue along the Snake River and land on a grass strip in Washington state, only fifteen miles farther, to say we had. Then we backtracked to the Salmon River and back to camp ourselves. We encountered some forest fire smoke just west of Yellow Pine that made canyon flying a little challenging, but we made it just fine and enjoyed an unusual sunset due to the smoke in the mountains as we tied our planes down for the night.

Before dinner that night at the "Corner—Great Food & Brew," we took a group photo as we noted the yellow and red trees lining the lanes, signaling the coming of winter. Tomorrow, we would head south, a day earlier than planned, in advance of the winter's first major snowstorm. But this evening, Buddy, Magellan, Crispy, Tater, Moon Pie, Gore Dog, Prophet, and MacGyver headed inside for a nice meal, fellowship, and then a good night's sleep.

Dave's C-170B had developed a mechanical problem, and Chip and Greg decided to stay with him until it was repaired. That took longer than expected, so they decided to fly straight back to Bentonville, AR. The rest of us headed south toward Nevada and Utah. We stopped in Wendover, UT, and refueled at an old Army Air Corps base for B-29s, which dropped the atom bombs ending WWII. We grabbed their loaner car and headed to an excellent Mexican restaurant just off the airfield. When it was time to head out, I noticed the Bonneville Salt Flats were just to the east of the field, about five minutes. We tried to do some quick research about the rules or possibility of landing on them, but hadn't found anything too definitive when Craig piped up and said, "Let's just land there!" So we did!

We got out and viewed the hard-packed table salt, as flat as a board, for as far as you could see. We took photos of each other and our airplanes and savored the last few minutes before taking off for Salt Lake City, then south to Price, UT, for the night.

The next day, we flew down the Green and Colorado

Rivers (Canyonlands National Park) to Lake Powell, Four Corners, and Santa Fe, New Mexico, for the night. What rugged beauty and grandeur! The desert Southwest is full of mystique and charm. Seeing its vastness, colors, and symmetry from the air was a humbling, rare privilege.

We decided to splurge and spent the night in a nice hotel downtown. We walked the streets of the artsy old cattle town with upscale shops and southwest charm. Then, we watched an incredible sunset from the upstairs Bell Tower Bar in the historic La Fonda Hotel overlooking the plaza and the end of the Santa Fe Trail.

The next morning, as we climbed out of Santa Fe, my Garmin GPS showed Bentonville, Arkansas, to be 548 nautical miles, and I was flying 124 knots with a nice tailwind. So the trip, if we didn't stop for gas, would take 4 hours and 24 minutes. Harper, in his C-180, did need gas, so he peeled off from our formation and eventually headed to his destination, Berryville, AR. Presley and David had already headed to Little Rock and Mississippi before Santa Fe.

On the last leg home now, Craig and I navigated some weather over Enid, Oklahoma, flying formation as we did the entire trip. We were friends from USAF class 79–06, Vance Air Force Base, Enid, Oklahoma, 40 years ago. And here we were again above the same airspace. The irony seems synchronistic and mysterious. Who knows where the winds of life and friendship will blow?

It was a dream trip with excellent weather, magnificent scenery, and worthy company. We flew about 2500 miles, a little farther than from NYC to Los Angeles, over nine days with 30 hours of flying. But then, "Life is not measured by the number of breaths we take, but by the moments that take our breath away" (Anonymous). It was that kind of adventure.

I didn't know it then, but this trip, as beautiful as it was on its own merits, along with the Alaska trip, prepared me for the next big flying adventure—flying to Honduras with a friend. Something else I never saw coming….

****

"Delight yourself in the Lord;
and He will give you the desires of your heart."
(Psalm 37:4)

"Even to your old age I will be the same,
And even to your graying years I will bear you!
I have done it, and I will carry you;
And I will bear you and I will deliver you."
(Isaiah 46:4)

"For of His fullness we have all received,
and grace upon grace."
(John 1:16)

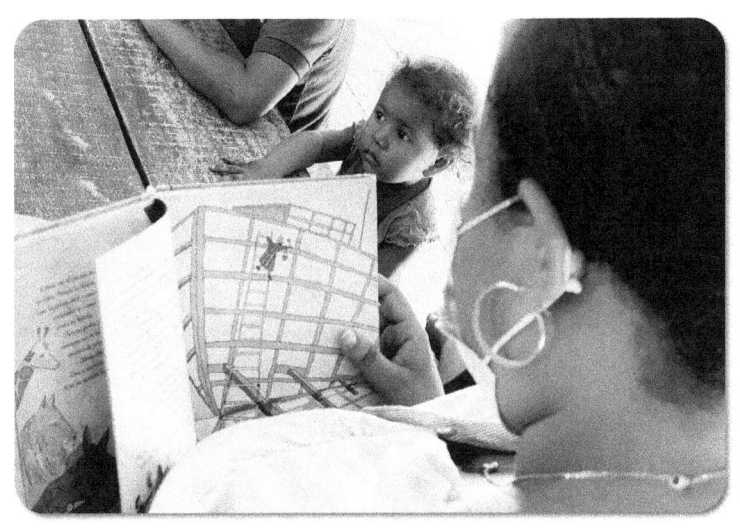

CHAPTER SEVEN

Flying Adventures — Honduras

"If I rise on the wings of the dawn, if I settle on the far side of the sea, even there your hand will guide me, your right hand will hold me fast."
(Psalm 139:9-10)

Journaling

Yesterday I located my journal from the Honduras trip. I'm so thankful that I journal. It's good to recapture the freshness of the experience. It's a bit like a photo for me. It causes time to stand still. It also brings back or triggers a flood of memories surrounding that time that couldn't be retrieved otherwise.

I'm thinking now about how I started an earlier book, *God Came Near*, with the lyrics of a Jim Croce song, *Time in a Bottle*.

> *If I could save time in a bottle*
> *The first thing that I'd like to do*
> *Is to save every day*
> *'Til eternity passes away*
> *Just to spend them with you*
> *If I could make days last forever*
> *If words could make wishes come true*
> *I'd save every day like a treasure and then*
> *Again, I would spend them with you*
> *But there never seems to be enough time*
> *To do the things you want to do*
> *Once you find them....*

Savoring the gift of time, the gift of life, the gift of love, the gift of friendship and adventure, the gift of beauty, all the gifts of God—that's what taking some time in solitude and silence to read, think, and record thoughts help me to do.

It's called journaling, and it's a spiritual discipline, habit, or rhythm like some of the others that draws one into a place of quiet listening for God's still, small voice, and many times, a dialogue with his Holy Spirit in stillness.

"**Be still, and know that I am God. I will be exalted among the nations, I will be exalted in the earth!**" (Psalm 46:10 ESV). "The Lord of hosts is with us; the God of Jacob is our fortress. Selah ["Selah"means stop and think about that]" (Psalm 46:11). "Be still and know...." If you're not still, you won't know.

I digress but with a purpose. I want to extol the habit of journaling to you. It slows one to the speed of life and being. It allows one or causes one to be alone with your thoughts and the Holy Spirit. It increases your spiritual sensitivity and the ability to hear and move in the spiritual realm. I usually do it before, after, or while I'm reading my Bible. But not always. This discipline or rhythm is a close cousin to solitude, silence, and meditation. In fact, that's what it is—meditation with a pen in your hand or nearby as you read, slowing to ponder questions arising or revelations and insights as they come. Just like one learns to canoe with a paddle in your hands, you learn to journal with a pen and paper in your hands. Give it a go. You'll discover how it works for yourself. It's more of an art than a science, and it might become a joy to you as you refine and make it your practice. It's simply, habitually taking time to think in silence, with a pen in your hand and paper nearby, writing some of your thoughts, then listening and recording others that might come to you.

Honduras 2021

In the fall of 2020, with the pandemic still raging, in the news at least, with the world seemingly perplexed at what to do, I was sitting on the patio at our mountain-top cabin with my journal, my Bible, and a cup of coffee. I paused for a sip and gazed at hundreds of square miles of green fields and forest below, with blue mountains stretching to the horizon from east to west. My phone, which lives on a silent ring, began to vibrate. I glanced at it and saw it was David Trapp, one of my Louisiana brothers, with whom I'd gone to Honduras on missions.

It made my heart smile that he was reaching out, and after a quick hello, he blurted out, "Can your airplane make it to Honduras?" Smiling inside at the outlandish, passionate question, I responded, "Yes, the airplane has been to Alaska. Why do you ask?" "Well, we want to send a couple of guys down there to see about drilling a water well in a village and to discuss plans for succession with Dario, the local pastor. We would pay for your gas and expenses. It would probably be cheaper than buying airline tickets."

Still smiling inside and happily flabbergasted at the way these kingdom brothers move freely in the Spirit, I replied: "It's possible. There would be a few governmental hoops to jump through, but they will work out if the Lord is in it. Give me a few minutes, and I will compute the distance, flying hours, and the approximate cost of fuel. I'll call you back, and you can decide if it's feasible." Then we hung up.

I sat there, still shocked and dumbfounded by how these spiritual adventurers are guided by the Spirit. I had the thought that in my last church, which had sponsored a few mission trips to Belize, this type of action would require numerous meetings and many months of discussion.

Within an hour I called him back with an estimate for fuel based on the most direct route, staying over land. Some people are reluctant to fly over the Gulf of Mexico or long stretches of water in a single-engine airplane. I doubt they would've objected but decided to take that option off the table. Their immediate response was, "Let's do it!" So, I started the planning with a list of all that needed to transpire before the trip. I had a fairly good checklist from the Alaska trip. But how might flying in Central America be different from Canada?

Among the biggest show-stoppers was my airplane's FAA registration, which had expired. My friend David, who was most responsible for the mission, didn't have a current passport either. With the COVID-19 bureaucratic slowdowns, both of these were big obstacles, and there was no crossing international borders without them. In faith, we continued to make preparations.

Most of my backcountry pilot friends were of little help. They wouldn't consider flying to Mexico due to the narco violence and media perception of lawlessness and corruption in the government. I told them they watch CNN too much, and if they did, they wouldn't go outside their houses. I surmised there were people who flew to Central America regularly, and I searched the web to discover the Baja Bush Pilots Association in Arizona. I joined so I could have the benefit of conversing with pilots who flew into Mexico and Central America on a regular basis. They were a big help and told me places to avoid, but in general, it was safe and enjoyable. They also had publications with current rules, frequencies, and boots-on-the-ground information on how things worked. They were a beautiful and welcomed part of the puzzle—recent experience from fellow pilots who have been there.

I called with my list of questions, and they put me through

to the top guy. He was friendly and helpful but very matter-of-fact, so I kept firing questions, and he fired back answers, leaving little room for questioning or chitchat. "Where are you going?" "Honduras, landing at San Pedro Sula, then flying around within one hundred miles or so of there." "Good, you'll love flying in Honduras. How are you going to get there?" "Well, we're planning to cross the border at Brownsville, Texas, and overnight the first night in Tampico or Veracruz." He interrupted, "Veracruz." "OK, thanks." "Then where are you going?" "Flores, Guatemala." "Why are you landing in Guatemala?" "Because it's on a straight line to our destination, the shortest distance." "Yeah, but you'll have to pay more landing fees and do more paperwork. Why don't you fly to Tapachula, Mexico, in the southwest corner, because you've already done all that in Mexico? Then you can refuel, maybe spend the night, and overfly Guatemala to your destination." "OK, thanks." That's how the conversation went; at least our plans were now in wet cement. After a few quick questions about security, air traffic control, and how customs and immigration work, we hung up.

Just before we did, he added, "You'll be calling me back!" I thought to myself, "This guy is a seer of sorts, very sure of himself and knowledgeable, but I doubt I'll call him back." But I did so—several times.

"Do I need to be concerned about the drug cartel stealing my airplane?" "No, not if you stop in the places we discussed, and besides, they won't steal a Maule. It's not the kind of airplane they like." I wondered why. Because I thought it would be a perfect drug-running airplane. It can haul all the weight you can put in it and land or take off from almost anywhere with just 300 feet to 600 feet of fairly level ground. But Mr.

Baja, as I came to call him, was so matter-of-fact and short I didn't question him. "Do I need to think about hiring a local security guard when I park the airplane overnight at some of these remote fields?" "No, we've never had anything stolen down there."

"I was a military pilot, and I know how to hide or not be detected by radar. Should I turn off my transponder and try to fly stealth through their airspace?" "No! They will think you're a drug runner for sure if they detect you. Turn on every electronic identification device you have. And be ready to be met in Tapachula by a 19-year-old soldier with an M-16 and a German shepherd. They will ask you to unload all your cargo and bags on the ramp and step away while they search the airplane and the dog sniffs your baggage. Then you're good to go, fuel, file a flight plan, and take off again." "Speaking of fuel, should I shop for the places with the cheapest aviation gas?" "No, gas is the same price at every airport in Central America. It's a monopoly. I think the price is about four dollars per gallon at the moment." After my questions, we enjoyed a little chitchat about his favorite airfields, places to visit, restaurants, and hotels along the route.

July 4, 2021

The planning was all done, and the preparation was complete. However, a week before departure, I still hadn't received my aircraft registration from the FAA in Oklahoma City. In what can only be explained as "an act of God," on the last business day before our scheduled launch on July 4, I made yet another phone call, got a knowledgeable human on the line, and someone with the authority to do so faxed me the required document.

David had not received his passport, and now it appeared that he wouldn't get it in time and be joining us on the journey. He was sad but OK with it. In hindsight, this was likely a blessing in disguise, as I learned later he was prone to motion sickness. He was also more than 6 feet tall, and I had clearly explained to David and Michael that the Maule could make the journey with no concern. But it would be a little bit like making the journey in a Volkswagen or sports car. The cockpit and cabin are adequate for medium-sized people but not so much for tall guys. He would have been cramped.

On July 4, I flew early from our cabin with my wife to Branson, Missouri, for an annual family reunion organized by my lovely and lovable aunt Joan, my mother's sister. After lunch, I dropped my wife back at our home airport in Springdale, Arkansas, and then flew to Monroe, Louisiana, to spend the night with David and Betsy. Before meeting them, I refueled the airplane and put it to bed in preparation for a dawn take-off the next day with Michael Clark for Honduras.

We were airborne at 7:30 AM and flew across Texas, passing just south of Houston and turning the corner over Corpus Christi. In fact, we flew directly over the aircraft carrier at the naval air station, then touched down at Brownsville, Texas, just after noon. The civilian aviation facility is in the old Pan Am terminal, which has many interesting memorabilia from that era. They gave us the keys to their loaner car and directions to a delicious local Mexican restaurant. We ate lunch while they fueled our plane and filed our flight plan to Veracruz.

We departed and arrived in Veracruz at 7:45 PM. Two

and one-half hours later, after being led from one office to another and paying this fee and that fee, which we were told to expect, Inspector Jesus, who was nice, said we were finished. It was good patience training. We hailed a taxi and made our way to the Hilton Garden Inn by the bay. Our room was hot, so we turned the air conditioner to max cold, went outside and sat by the beach in the breeze, debriefed our day, and planned our coming days as much as possible until a 1:00 AM bedtime. It was a long but great day overall. We both remarked that we felt the blessing and presence of the Holy Spirit.

We were up at 7:00 AM, had breakfast, took a taxi to the airport, paid more fees, and were airborne at 10:30 AM. While filing my flight plan, I learned that our planned airport in Honduras, La Ceiba, was closed for repaving the runway and would be unavailable the whole time we were there. We would need to cancel some reservations and make some new ones, but that is nothing new to travel or missions. We hoped to make a Honduras landing at about 5:00 PM if the breadcrumbs for our mission kept falling into place.

The flight over the mountains to Mexico's Pacific coast was beautiful but increasingly cloudy the further west we went. We found a clear area in the clouds near the coast and let down below the clouds for a low-level flight over about fifty miles of the Pacific coast beach. It was sparsely populated with no roads, and we flew about 100 to 500 feet above the ground or waves. The watercolors and beaches were breathtaking in their beauty. We saw only one beach resort, which was deserted due to the pandemic.

The flight into Tapachula, Mexico, was uneventful, with less bureaucracy and more help than Veracruz. The fuel guy charged us about $50 too much for gas. When we tried to tell the officials inside, they shrugged their shoulders and said, "Bad people." However, we had no recourse. We paid cash because their credit card machine was broken. And we needed to be on our way to make San Pedro Sula by 5 to 6 PM to get to Trujillo, our newly-planned place to spend the night.

By midday, the clouds building on the front range of the Guatemala mountains from the moist, warm Pacific Ocean were becoming significant. We had seen them as we descended to the clear areas along the coast. So, on departure, I figured we would climb to 7500 or 9500 feet and see if we could get around the mountains on top of the cloud deck. The weather forecasted along the Caribbean coast and at our destination was good for the rest of the day. As long as we had an escape route back along the Pacific with clear skies, we could return and spend the night in Tapachula. The weather guy in Tapachula, where I filed my flight plan, commented, "Not many people try to fly over the mountains in the afternoon." That gave me pause as I wondered if the Lord was trying to tell me something. But the plan for going forward looked reasonable, and the escape route for returning looked good. I told Michael we might fly for two hours toward Guatemala City and Honduras and then return to spend the night here. He said, "I'm with you, Boss."

I decided to try it. The cloud tops were low enough that we kept flying southeast with an escape route to the southwest. A reasonable distance away off the right wing, the sky was completely clear, and we could see the Pacific Ocean behind us, with the beach line extending seemingly all the way to El Salvador. We continued climbing to 10,500 feet, then 11,500 feet to stay on top of the rising clouds and away from several fully-blown thunderstorms with very high tops and lots of lightning. We had sketchy radio contact with Guatemala Radio. I hadn't heard anything from them in quite a while and doubted if they had radio or radar coverage to watch us in this high mountainous terrain. Flying into the clouds now was out of the question because some of the mountains in the area are more than thirteen thousand feet high.

There is something surreal, peaceful, and invigorating about flying in this unforgiving environment of mountains and clouds. You're far from anything familiar. You have to rely on your airplane, piloting skills, experience, and judgment about fuel, weather, divert options, communications, regulations, and many other things as you react to what you see and stay aware of what you might not see that could hurt you. It makes you feel alive, humble, and grateful for what you've been able to do, see, and experience.

I had to fly more southeasterly than I wanted, so I could stay out of the clouds. When we could finally return to our course for San Pedro Sula, we rounded a big thunderstorm extending to the heavens from the mountaintops. A controller suddenly came on the frequency and asked for our altitude. We were at 10,500 feet at the time in the clear with towering cumulus clouds all around us. His radio transmission was almost as frightening as it was reassuring, coming out of the blue: "N188DL (spoken as "November one eight eight Delta Lima"), do you see the mountain and volcano to your left?" At the time, we didn't, but in a few seconds, we flew into a clear area, looking straight down into the smoking cauldron of a massive volcano about 1000 feet below us! I responded, "Guatemala Radio, N188DL has the volcano and mountain in sight." He responded with, "Maintain VFR," which means, in layman's terms, "Don't fly into any clouds in your area; there are rocks in those clouds!"

It was impressive, to say the least! The site was magnificent and inspiring, and it was beautiful with its setting of blue-green mountains and bright white clouds peacefully towering around them, obscuring the mountaintops all around. A few seconds later, for the first time in a while, we saw a large patch of ground, and at the center of it lay Guatemala City!

Whew! A sense of relief and relaxation came over me as I knew we could at least land there if need be and spend the night without returning to Tapachula almost two hour's flying time behind us. And there was the promise we'd be able to continue to Honduras, which had come to look quite doubtful.

With a place of refuge in view, we continued our descent and committed to some scud running eastbound. This is low-altitude flying between the clouds and the ground if the visibility is good enough. I was comfortable doing that as long as I had suitable weather ahead, where it became clearer, with space between the ground and the clouds to fly comfortably and a clear path to return to the airport if the weather in front of us deteriorated. We continued onward. We were about one and a half hours from SAP (San Pedro Sula) but on the east side of the tallest mountains, with the weather improving.

Another remarkable thing occurred just after the controller told us about the volcano. I got a WhatsApp message from Gilberto, our mission travel contact in Honduras, asking if we were still planning to overnight in Trujillo. I texted that we were running late flying around the weather and would spend the night in San Pedro. He replied that it was a good idea and that he would cancel our room in Trujillo and get us one near the airport in San Pedro. And he would pick us up himself. I pinched myself and thought, "Did I just get a WhatsApp message among thirteen thousand-foot mountains in the middle of Guatemala when there was hardly a cell signal five short years ago? Technology is advancing at an amazing rate!"

I'm fifty miles east of Guatemala City now, following a major river and highway system to lower and lower terrain, thinking we'll make it from here. I also thought, "We should've left Veracruz at first light, say 6:00 AM, before all the clouds built over the mountains!" But we would have been running on only about four hours of sleep and needed to rest with some margin in our journey. Father is continually pointing out this to both of us as we run! Still, He helps us run and is continually with us. Grace.

The last hour of our flight was one of relaxed beauty and peaceful awe as we viewed this special part of creation. We followed mountain-dividing rivers and roads to lower terrain as we headed toward the coastal plains and the Caribbean Sea. The clouds were about 4500 feet above the ground, obscuring the mountains on either side of us, but a broad corridor of clear, if sometimes hazy, air lay in front of us. Bold and frequent lightning strikes from cloud to ground seemed close to our flight path on our right. They were powerful yet peaceful—a picture of when God comes near. There were one, two, and three brilliant rainbows on our right side, with one double rainbow as the valley widened and multiple rivers came together as one below us. Off to our left were mountains in the distance and Belize just a few miles away. We crossed the Guatemala and Honduras border, turned southeast into some lower but impressive mountains, and headed straight toward San Pedro Sula.

> Beauty. Grandeur. Simplicity. Peace. Joy.

We exited the mountains to the plains, and over San Pedro Sula airport we entered a left base turn and landed on Runway Four with a gentle breeze straight down the runway. After a smooth, short landing, we exited the runway and taxied immediately to the general aviation customs area, which was newly renovated in the old terminal building and the home of the Honduras Aero Club with its big, beautiful sign out front.

I had flown into San Pedro Sula several times before on the airlines as a passenger on mission trips and noted that sign. I even dreamed I might get checked out in one of their airplanes and fly around Honduras. I searched the web for a contact and information without success. And now here I was, flying my own airplane, sitting peacefully on the ramp with the promise of flying around Honduras the next few days on a kingdom mission to serve, love, and follow the Spirit's leading with His provision and empowerment with a friend. It was a real-life picture of being a son, a child, a servant, a friend of the King! My definition, understanding, and experience of grace continue to expand as I journey and abide with Him.

From my journal before falling asleep: "I feel so blessed, so humbled, so happy, so at rest, and at peace. Thank you, Lord! That seems small, once again. But my heart is full, and I offer thanks to You. It's all I can do. As I'm coming to believe, it is all You require, and pleases You. Ephesians 2:8-9."

We Made It!

From my journal the next morning: "July 7, 2021, 0600L up drinking coffee, worshiping, journaling. After a long day of flying yesterday, spectacular but physically and mentally draining, Michael and I had a nice dinner at Larsons, beside my favorite little hotel near the airport."

"Gilberto picked us up with his wife, which was a tremendous blessing (maybe a $1500 blessing—a story for later). Provision and leading will be the storyline of this mission and adventure, or so it seems. Our drive to the hotel from the Aeropuerto was seamless. Our comfortable room was ready, and the adjacent restaurant, which appeared to be closed due to the pandemic, was actually open for hotel guests. We had a delicious meal over conversation with a delightful waitress who turned out to be a believer."

"Michael asked if he could pray for her as he paid our bill. She said yes. 'What is the biggest, most pressing thing in your life where you need help from the Lord?' 'My sister is having surgery tomorrow. Please pray for my sister.' We both did, right there in the restaurant. Then Michael asked, 'Where is your sister?' 'She's in the hotel next door (our hotel). She's the manager.' Michael said, 'We'll go over and pray for her right now.' This we did with her being very receptive, and the beautiful young woman, impeccably dressed, held her hands out, palms up with tears eventually running down her cheeks. It was a holy moment of a normal Christian life by the front desk with her employees looking on and listening. Thank you, Lord, for the simplicity of listening to you and saying and doing what we hear."

"The thought comes to me now, 'As spiritually sensitive

as Michael is and effective as the Holy Spirit is in him, there is no telling how powerful he would be if there was more margin, stillness, and solitude in his walk and life! We'll see if I'm led to tell him or suggest such as we journey.' It's been a treat for both of us as we're very compatible and becoming even closer friends and brothers."

"In a few hours, we'll see what awaits us in Olanchito. That will happen at about noon instead of the planned 8:00 AM. I think the Lord is slowing us down on purpose to the speed of Honduras, the speed of relationship, the speed of spiritual life."

"Being. Listening. Yoked. Abiding…in His grace. Forever. Amen."

"It's time to eat, write in Dario's gift books, shower, and amble to the airport at 9 AM to see what awaits us today."

Olanchito, Honduras

Olanchito is a five-hour drive from San Pedro Sula but only a thirty-minute flight over the mountains. We land at the private Dole Pineapple airfield with permission obtained because of the pastor's excellent reputation in the community. It's near Coyoles, about ten minutes from Olanchito. I try to park out of the way in the grass and away from the immaculate crop dusters, but they marshal me right up front to a place of honor and tell me to leave it there. "It will be fine, and we'll move it if we need to do so."

We express our thanks for their hospitality and shake hands with everyone coming out to check out our plane. Pastor Dario then drives up, greets them in Spanish, and whisks us into town to their church, where there is a little reception for us with hugs and smiles all around. Michael gives them greetings from our churches and people they know. Pastor Dario tells the congregation a little bit about our purpose and mission there. We pray over our time together and share a meal they have prepared. It was an enjoyable time of hospitality, fellowship, and goodwill.

In the early afternoon, Pastor Dario, his associate pastor, Leonardo, Michael, and I met privately in the church office. Michael is the representative of Covenant Life Fellowship of West Monroe, Louisiana, a church that has had almost two decades of relationship with this Olanchito church. I've been on a few mission trips here, so I know everyone, but I'm mainly there to observe, pray, and counsel if needed, and as the pilot. Michael hadn't shared much of the agenda with me. I was very impressed at how focused and deliberate he was as they launched right into discussion and church business.

The church was recently broken into, and their sound equipment was stolen. It was somewhat antiquated, but it was all they had. Numbers were thrown around about what was needed, the cost of replacement, and the priority of what should be purchased. Other church needs were discussed. Then, before I knew it, Michael and the pastors had agreed on the priorities, and Michael started counting out several thousand dollars in stacks of one hundred dollar bills for each need to be met. I've never seen anything like it, but I wasn't shocked either. That's how these brothers roll—Spirit-led and generous, with deep trust centered around Christ and His kingdom.

It was approaching dinner time, so Dario drove us to the airplane. On the way, we talked about his plans for succession. We both encouraged him not to wait too long to turn the reins over to his successor so he could help him if he stumbled or had troubles. But we also reassured him that we knew that God had made him Pastor and invested that spiritual authority with him, so it was his decision to make. With the conclusion of this discussion and the day's activities, one-half of our mission was complete. Unknown to us, we had a big treat in store for dinner and our night's lodging.

Trujillo

The staff at the Dole Pineapple airstrip treated us like royalty. They said we were welcome to visit anytime, and when we returned tomorrow, we would park in the same place right up front, where they had chocked the plane and placed protective cones around it. The flight to Trujillo would take about thirty minutes. On my first mission trip to Honduras a few years before, a veterinarian we called Bro. Dr. Jay in our group had scouted out some places to bring veterinarian students later on a public service, educational, animal husbandry mission. At dinner one night, he exclaimed to me: "Dwayne, I went to a city today on the coast named Trujillo, and they have a runway right in town, on the beach practically!" That made my spirit jump, and ever since that time, I've hoped to see it and maybe fly there someday. Today was that day!

I had been making all our hotel reservations through web research and phone calls until now, but with so many changes, from runway closures to weather in the mountains of Guatemala, I decided to let Gilberto, our mission travel agent, take over. I reasoned that WhatsApp worked very well for communicating with him. He knew the lay of the land for the best accommodations and could negotiate better prices than I could, being a native. He agreed. He was always quick to answer and act.

When I asked him about Trujillo, he said it was an excellent location, with a very nice hotel right by the runway near the water. It was reasonably priced, and because it was so remote, natives used it more than tourists. All this was music to my ears, and we had him book us a room. He added, "Oh, I must tell you, we have to call the authorities because they must have notice to clear the runway for you. But I'll do that." I thought, "That's wonderful! What a country!"

Well, it almost went that way. From about ten minutes out, the scenery became more and more beautiful, with sandy beaches, palm trees, and green mountains tumbling down into the turquoise sea. Then, we spotted the colorful, picturesque town perched on a steep mountainside extending from the top of the mountain to the sea. And there, near the water, was the runway between the hotel by the water's edge and the city. Perfect, except that it appeared to be full of people and vehicles!

So much for local authorities clearing the runway and things going exactly as planned! Gilberto told me previously that the locals also used the runway for jogging, walking, strolling with baby carriages, and even racing their motorcycles. What was I to do? Well, the fighter pilot came out in me a little bit. I reasoned that they knew it was a runway, and I just needed to let them know there was an airplane in the area. So I told Michael, "I'm going to buzz them so everyone will know we're here, and they'll probably clear the runway and stay clear." He nodded quizzically as I went into a steep, fast dive for the near end of the runway, with my landing lights and all my lights turned on, leveling off maybe ten to twenty feet above their heads. Flying about 150 MPH along the length of the runway, I pitched up to a normal left downwind over the water, slowed, put the flaps down, turned base to the final approach, and landed. No one was seen on the runway or anywhere near it.

We taxied a short distance to about fifty feet from the hotel entrance, swung the tail around toward the wall that separated the runway from the hotel, shut down the engine, retrieved our bags, and walked thirty paces into the beautiful hotel lobby for check-in. It was a dream.

After checking into our pleasant room with windows and a balcony facing the bay, I went back out to tie the airplane down for the night, and we had a nice dinner at the classy hotel. The place had a colonial feel with big stairways, lots of wood, and high ceilings, with the air of a more peaceful and civil time. The staff was friendly with an air of respect and honor for their guests. The food was delicious, and our dinner and breakfast were served in an elegant dining room decorated with wall murals of Christopher Columbus and his exploits.

Christopher Columbus landed in Trujillo on August 14, 1502, during his fourth and final voyage to the Americas, and wintered here with his ships and men. At one time, Trujillo was the capital of Honduras. However, it turned out to be too remote and hard to defend to remain the capital. Its beautiful hotel was now a hospitable respite for travelers and local people coming to rest and relax in its beautiful mountain and sea atmosphere.

Michael and I reminded each other at breakfast of what we had said over lunch in Brownsville, Texas, before venturing into Central America and looking to do the Lord's bidding in Honduras. We felt His pleasure, a sense of mission, and an awareness of His grace surrounding us. We said we would be good stewards of the King's money and faithful to the church that sent us, but we would enjoy our journey as sons of the King, which indeed we are. We certainly felt His grace in Trujillo.

Water For Bethany

After breakfast, we leisurely read, journaled, and ambled to the airplane to fly back to the plantation airstrip near Coyoles and Olanchito. Between the two towns was the small but growing town of Bethany. Pastor Dario's church had established a church plant there, and the building used by the church was doubling as a school.

We met two beautiful and charming young women, Mary and Yelina, recent college graduates who were the teachers, as they rode up on Mary's moped to begin class for the day. The facility was very humble but adequate. It gave young kids in this village a chance to learn to read, write, and do some arithmetic, which would put them in a better position for their future. They would also learn about God and history from the Bible to nurture their souls and spiritual beings.

The Louisiana brothers had learned that there was no water in this village. The villagers collected rainwater, but it was inadequate. People hauled water from the city or a nearby river. A commercial truck came around selling water every day, and even though the cost was reasonable, it was more than most people could afford. We were there to survey the situation for a well's feasibility, plumbing, and electrical availability and hear the pastor's heart on the situation. We also got to see these young teachers pour their hearts and abilities into teaching young children who were among the poorest of the poor. It was humbling to be there and witness the poverty as well as the love and hope. We put our hearts into doing what we were tasked to do, praying as we went that it would work out and that God would provide water and a better life for these little ones.

The Spirit was with us and blessing our mission there. In my quiet time that morning, I journaled the following verses:

> "**Surely God is my salvation; I will trust and not be afraid. The Lord, the Lord himself, is my strength and my defense**; he has become my salvation. **With joy you will draw water from the wells** of salvation. In that day **you will say: 'Give praise to the Lord, proclaim his name; make known among the nations** what he has done, and proclaim that his name is exalted. Sing to the Lord, for he has done glorious things; **let this be known to all the world.** Shout aloud and sing for joy, people of Zion, for **great is the Holy One** of Israel among you.'"
> (Isaiah 12:2-6 NIV)

We measured distances from electrical poles, estimated the necessary plumbing supplies, talked to several people about their ideas, took photos of the site, got the contact information of well-drillers in the area, and listened to the school class conducted while we did our work. We met some of the neighbors and prayed for them in their yards or homes. We were finished by noon, and I asked pastor Dario, if there was any other use he might have for the airplane while we were there. I offered to fly him and his sweet wife to Tegucigalpa to visit their family if they wanted. It's a ten-hour bus ride and only a one-hour flight over the mountains. There wasn't anything more he could think of at the moment, and he thanked us for the offer and for coming.

Ever spiritually sensitive, Michael asked the pastor, "What is the biggest need in Mary's life?" "That moped! She bought it new, and the payment takes a large part of her meager salary. It's like a chain around her neck." "How much does she owe on it?" "Three hundred seventy dollars," he replied immediately as he stepped out of his Toyota 4WD pickup to speak with a friend who waved us down. Michael and I looked at each other and said at the same time, "We're going to buy that moped for her." We did not have that much cash left individually, but we pooled our money, and Michael gave it to Dario when he came back to the truck and told him what we wanted to do. He smiled broadly and happily and said he'd take care of it.

Pastor Dario mentored several young high school and college kids who translated for us, led worship and helped with youth activities when we came on mission trips. We knew them well and asked if we might treat them to lunch at a restaurant in town to encourage them and catch up on their lives and dreams. The pastor started making phone calls as we drove toward town to meet them. I asked Michael where he wanted to spend the night, as we appeared to be finished with our mission and could start home the next day. I mentioned San Pedro Sula, Tegucigalpa, and Roatan as options. He jumped at Roatan, as he was a diver and had heard lots about the place. I texted Gilberto, and he said, "I don't know anything about flying your plane there, but I can get you a hotel with transportation to and from the airport." "Perfect, do that, and I'll figure out the rest."

Our lunch with the pastors and young people was lively

and joyful as they were full of life and sharing about Jesus in their culture. When we finished eating and saying our goodbyes, Pastor Dario said he was taking Mary to the bank to pay off her moped, and Lao could drive us to the airport for our afternoon departure. The kids wanted to go, so they piled into the back of the pickup, and off we went.

Unfortunately, the kids were not allowed to accompany us to the airplane due to security restrictions. Instead, they jumped out and waited by the fence where they could see us start up and fly away. I told them I'd fly right over their heads for a good look and did so. Now, we were flying out to the east again toward the coast with a smile on our lips and hearts. These people are like family. And the Lord is in their midst.

We're reminded of the verse David Trapp gave us the morning we left Monroe: "And **if anyone gives even a cup of cold water to one of these little ones** who is my disciple, truly I tell you, that person will certainly not lose their reward" (Matthew 10:42 NIV). Another verse that has come to us repeatedly is: "**If I rise on the wings of the dawn**, if I settle on the far side of the sea, **even there your hand will guide me**, your right hand will hold me fast" (Psalm 139:9-10).

Roatan

Roatan is an island about forty miles off the northern coast of Honduras. Its white, sandy beaches, beautiful blue waters, size, and location have made it the Hawaii of the Caribbean. Gilberto made our reservations at the Henry Morgan Hotel on the West End beach with free transportation to the airport. The flight from Olanchito was gorgeous, with about 30 minutes over land and 20 minutes over water. We tied down the plane, made our way through customs, enjoyed the scenic ride to the fancy hotel, enjoyed a fabulous island buffet dinner, and then sat out in the evening sea breeze, rehearsing the day's activities and listening to the gentle surf before turning in early to get some needed rest.

After breakfast, we took a water taxi to Fosters and the shops in that area to buy some souvenirs and enjoy viewing the shoreline from a boat. At 1:00 PM, we took off and flew the length of the island and back at 500 feet above the ground, admiring the island's beauty one last time before departing toward San Pedro Sula. A few years back, I visited Roatan on a mission with a sister church in Fort Smith, doing some children's ministry and putting a large collection and water distribution tank in a church and village on the island's east end. It was an extreme joy to revisit the island in such an unusual and intimate fashion with a friend, flying my own airplane.

Wearing our lifejackets, we climbed to three thousand feet and enjoyed a nice tailwind on the 50-minute flight to San Pedro Sula. Baja Jack had told me, "Wear them! It will be confusing, and you might not have time to put them on if you end up in the water." Michael flew half the time on the way there and much of the trip. I started our journey, letting him fly a little bit to see what it was like and answer any questions he might have. But he was so inquisitive and good at it that I just kept giving him pointers and letting him fly. He was a natural! Of course, I made all the landings, but he took it down to fifty feet a few times.

At San Pedro Sula, we relaxed while fueling, adding oil, and cleaning our windshield. We filed our flight plan so we could blast off as soon as the airport opened for immigration the next day at 7:00 AM. We went back to the micro-hotel again and had a beautiful dinner and debrief at Larson's restaurant. We discovered Karen was fine after her surgery and returning to work on Monday. It was a beautiful day of rest and flying, with flying preparation for the long trip home beginning tomorrow.

Weather and circumstances permitting, our plan was to fly from San Pedro Sula to Tapachula, Mexico, for refueling and customs, then on to Puebla, Mexico, to spend the night. We'd see how far we could get toward home the following day. The adventure and beauty of Central American flying continue. We both feel so grateful to the Lord. What a dream trip and mission adventure! We are humbled and pleased. "Grace upon grace," a phrase found in John 1:16, couldn't feel more accurate and true.

I called my wife, who was at our cabin enjoying some time with our friends Flora and Michelle. She was also helping our Fort Smith friends, Adam and Angie, get into our house in Northwest Arkansas to spend the night after a wedding. I made a spreadsheet to help Michael with expense recording and reporting to his church about our trip. It was time to ease back into home life and thinking, still two thousand miles away, and to check in with the wife. Overall, it was a calm, restful day of recoup and recovery after two successful mission days and before beginning the two-day or three-day trip home at 6:40 AM tomorrow. Our heads hit the pillow with grateful, peaceful hearts, yet we anticipate tomorrow's travel sights and adventures with excitement.

Guatemala and Puebla, Mexico

From my journal on July 10: "I am up at 5:30 AM in the hotel lobby to drink coffee and write. Isaiah chapter twelve continues to ring in my ears for our trip as I read and meditate on it and note a few thoughts. We start for home today, and international flight planning duties now distract me from my quiet time. We'll fly from San Pedro Sula over Guatemala to Tapachula, Mexico, then to Puebla and spend the night. It's about a seven or eight-hour flight, and we need to get an early start to avoid the clouds and storms that form every afternoon over the 13,000-foot mountains and jungles of Guatemala. There will be mountains and clouds between Tapachula on Mexico's Pacific coast and Pueblo near Mexico City, too. Hopefully, we'll be able to pick our way through them or return to Tapachula for the night. We carry about 6 to 7 hours of fuel to begin every leg, so we have options."

Oh no. I just checked in on Michael to see if he's up and learned that our driver's car wouldn't start. We must call a taxi, and the famous Central American delays have already begun. Everything goes smoothly at the airport as the customs and airport operations personnel know us by now, and we have a good camaraderie with them. Soon, we're climbing out on a perfect weather day. The scenery is beautiful and surreal. We can see Guatemala under clear skies now as opposed to our ingress. The greens and blues of mountains and jungles are as pleasing to the eyes as the multicolored villages and cities that dot the land with its steams, jungles, towering mountains, volcanos, and waterfalls.

Landing in Tapachula on the Mexican-Guatemalan border was easy for us this time. We cleared customs and immigration with the drug dog inspection, filed our next flight plan, and fueled. As you may recall, this was the place where we experienced our only known attempt at bribery or extortion when the guy charged us $50 too much for fuel. We had them fill us up, and then when they told us their credit card machine was broken, and we needed to pay cash, I refused. I was going to make a little fight or fuss about the previous transgression, but in the end, I would do whatever they said. It was their country, and we wanted to get home. To our great surprise, they said, "OK, you can pay for the gas when you get to Puebla. Their credit card machine works."

Michael and I looked at each other incredulously, got in the airplane, and flew away. One of my big takeaways from flying in Mexico is that there are many more mountains than I ever dreamed. The country is also longer and larger than I imagined when I experienced it up close and personal. The clouds from the Pacific Ocean were there and growing as the afternoon progressed, but we were able to pick our way around them and landed in Puebla in the early afternoon.

Puebla is the fourth largest city in Mexico, after Mexico City, Monterrey, and Guadalajara. More than twenty years ago, I flew there somewhat regularly as an American Airlines Fokker-100 captain. I always loved it. It was what I imagined old Mexico to be—lots of farms and ranches with animals working the fields, men with sombreros and hand tools, coming and going from small villages with pastel, colorful homes. TripAdvisor says that the area has somehow escaped the narco violence that plagues Mexico. Known for its culinary history, colonial architecture, and pottery, it has a Renaissance-era Cathedral with tall bell towers overlooking the central square. Quite by accident or grace, we stayed near the square.

We closed our flight plan, ordered fuel to fill the airplane for the next morning's flight, and called a taxi to drive us to our hotel. The place was gorgeous—an old nunnery or convent converted to a hotel in the center of the city. It looked like it could have been designed by Ralph Lauren, with its tasteful, beautiful furnishings celebrating the area's strong, traditional, timeless, and cultural history.

I asked if I could pay now to expedite our checkout because we anticipated an early departure for the airport the next morning. The charming lady at the desk said, "Of course," and told me the amount. It was about twenty percent more than I had been quoted when making the reservation. When I inquired why, she looked at my reservation and told me that was a different hotel with exactly the same name about twenty minutes away. Well, this hotel was knock-dead beautiful, right downtown, and we were here, tired from a day of flying. "We'll be delighted to stay," I humbly told the gracious host, "and the rate is quite reasonable."

We walked around the architecturally impressive colonial city center, had a delicious five-course meal in a charming restaurant, and watched the people of a more laid-back culture enjoy their evening. Then, we returned to our hotel and explored its interior, finding it to be even more special, elegant, and beautiful than we initially observed. We fell asleep at 8:36 PM. I noted the time we crawled into our beds in my journal and then found it on the floor with my glasses at 7:00 AM the next morning, waking a bit late after setting no alarm.

So we arrived a little bit late at the airport, but it wouldn't have helped if we had arrived at 7:00, 8:00, or 9:00 AM because the necessary authorities were not there. We took off at 11:00 AM, which was three hours later due to procedures that would have taken fifteen to thirty minutes in the States!

I almost felt the Lord saying, "How are you doing at extending grace?" and, " You should consider slowing to their speed and thinking about their pace." The people we were dealing with were childlike and sincere, and I knew they were doing their best. But I was having a little trouble reconciling the fact that we were at an international airport, and almost no one spoke English. And we had paid an extra hundred dollars for immigration personnel to come out and meet us because it was the weekend. The first thoughts I had prevailed in the moment, and I settled down in my spirit to await their arrival and slow to their speed.

We taxied to the active runway, which is at a height of 7300 feet above sea level, under splendid clear skies and a desert temperature of 70°F. Two massive, snow-covered, active volcanic mountains were nearby as a backdrop when facing west toward Mexico City, which was only 100 miles away. Beautiful! Exquisite! Peaceful! Surreal!

But alas, we needed to get going! We had a long day of flying ahead, and as the sun hits the earth, clouds will form quickly, producing thunderstorms and mountaintop obscurity. There are many mountains between Puebla and the Caribbean! And they are high! Indeed, the Maule didn't leap off the ground or climb like a homesick angel, as is her norm nearer sea level pressures. I was slightly surprised, but I shouldn't have been. At 7000 feet elevation, full of fuel, close to maximum takeoff weight, climbing to 2500 feet above the terrain already had us at 9500 feet above sea level. Light aircraft with reciprocating engines produce a lot less power at these high altitudes, and the wings produce less lift.

Some of the most beautiful scenery of our entire trip was experienced on this leg of the journey. We flew over the high desert, with volcanic fertile fields, then headed into the alpine mountains between Puebla and Tampico. There was some scud running with the ever-rising terrain a factor. I elected to stay beneath the clouds as long as visibility combined with cloud and terrain clearance allowed, with an escape path directly behind if I needed one.

It looked like I might be able to climb above the clouds if suitable holes or breaks in the overcast presented themselves. Climbing in the clouds with so many mountains around was out of the question. There continued to be occasional breaks in the clouds above as we proceeded and viewed some of the most rugged mountains and canyons I've seen on the planet not far beneath us. These mountains were dotted with colorful villages and brightly painted churches with adjacent cemeteries at their centers.

Finally, with mountains all around shrouded in clouds, there appeared a big, open, clear space to attempt to climb to get on top of the clouds, which looked to be about 10,000 to 12,000 feet above sea level. So I began to climb to get on top where I could see the mountains if they poked up through the clouds and fly around them. I had to make one 360° turn, gaining altitude to get on top of the clouds at about 11,500 feet. We eventually climbed to 12,500 feet to stay on top of the clouds, where we could see the mountains that were higher than that. We flew there for an hour, then began a slow descent back to 9500 feet as we approached the coastal plains at Tampico.

We were enjoying a 20-to-30-knot tailwind already, which we would enjoy all day! That's fantastic and not normal. It meant we were not moving along the ground at the Maule's normal pace of 135 mph, or even less if we had a headwind, but often at 165 miles an hour to 180 mph. This makes a huge difference when one is flying for 10 or 11 hours. During this time, I uttered several silent prayers thanking the Lord for this tailwind. And for the wind of His Spirit, the tailwind of His grace, power, provision, and favor.

Getting through U.S. Customs at Brownsville, Texas, was a breeze. We decided not to fill up with fuel there or eat lunch but to continue on to Lake Jackson, Texas, where fuel was cheaper—$4.10/gallon v.s. $5.65/gallon. There was a cafe right on the field where we parked after refueling and walked inside. It was a great meal and rest stop made feasible by the tailwind!

Then, I let Michael take off and fly through Houston's airspace to Monroe, Louisiana. The flight took only two hours and ten minutes with the big tailwind! Michael loved flying the Maule and had an incredible aptitude for it, flying at least half of the entire 34-hour journey. I took over at about 3000 feet, flew the pattern, and landed.

His beautiful, smiling wife, Amy, greeted us along with the sole airport attendant, who said they would close in ten minutes. As I said bye to Michael and Amy, he filled the plane with fuel. I added a quart of oil, cleaned the windscreen, and departed just before sunset.

It was an incredible sunset with a moonrise near Venus, oranges and blues amid white clouds, and the blackness of deep space beyond the stars. Directly along my flight route was a large area of thunderstorms near Hot Springs, Arkansas. The tops didn't appear too high, and I thought briefly about flying over them at 10,500 feet to 12,500 feet. But the very frequent lightning, cloud to cloud, inside them, although beautiful and awe-inspiring, was too ominous for flight above or below them. I decided I'd fly around them to the west to ensure a safe distance from the lightning, hail, and severe turbulence often associated with thunderstorms, which have been known to tear airplanes apart.

I flew almost to Texarkana into the sunset before I could turn the corner where there was no lightning and passed along the cloud tops at 12,500 feet. I briefly climbed to 13,500 feet, the highest I had ever flown the Maule, and headed directly to Springdale, Arkansas, passing Mena off my left and Hot Springs off my right, about equidistant. With the big tailwind decreasing but still pushing me along at a good clip, I was soon over Booneville and then over I-40 east of Fort Smith where the lights at Fort Smith and Russellville were visible off my left and right sides, and the glow of Northwest Arkansas lights was visible over my nose on the horizon. I descended to 6500 feet over the Boston mountains to stay beneath some higher clouds, keeping visual contact with the ground and avoiding the threat of hypoxia at the 12,000-foot and higher altitudes.

The Fayetteville and Springdale air traffic control towers were closed for the night. I didn't talk to anyone from Monroe onward, so I made a peaceful, silent approach and landed at Springdale at 11:00 PM. Wow! What a day! What a peaceful, smooth flight with an awesome and awe-inspiring power display off my right side as I neared the end of this journey home.

I've often enjoyed these storms, feeling they were tokens of God's presence, power, and blessing. They make me feel His favor and remind me of His great power to protect, keep His promises, and love His children and creation.

I pulled into my garage at 11:30 PM and got a big hug from my beautiful wife, Elizabeth, who greeted me at the door. Soon thereafter, I crawled into bed and received a text from Doug Lamb, one of my best friends, a former fighter pilot, the guy who sold me the Maule and flew it to Alaska with me in 2017. He had followed our flight progress on the web via our inReach satellite device all day. His text read:

> "This has been an incredible day for Maule Aviation, Dwayne Bell. You flew all the way from Mexico City to Springdale in one day and didn't start the flight until late morning!! You and your Maule are unstoppable! Richard Branson has no bragging rights over your feat today! Welcome home, my friend and Maule aviator extraordinaire."

I would later learn that Richard Branson the billionaire became the first civilian to travel to the edge of space, some 53 miles high, with a few others in a winged aircraft on this same day, July 11, 2021.

I texted, "Thanks, friend! :):)" and then fell asleep. His noticing meant a lot to me!

The following morning, I received a text from Joe Carruth, a close personal friend whose life is given to prayer, worship, and knowing God:

> "Praying for your safe return and looking forward to seeing you. This verse seemed to be for you this morning: 'By this my Father is glorified, that you bear much fruit and so prove to be my disciples'" (John 15:8 ESV).

Later in the morning, Michael and I text each other verses, details, and thoughts about the trip. We both agreed it had been an Ephesians 3:20 adventure, "Above all we could think or ask." Years earlier, Charles Duke, an astronaut who walked on the moon, wrote that reference on the inside cover of my Bible. It says, "Now to Him who is able to do far more abundantly than all that we ask or think, according to the power at work within us" (Ephesians 3:20).

I wrote this prayer in my journal that morning: "Father, as we bask and meditate on all we saw and You did, continue to open our eyes and hearts to see what You would show us or say to us. Your servants are listening."

****

> *"And if anyone gives even a cup of cold water to one of these little ones who is my disciple, truly I tell you, that person will certainly not lose their reward."*
> (Matthew 10:42 NIV)

> *"But we request of you, brethren, that you appreciate those who diligently labor among you, and have charge over you in the Lord and give you instruction, and that you esteem them very highly in love because of their work. Live in peace with one another."*
> (1 Thessalonians 5:12-13)

CHAPTER EIGHT

Flying Adventures — Aircraft Delivery

"None of us will ever accomplish anything excellent or commanding except when he listens to this whisper which is heard by him alone."
—Ralph Waldo Emerson

We're Going to Get That Airplane!

This flying story is the home plate of a home run of flying adventures in the last ten years. The first base was Alaska, the second base was Idaho and the western US, then the third base was Honduras and Central America. Now, I'm about to pick up an airplane with a friend from the factory in the Pacific Northwest and fly it back to Arkansas with its new owner. I still muse, "You can't make this stuff up!" Or, "Has this really happened to me?" Deep inside, I smile and know it's "Grace upon grace" (John 1:16b). These adventures involve faith, flight, fellowship, and friends. That's what makes them so special.

My friend Jim is just a few years older than me, and he mentored me as a young F-4 pilot in our fighter squadron and as a new pilot at American Airlines. For several years after he retired, my friends and I badgered him to buy an airplane and join us in the fun we were having. We reasoned that he could afford it, knew how to fly, and it would be useful for him to visit his elderly parents across the state from us. But for some reason, he wouldn't do it, so we gave up pressuring him and just took him with us whenever we could.

So I was shocked earlier this year when he called me and said, "I just bought an airplane." "What kind of airplane?" "A Vashon Ranger manufactured north of Seattle." "How are you gonna get it here and get some training?" "I'm having a pilot from the factory deliver it here, give me some instruction, and then I'll buy him an airline ticket home." I thought about it momentarily and then blurted out, "You are not! We are going to fly up there and get that plane! This is an earth event—getting a new airplane from the factory! We will fly out there on American Airlines and fly the plane back ourselves, familiarizing you with the airplane and savoring another sightseeing and friendship adventure." "Would you do that?" "Certainly!" And the stage was set.

Reservations

I knew Jim would have some reservations. Even though he was a very capable pilot with fighter and airline experience spanning four decades, it had been a long time since he flew light airplanes in the general aviation environment. He would have to learn to do his own flight planning, get his own weather, relearn the rules, find out what might have changed, and knock the rust off of his flying skills. I would have the same concerns if I were in his shoes, but I had been flying in this environment for the last ten years. So I reasoned that I could help him, and we could have fun with it, plus experience seeing a lot of the United States from the air in a beautiful way we both enjoyed. He would spend the money for delivery anyway, so we could enjoy the flying, get him off to a good start with his new airplane, and make a memory. I would want someone to do the same for me.

We are kindred spirits in travel and adventure, not to mention our love for flying. We have traveled together to Machu Picchu, Greenland, Iceland, took an Amtrak across the northern United States and back through the Rocky Mountains and the Great Plains to Chicago, flew to Alaska in small airplanes, rode ATVs in Colorado, and climbed Mt. Fuji. We like hanging out with each other and with Doug, Ken, and others who accompanied us on some of these adventures. We are comfortable travel companions with deep trust in each other and grateful for our relationships with each other and God.

Seattle Bound

This turned out to have a double meaning. As noted in my journal on January 20, we were bound for Seattle for what we thought would be a three-to-four-day school and then fly home. But due to weather and staffing shortages at the Vashon Ranger facility, we were bound in Seattle for twelve days. It went like this.

Jim, aka Shep, and I had flown to DFW the night before to get on the first AA flight from DFW to SEA, which had thirty empty seats when we went to bed. Being retired pilots, we can fly free for life anywhere American Airlines flies. But there must be empty seats available. At 5:15 AM, we checked in the computer, and the flight was now oversold! We had a backup plan to fly to Portland, Oregon, and drive 2 1/2 hours north, but we ended up getting on our original flight to Seattle.

The real situation when I deplaned last night at DFW was Taylor, her six-month-old baby, and her mother trying to get to our cabin against our better judgment and advice. They had stalled on a steep, ice-covered hill about halfway there. They started walking in the cold (12 degrees Fahrenheit), night to the cabin, not realizing it was still three miles away with more icy hills ahead. A few phone calls later, I got them walking back to their car for warmth and protection. I called Rob to mobilize neighbors Warren and Gary, who had a four-wheel-drive truck with chains, and they rescued the girls and child and took them to our cabin for the night after deciding it was too dangerous to move their cars on the icy slope. There was more freezing rain and cold weather in the forecast. They would try to get their cars off the mountain the next day. At least the ladies spent the night safe and warm in the cabin instead of in their car.

Now, we were airborne on our way to Seattle. Shep is excited about getting his airplane. And it is the perfect plane for him. It is all metal, with a proven engine, tricycle gear, modern avionics, a stick, autopilot, and flight characteristics that are friendly enough for a trainer yet rugged enough to fly into the backcountry for camping. He sat in one a few times on our trips to Oshkosh and knew it fit his frame with plenty of space. It was an economical trainer with backcountry capability, built for trouble-free flying. His purchase narrowly preceded a price increase of twenty thousand dollars, so it was a good investment.

I noted in my journal, "Getting the plane home should be a pleasure and a fun, flying, and learning experience. There is a day of ground school, beginning Tuesday, followed by two days of flight training, and then we depart the Pacific Northwest for Northwest Arkansas and home. The weather at this time of year could determine our route. The shortest distance is to cross the Rockies near Spokane, Washington, then cross Montana, Wyoming, and the Great Plains, but it's winter. We keep smiling and saying to each other, 'What could possibly go wrong?'"

Arlington, Washington — Vashon Assembly Facility

On January 22, at 7:30 a.m., we wake up at our hotel, have coffee, and head to the Buzz Inn for breakfast. From there, we drive the short distance to the airport (KAWO) and check the front door to the Vashon hangar. It's open, so we step inside and greet some of the employees who are beginning their lunch break. They invite us to look around and see the operation for ourselves, unescorted.

We spend a very pleasant hour exploring the facility, taking photos, and touching N188JS for the first time. She's a beauty! Toward the end of their lunch break, the maintenance assembly supervisor, Ryan, joined us and answered many questions giving us insight into the genesis of the company, the manufacturing process, and some of the components. It seems like a top-notch outfit with a great product at the right time and an eye toward the future and longevity.

Shep seems pleased. I know I am, and to be a part of the acceptance, delivery, and flying her home to Arkansas seems like an approaching dream come true. We're keeping Doug and Ken, our Alaska adventuring pilot friends, in the loop with what's going on by texts and photos. My daily Bible reading contained this verse: "You have given him his heart's desire, and You have not withheld the request of his lips" (Psalm 21:2). This could be a verse for Shep. I know it is a verse for me. It's for both of us, and we know it.

Spiritual Interlude

I'm enjoying reading and journaling when I'm not at the airport with Shep. I continue to be amazed at how the Holy Spirit moves on the gospel writers to tell the story about Jesus and the church's birth in Acts. Herod had James, the brother of John, put to death with the sword. Peter was arrested, and four squads of soldiers were used to guard him. The church was fervently praying for his release. The Jewish people were expecting another sword execution.

An angel of the Lord goes into the prison to get Peter at night. Peter thought he was seeing a vision. Apparently, they were used to visions and expected them. Would we be? I wonder what it feels like for an angel to strike you in the side? The angel led him out into the street and then disappeared. Peter made his way to the house of Mary, the mother of John Mark, where they were praying.

Herod ordered the guards executed. He then went to Caesarea, where he died of worms, by God's hand. "But the word of the Lord continued to grow and to be multiplied" (Acts 12:24). Just the facts!

Ground School

The next day, we enjoy brunch at the Buzz Inn and arrive for ground school as scheduled at noon. Kurt is just taxiing in with Ron, a United Airlines captain who purchased N367VR. He plans to return to Lakeland, Florida, with his teenage daughter as soon as possible. Their training was delayed by the weather last week.

We begin ground school at about 2 PM and continue until 10 PM—the whole eight hours, without any breaks, except to walk out individually and use the restroom! Kurt is very good at what he does. He's passionate, engaging, knowledgeable, humble, and has a heart to equip and serve.

There's a lot to know about this little jewel. Kurt hit the highlights, the important operational stuff, and the ridiculously good avionics suite. He dove deep where it seemed important and answered our questions as they arose. We left the session tired but exhilarated at the information shared, learned, and hopefully digested. We drove by the Jack in the Box for tacos, brought them back to our room, and stayed up two more hours talking about it! Then we fell peacefully asleep.

Flight Training

Even with a short night's sleep, Shep beat me up the next morning, was dressed, and had coffee waiting for me when my eyes opened. He was going to run by the hardware store for a different phone cord and some foam padding for the cargo compartment of his plane before reporting for flight training at 10 AM. I stayed at the hotel to journal, read, and take walks. In the early afternoon, I noted that the normally overcast sky had changed to broken clouds high enough to fly with some blue sky peeking through. But the clouds were moving in and out, and the ceilings were not consistently high enough to fly, so there was more sitting around than flying for Shep.

This was the case for the next few days, and then the weather cleared enough for him to fly three times in one day. He's still unhappy with his landings, but everything else is going well.

I've been flight planning every day and looking at the weather to choose the best route for our flight home. I've flight planned three primary routes: [1] a northern route through the Rockies and over the Great Plains, [2] the Reno NV—Las Vegas NV—I-40 route flown by Ron and his daughter when they departed a couple of days ago, and [3] a southern route west of the mountains through California south to Bakersfield, then east paralleling I-40.

Over dinner and during the evenings, we discuss the pros and cons of all the routes, considering the weather, terrain, and the shortest distance. It's starting to feel like Shep is making his decisions based on feelings much more than I imagined—not that this is bad. He has a little unfounded fear of mountain flying, and it's understandable due to his inexperience with general aviation and mountain flying. I was like that too before 2019, when I flew to Idaho, Colorado, Wyoming, and Utah.

So I need to quit flight planning and let him decide what he wants to do. Then we'll plan and fly that route. It's roughly 15 hours to fly the northern route, 17 hours for the Reno option, and 19 hours for the southern California option—without wind consideration, which changes daily. But what does a couple hours flight time mean between friends? Especially when you're getting to look down on the earth from above and play with new avionics and a new airplane. I pause and thank the Lord silently for the opportunity and experience.

My good friend Mark Barnes has called a few times, hoping we can come spend the night with him and his wife in Spokane, Washington. I promised I'd come soon for a visit, whether we get to stop by tomorrow or Sunday or not.

The weather forecast along these routes changes daily, as do Shep's flying schedule and opportunities. The weather and Kurt's vacation schedule collided, causing Shep to get a new instructor for the remainder of his flying training. We're not sure when we'll finish. We're already on day seven of our planned four-to-five-day adventure.

Neither of us wants to spend an extra day, but if we finish tomorrow, it might be prudent or desirable to fly out Sunday, which could change our thinking on the routing. The weather near Spokane, Washington, looks iffy, but it's clear across the plains. The Reno route weather is forecast to be great all the way, so that's a good option, but Shep is uncomfortable with a few mountains along the route, and there needs to be more diversion airports to suit him. The best decision now is to go south, 50 miles short of LAX, before turning N188JS eastward and home. But wait, a widespread weather system is blowing into southern California just behind our projected time to pass through. It could be close, and we might get stuck on the ground there for a few days.

For now, we're stuck here. The weather is iffy the next couple of days through the weekend. And there are no instructors available to fly with Shep anyway. So we make the best of it and drive to the Puget Sound over the weekend. We visited the Navy Whidbey Naval Air Station, took photos, and enjoyed the nearby ocean. I have wanted to see it ever since I didn't get to come with our F-4 Squadron early in my fighter career. We paused in Deception Pass State Park and had a memorable, delicious salmon dinner in the quaint coastal town of Coupeville—grace, a gift.

Day 10 — Finished

On day 10 we were up at 5:45 AM to shower and head to the airport by 7:30 AM. Against all odds, Shep got checked out and all the paperwork done by 3:33 PM. Ben, the instructor pilot, and I looked at the weather and decided the northern route was better than the others, and now was a good time to go, overnighting in Spokane. The weather the next two days was excellent, with a high-pressure area over the central USA and no blizzards or drifting snow on the High Plains.

Shep didn't want to do it. He was tired from the days flying, and that's understandable. I offered to fly us to Spokane while he rested. I think he's still leery of flying through the Rockies, even if that's the route he favored when we arrived here. Oh well, it seems like we're going south.

I told him I wanted to go north once more, and I couldn't imagine better weather than this afternoon with a good forecast for tomorrow. He just shook his head no. Well, there's nothing better for me to do than get over it—the lack of trust in me, the fear of mountain flying, or whatever is driving him—and enjoy the flight home.

I went for a walk in the parking lot to shake it off and ponder why we were not doing what we set out to do, the way we set out to do it, when all the circumstances indicated we should. It could be a feeling he has to warn us about some unknown hazard or threat. Most savvy aviators have learned to honor those feelings in the interest of safety. I called Elizabeth and told her what was going on. Our wives were growing restless, too, because of the longer-than-expected outing. But Elizabeth talked me off the ledge, reminding me of my purpose for coming and telling me to let it go, be grateful, and continue to enjoy the journey and time with Shep. The Spirit helped me to be at peace.

Earlier in the Day

The two landings I got with Ben earlier in the day were beautiful, and the airplane flew like a dream. This was the first day with sunshine and high ceilings revealing the surrounding terrain, which was magnificent! Mount Rainier was in full view to the south, with lower mountains and spruce forests.

The Pacific Ocean was visible to the west among the San Juan Islands with their rolling mountain tops. It was knock-dead beautiful!

The day started with the most beautiful and different sunrise I had ever seen! It was pink, blue, and orange, with snow-capped mountains in the distance. I took some reasonably good photos.

While Shep was getting his one hour of solo time, I filled up the rental car with gas so we could drop it off quickly if he decided to begin flying home. When everything slowed down a bit with his no-go decision, Ben changed the nose tire due to a small shimmy, and we adjusted our rudder pedals for our sitting height. I put my headset, inReach satellite tracking device, and tie-down ropes into the plane for the following day.

We also reviewed some of the avionics updating procedures, but with twenty hours of flight time staring us in the face tomorrow, we'd have time to experiment and learn how it worked. Besides, the airplane flies easily without it.

Ben said he would meet us at sunrise to see us off in the morning. So we headed back to the hotel and dropped the rental car off just before they closed. They drove us to our nearby hotel, where we had dinner and went to bed.

Mounting Up with Wings Like Eagles— Going Home Day

Reason had returned to me. I have been flying in the general aviation environment for ten years now. I remember how different and unusual it was and how delightful it was to transition back into the general aviation world of little airplanes, where we started fifty years ago. But that it took some time—time I might not be giving Shep.

I wanted to help my friend who mentored me in the fighter and airline journey to get familiar with and enjoy the new flying environment as quickly and painlessly as possible. We speak the same aviation language and share similar experiences. It was a simple "Do unto others as you wish they would do for you" for a friend. And have some fun while savoring the joys of an earth life while doing it. I needed to keep that mindset and mission at the front of my mind and follow the breadcrumbs that the Holy Spirit laid out for us.

And I needed to do so "with a very good will," as the pilgrim in *The Pilgrim's Progress* was fond of saying whenever he joined up with a fellow pilgrim for parts of their journeys. Our Uber driver picked us up at the hotel at 6:00 AM and arrived at the factory at 6:30 AM. People were already at work assembling more Vashon Rangers. There are nearly 100 of these planes flying now.

Ben greeted us and assisted us in any way he could. Soon, he opened the hangar door, and Jim pulled the airplane onto the ramp. We were quickly airborne south, beginning 20 hours of flying that would seek to take us across the lowest terrain on our way home. We were also in a bit of a race with a major winter storm forecast to move into southern California about the same time we were to go through two days from now.

As it turned out, our plan was already falling apart. We ran into some low clouds between Seattle and Portland—a scud layer we call it. We were being forced to land somewhere in the clear and wait for the low clouds to rise, move, or dissipate. That could take hours or all day in the Pacific Northwest. Or we could climb above the low clouds and lose sight of the ground, hoping it was just a local situation and we'd be in clear weather farther down the road. Or we could fly near the ground in low mountainous terrain unfamiliar to us with three miles of visibility until we were past it. If the visibility deteriorated and we couldn't assure terrain clearance, we would have to do a 180° turn and fly back to better weather conditions or climb up through the clouds on instruments until we were on top at an altitude ensuring terrain clearance. We chose the latter as our best option.

We quickly reached the top of the solid cloud layer, and further south it was completely clear as we passed Portland, Oregon. We flew over extremely mountainous terrain in Oregon for the next two hours, with few places to land. I don't think either of us was anticipating that. The Rockies of Idaho and Montana are higher than these, but the distance to get through them was much shorter, and there was an interstate below for an emergency landing if necessary. This environment prompted me to tell Shep what a backcountry flying course instructor told us: "If you're worried about your engine quitting, you shouldn't be flying in the backcountry." We landed at Redmond, Oregon, for fuel and our first rest stop.

Airborne again for the second leg of our three-leg day, we flew over the same high terrain, majestic and vast, for three more hours, passing overhead Klamath Falls before crossing into northern California. We flew by snow-topped Mt Shasta, elevation 14,162 feet above sea level, and made our way to our next fuel stop, Redding, California. The Sierra Nevada mountains were breathtaking, but we were ready to enter the Sacramento and San Joaquin Valleys. This terrain, much lower and flat, was also vast. We flew over it for hours, passing over Chico, Yuba City, Sacramento, and Stockton before we reached our overnight destination of Modesto. We both had a new appreciation and understanding of the bread basket of California, which you don't get when you look at a map or read numbers. The acreage of agriculture we flew over at 500-1000 feet above the ground was mind-boggling.

Shep had recently reconnected with an old Air Force buddy by phone who lived in Modesto. He insisted on picking us up at the airport, driving us to a delicious Mexican dinner, then to our hotel, and picking us up the next morning after breakfast, delivering us back to the airport. It was a pleasure to hear these two reminisce about pilot training, flying fighters, and their Air Force careers—also where their dreams and aspirations had taken them. This pilot was now an FAA examiner, owned a pristine C-170, and had flown it with a friend to Oshkosh the previous year. So we had lots to talk about!

Beating the Storm — Avoiding Military Airspace

We climbed out the next morning early to beat the storms forecasted to move into the Los Angeles area by noon. It was clear with excellent visibility at Modesto. We could see some of the San Francisco and San Jose skyline, which are fifty miles to our west. During the next two hours, we flew over Merced, Fresno, and Bakersfield before turning the corner to head east about fifty miles north of LAX. We could see the clouds building over the Pacific, and Los Angeles wasn't its normal cloud-free self, so we had beaten the weather into the area and now would be heading away from it, traveling much faster than it was. We stopped for fuel and a rest break in Lancaster, at General Wm J Fox Airfield, just north of Palmdale, twenty miles SW of Edwards Air Force Base.

We experienced severe turbulence in the 8,000-foot mountains at the south end of the Sierra Nevada range. Winds from the Mojave Desert flow through the mountain passes like a venturi. I ask myself, "What flying conditions will we not experience during this adventure?" We had stuck our noses in what turned out to be a boxed-in canyon, trying to decide whether to fly around the mountains or climb over them with the strong winds impeding our progress. We flew south around the end.

In the eclectic little restaurant at the remote desert airfield, models of SR-71s, U-2s, YF-117s, and all sorts of spy and test airplanes that had their beginnings nearby were displayed. Photos of the pilots who flew them were hanging on the walls, complete with signatures and best wishes to the cooks and staff who regularly served them meals when they could escape their top-secret work nearby. We enjoyed a fantastic breakfast.

Those familiar with the military will recognize the names above as secretive research and test facilities for the military, USAF, and NASA. There are many restricted flying zones in the area where general aviation aircraft are forbidden to fly. But with excellent, inexpensive software available, like ForeFlight for iPhones and iPads or the leading-edge Dynon glass panel avionics suite in Shep's Ranger, these are depicted and easy to avoid, showing the boundaries and your aircraft's location. The same is true of FAA-controlled airspace.

We had just flown over some of the most populated areas of the US at a thousand feet above the ground and altered course a few times to skirt military and ATC-controlled airspace without talking to anyone except the control towers of the airports where we landed. We only had to know the rules and know where we were. If Shep had been worried about this facet of general aviation before, he wouldn't be anymore. What we had just accomplished surprised me also for its simplicity and peaceful flying.

We flew eastward toward Kingman, Arizona, on our second leg of the day. We passed overhead Barstow, California, and a lot of desert before crossing the Colorado River into Arizona at Bullhead City. It was Shep's leg to fly with me talking on the radio, just like our former airline routine. Shep demonstrated a good bit of airmanship when the winds were discovered to be different from the previous hour's weather reporting. He noticed our ground speed was quite high for flying into the runway in front of us, so he flew a low-altitude circling approach and landed into the wind in the opposite direction. It was a good landing. He was getting to know his airplane.

On the third and last leg of the day, the desert gave way to high desert and then alpine topography as we overflew Flagstaff, Arizona, just south of Humphreys Peak at 12,633 feet elevation. We flew directly over the runway at 3000 feet above the ground. It's a beautiful and interesting city. From there, we flew about twenty miles north of Winslow, Arizona, and into Gallup, New Mexico, where we spent our last night on the road.

We landed just before a beautiful sunset and enjoyed it while we tied down the airplane. We tried to get an Uber for the 5-mile drive into town and our hotel. When we discovered this wasn't going to work, we tried to get a taxi. That was going to take an hour. So, with his legendary travel negotiating skills, Shep talked the airport guy into giving us a ride on his way home from work, handing him a nice tip as we said goodbye. It was an adequate hotel, with a good restaurant next door. And we rested well from a long, satisfying day of flight. Shep called the taxi company before bedtime and arranged for them to pick us up at dawn for a ride back to the airport.

Last Day of the Epic

The taxi was there, and we witnessed a gorgeous sunrise on the drive and during our airplane preflight. Gallup is in the high desert. The airport's elevation is 6472 feet above sea level. And it's winter. We had hoped for a dawn lift-off because we believed we could make it home with an early start and a tailwind. But we discovered the airplane was covered with thick frost. To his credit, Shep went inside the airport operations area, found a stiff broom and a ladder, and started deicing the wings.

At first, I didn't think this was necessary. But, when I saw the copious amounts of ice accumulating under the wing as he scraped it off and considered the high-density altitude, it was absolutely the prudent thing to do. I gave him my gloves, added a quart of oil to the engine, put away our tie-down ropes, and situated our water bottles while he finished. Frost is heavy, and it disrupts the airflow over the wing, resulting in less lift. With its 100 hp motor at high altitude and maximum weight, our airplane would need all the lift and thrust it could generate. Our slow climb out just over the city's rooftops thirty minutes later would demonstrate that in terms we could understand.

We flew over the high desert for half the day, with terrain from 6000 feet to 9000 feet above sea level below us. We flew directly over the airport at Santa Fe, New Mexico, elevation 6349 feet, before crossing over the 10,000-foot terrain of the Pecos Wilderness Area and back over the high desert at Las Vegas, New Mexico. We crossed into Texas SW of Dalhart, stopping at Dumas for our last fuel and rest break and enjoying lunch at the runway cafe. We crossed into Oklahoma SW of Woodward and flew over Stillwater. With the nice tailwind, we made it to Fayetteville, Arkansas, to drop me off in time for Shep to continue to Fort Smith and home before dark. Today, we completed a journey of 2092 miles, taking twenty hours and twenty-eight minutes of flight time, burning one hundred forty-five gallons of gas. That's one summary of the epic journey.

Afterword

From my journal, February 2, 2024: "6:15 AM, up to journal, listen, read, and reflect."

"Noah found grace in the eyes of the LORD" is a phrase that came to me early this morning as I slowly awakened—home in my bed after twelve days on the road with Shep to fetch his Ranger-7 airplane from the factory near Seattle. What grace we have experienced in our lifetime! How much favor, joy and life has the Lord allowed and caused us to experience!

We reflected on it together somewhere between Gallup, New Mexico, and Dumas, Texas, east of Santa Fe, at 8000 feet with a 25-knot tailwind on a clear, beautiful winter day heading for Fayetteville, Arkansas, and then Fort Smith for Shep.

Beautiful, peaceful college freshman Savanna met us at the Fayetteville airport. She is Shep's oldest granddaughter. She seems like a lovely young lady inside and out. Maybe a picture of grace.

As I reflect now, the trip took us twelve days, mainly due to weather and training delays in the Pacific Northwest. It took us twenty hours of flying and three full days to arrive home. We arrived pleasantly tired but fulfilled and joyful at the success and experiences. My heart is full and most grateful for this grace I never saw coming. I can say no more.

I appreciate friends like Shep, who refuse to settle and continue to enjoy adventure and relationships into their graying years. They wait on the Lord, who renews their strength, and mount up with wings like eagles (Isaiah 40:31).

****

"None of us will ever accomplish anything excellent or commanding except when he listens to this whisper which is heard by him alone. Whatever you do, you need courage. Whatever course you decide upon, there is always someone to tell you that you are wrong."
—Ralph Waldo Emerson

"Do what you fear and your fear will die."
—Ralph Waldo Emerson

"I would have despaired had I not believed that I would see the goodness of the Lord in the land of the living.

Wait for and confidently expect the Lord; Be strong and let your heart take courage; Yes, wait for and confidently expect the Lord."
(Psalm 27:13-14 AMP)

"Even to your old age I will be the same, And even to your graying years I will bear you! I have done it, and I will carry you; And I will bear you and I will deliver you."
(Isaiah 46:4)

"He makes the clouds his chariot; he rides on the wings of the wind."
(Psalm 104:3b ESV)

"For of His fullness we have all received, and grace upon grace."
(John 1:16)

CHAPTER NINE

Growing Older — Grey Eagles

"You shall rise up before the grayheaded and honor the aged, and you shall revere your God; I am the Lord."
(Leviticus 19:32)

> *"Even to your old age I will be the same,*
> *And even to your graying years I will bear you!*
> *I have done it, and I will carry you;*
> *And I will bear you and I will deliver you."*
> (Isaiah 46:4)

> *"But they who wait for the Lord shall renew their*
> *strength; they shall mount up with wings like eagles;*
> *they shall run and not be weary;*
> *they shall walk and not faint."*
> (Isaiah 40:31 ESV)

Since this is a book about God staying near in the later decades of life, I think I should address the elephant in the room. Actually, it's not an elephant but an expected surprise. God keeps His word, and much grace is revealed for the moment in this season of life—just like He promises and loves to deliver.

Grey Eagles

Grey eagles are a particular species of South American eagles, but the term also applies to aged people with the character traits often ascribed to eagles. Retired American Airlines pilots have an association named The Grey Eagles to maintain and continue the members' close friendships. Historically, the character traits and virtues ascribed to the eagle are strength, power, wisdom, and freedom. The eagle's ability to soar high in the sky was believed to be a direct connection to the heavens and a symbol of divine protection and spiritual guidance. A life lived with God will experience these things.

That's my observation and story—a story unfinished.

Yet I want to report on it now from the cleft of the rock where I'm writing—the cabin. And from this time in our lives, 2024 just past and beyond, as I've entered my seventies. Job, inspired by the Holy Spirit, records in the oldest book of the Bible that: "Wisdom is with the aged, and understanding in length of days" (Job 12:12 ESV). So if I have gained any wisdom, I want to pass it on to the next generation. One of the most pleasant surprises in this chapter of our lives, for both Elizabeth and me, is that we're surrounded by younger people who ask for our counsel and enjoy our company to get it. This is a blessing from the Lord in our chapter of life and the heart of the Lord for us to do. "Go therefore and **make disciples** of all nations, baptizing them in the name of the Father and of the Son and of the Holy Spirit, **teaching them to observe all that I have commanded you**. And behold, I am with you always, to the end of the age" (Matthew 28:19-20 ESV). "**One generation shall commend your works to another, and shall declare your mighty acts**" (Psalm 145:4). This continues to be both a joy and a challenge, requiring us to trust in the Lord for words of wisdom and His power to sustain us and send His Word on its way.

I feel that God has been very gracious to me and my family and friends as He was to Israel in their desert wanderings: "He found him in a desert land, and in the howling waste of a wilderness; He encircled him, He cared for him, He guarded him as the pupil of His eye. '**Like an eagle that stirs up its nest, that hovers over its young, He spread His wings and caught them, He carried them on His pinions**'" (Deuteronomy 32:10-11). And, "You yourselves have seen what I did to the Egyptians, and how **I bore you on eagles'**

wings, and brought you to Myself" (Exodus 19:4).

Other verses about eagles and relationships with others and the Almighty are: "Bless the Lord, O my soul, and **forget none of His benefits; Who pardons all your iniquities, Who heals all your diseases; Who redeems your life from the pit, Who crowns you with lovingkindness and compassion; Who satisfies your years with good things, so that your youth is renewed like the eagle**" (Psalm 103:2-5). "Saul and Jonathan, beloved and pleasant in their life, and in their death they were not parted; they were swifter than eagles, they were stronger than lions" (2 Samuel 1:23).

I don't feel like I'm 70. I feel like I'm 50. I think that's much better than being 50 and feeling like you're 70. I wished my close friend Shep a happy birthday last week, and he replied, "I'm seventy-six today. Statistically, people who have more birthdays live longer."

I'm happy to be where I am. It offers a unique perspective, and I want to share some stories and thoughts about it for your consideration and reflection, with a prayer that they aid you on your journey.

A Cabin In Time

If you read my second book, *God Came Near*, you might recall toward the end that I was hearing in the spirit that I should build a cabin for solitude, silence, and fellowship with family and friends. This was a big stretch for me. I never envisioned or wanted a second home with associated expenses and the threat to retirement income. But Elizabeth, my family, and I followed the breadcrumbs the Lord was putting down, and the cabin became a reality six years ago.

In the interest of transparency and telling the whole story, the cabin is a three-bedroom, three-bath house with a large great room, wood-burning fireplace, modern kitchen, modern electronics, WIFI, fiber optic Internet, and a large TV above the hearth that can be pulled to viewing height but is seldom used. Its 17-foot-high windows on the south side look out on the majestic, blue-green Ouachita Mountains as far as you can see from a cliff on top of a mountain.

Most friends who visit say, "This is not a cabin!" But it is for us, with many cabin-like design features. And it's used like a cabin for getting away in nature, for silence and solitude. Very few neighbors live on the mountaintop. Most come up on the weekends or for hunting season or family getaways. Access is gained by driving a five-mile, steep, crooked gravel road behind a locked gate. The residents here have each other's contact information in case someone needs assistance, but we are mainly here for isolation, nature, solitude, and silence.

The best way to get here is by backcountry airplane, which is how I found the place. There is a half-mile-long grass strip four hundred yards from the cabin that I didn't have to build. And, by miracle, I was able to obtain a one-acre lot to build a hangar for my airplane, giving me permanent easement and use of the runway. The only reason I'm sharing all this detail is to give glory to God for His gift to us. More miracles and details could be shared, but I think you understand. It's a dream come true—a dream I never saw coming.

I wanted our adult children to be involved to keep the family close relationally, and they were involved from the beginning. Before making an offer on the lot, we drove to the mountaintop from where we lived and decided we liked it enough to use it even if we didn't have an airplane. My son loves architecture and has an eye for beauty and design. After my wife drew what she wanted for the interior on a napkin, he practically designed the whole thing. It was a little modern for my taste, but when I protested that I wanted a real cabin, not glass, concrete, and steel, my daughter chimed in and said, "Dad, we're not calling it modern; we're calling it simple." My son added, "I can warm the interior with wood and light colors."

"But black exterior? That sounds like a millennial thing to me, and I'm not sure I like it." "It's a great color that blends into nature, making it almost invisible." The discussion continued, with a flurry of *Architectural Digest* photos and articles being pushed my way. And I learned that "black is the new black." The truth is I didn't care much about the look as long as it was strong, functional, low maintenance, and energy efficient. For me, it was more about the location, the beautiful view with nature all around, keeping the kids close, sharing with friends, having a venue for spiritual solitude and silence, and of course the runway. I'm joking about the runway—somewhat. It didn't hurt anything that it was part of the equation.

It turned out beautifully, as I trusted it would if Josh put his eye and touch to the task. Amanda chimed in plenty of times on granite and interior furnishings. Her husband, Chris, made fun of us as we bartered back and forth. It was a family affair. But during the construction, I had a couple of tense, fearful moments about the whole thing.

About halfway through construction, we had cost overruns like any project. They were significant at the time, and dark spirits were insinuating that I had made a big mistake. As I walked around the construction site by myself, looking at the view, I started to pray to the Lord that I was worried about it and wondered if I was spending too much of His money. Everything belongs to the Lord, but he graciously allows us to steward the amount He entrusts to us. How we do that says a lot about us, and what we believe about Him (1Chronicles 29:11-13, Matthew 25:14-30). Immediately, I had a strong thought that wasn't my thought—a way the Spirit often speaks to me—"I have a lot of money." I had to laugh, and my fears dissipated. I knew He had led, was leading, cared, and was happy with me and the progress. It wasn't a mistake, and He would provide. He was happy with my motivation and faith to risk doing what I felt He was leading me to do.

The second fear that rose against me was born from a comment from two of my best friends. They are pilot buddies and have had cabins for some time for getaways and recreation. They had encouraged me to build the cabin. While up to examine the construction progress one of them remarked, "You know, the kids say they will come, but they won't come." And the other one nodded his head in serious agreement. Inside, I screamed, "But you told me they would come!" Nothing needed to be said. It was a faith risk, and how the situation would pan out would soon be known. I will add a very personal note that I don't often share. While meditating one day and praying to the Lord about this situation and my recent fear attack, I had a strong thought that wasn't my thought: "I would build it just for you and Me to meet." I certainly don't think like that, and it undid me. It still does. Grace revealed.

The kids did come, even though they live far away. They came by themselves, together, and with friends. They came for family holidays and vacations. Josh worked from the cabin for a month during the early days of the COVID-19 pandemic. Amanda brought fellow physicians and researchers up for a writing retreat.

Our guest book illustrates we've shared the cabin with dozens of friends, family members, missionaries, and a few strangers who wanted to get away for a spiritual retreat. It was a special joy to access it during the pandemic, just the two of us, and sometimes with friends. There have been cousin retreats, sibling weekends, personal counseling and healing times, four-wheeler adventures, anniversaries celebrated, and the beauty of solitude, silence, and nature experienced up close and personal for all who've come—and rest.

One funny note needs to be shared so you have an accurate view of what the Lord gave us in the cabin. When we moved furniture inside six years ago, my son carried things back to the truck after my wife had carried them inside. "Josh, what are you doing?" "Dad, I know this is your second home, but I think it should be like an Airbnb for you and Mom to come and rest without family pictures on the walls or too much to do. It should just be about rest, nature, and the view. Others can come here too, and not feel like they are intruding—it's just about them, the view, nature, and God." And so it was.

God was faithful to us financially, and supported the risk. And He was faithful to us relationally. It's gotten a lot of use! "Let God be true, and every man a liar" (Romans 3:4) continues to be one of my favorite verses, and my experience. In the same genre are my life verse, Proverbs 3:5-6, and a few others: "Trust in the Lord with all your heart and do not lean on your own understanding. In all your ways acknowledge Him, and He will make your paths straight." "Delight yourself in the Lord; and He will give you the desires of your heart. Commit your way to the Lord, trust also in Him, and He will do it" (Psalm 37:4-5). After the fact, I would do it again. It's been above all I could ask or imagine.

If I were to put a verse over the door of the cabin or the hangar, it might read: "For of His fullness **we have all received, and grace upon grace**" (John 1:16). Or if it were a quote, it might be the one I used to begin the chapter "A Cabin in Time," in *God Came Near*:

"Hurry is not of the devil; hurry is the devil."
— C.G. Jung

One of the cabin's highest and best uses has been to support the ruthless elimination of hurry.

Avoid The Hezekiah Syndrome

With generations as disconnected from the grey eagles as the two after them are, primarily due to technology, the isolation of screens, decaying morality, disrespect for authority and age, there is a tendency for the grey eagles of my generation to enjoy the fruits of their labor and disregard the subsequent generations as hopeless. We're tempted to give up on helping them and let them go on their way, eat of their own devices, reap what they sow, and learn from the school of hard knocks. Is that wise? Or do you think this pleases the Lord?

One of the best kings in ancient Judah was Hezekiah. He was so excellent at a time when the bar was quite low that I hate to say anything negative about him. He was the 13th king of Judah during the time when Isaiah and Micah prophesied. He witnessed the destruction of the northern kingdom of Israel by the Assyrians. When Assyria came against him, he trusted God and saw a miracle as God Himself delivered Jerusalem from Sennacherib in 701 BC. He enacted sweeping religious reforms, re-instituting the worship of Yahweh and doing away with idols. He is considered a righteous king in the Books of II Kings and II Chronicles. To top it all, he is one of the kings mentioned in the genealogy of Jesus in the gospel of Matthew. His reign is summarized: "**He trusted in the Lord, the God of Israel; so that after him there was none like him among all the kings of Judah**, nor among those who were before him" (2 Kings 18:5).

But in his old age, he let his guard down and wasn't staying spiritually sensitive by practicing soul care. The king of Babylon sent an emissary to console and congratulate Hezekiah because they heard he had been ill and had recovered. Hezekiah received them and also showed them all the riches and treasures of the Temple and his own house. The prophet Isaiah dropped in and asked the king about the strangers and what he had shown them. The king reported that he had shown them everything. Isaiah told Hezekiah that was a huge mistake and prophesied that the Babylonians would return one day and carry the treasure away, a prophecy fulfilled in 586 BC. What was Hezekiah's response?

The Bible tells us what he said and what he was thinking: "Then Hezekiah said to Isaiah, '**This message you have given me from the Lord is good.**' For the king was thinking, '**At least there will be peace and security during my lifetime**'" (2 Kings 20:19 NLT). That thinking is what I'm calling the Hezekiah Syndrome.

You can decide for yourself. But I don't think God is that pleased with it compared to His heart and actions, as described throughout the Bible, and the mercy and grace He's shown each of us.

Embrace The Nehemiah Syndrome

A couple of grey eagles meet with three slightly-graying eagles next door every Wednesday at 7 AM. We call ourselves the Nehemiah group, and we've been meeting for five years now. It started when some State Farm agents asked my neighbor, a retired State Farm agent, to mentor them. They said, "We are so burned out. And we want the second half of our lives to count more than the first. Will you mentor us?" Ron, our leader, picked a study on the book of Nehemiah called *Holy Ambition* by Skip Ingram and asked me to join them, and we began.

We learned that Nehemiah was very successful in his time and place. In fact, he was the wine taster for the King of Persia, an empire that ruled the known world. He had frequent access to the king, and his job was to ensure some would-be assassin hadn't poisoned the king's wine. It was a bit risky, but it allowed him great privilege and the chance to live in an opulent setting. Still, his heart longed for and cared for his native land, their faith, and culture—Israel, the Jews, and Jerusalem. He would come to demonstrate a holy ambition.

He learned that some Jews had come to the capital of Persia, and among them was his brother. He immediately called for him and asked about the condition of Jerusalem and its people. The brother reported, "**The remnant there**

in the province who survived the captivity are in great distress and reproach, and the wall of Jerusalem is broken down, and its gates are burned with fire" (Nehemiah 1:3). I often think that's a fair description of the culture and the church in the United States of America, and the West. Our people are in great distress, our boundaries are broken down, and our gates to keep harmful influences out are burned with fire.

Nehemiah risked his life and fortune, found favor with the king, and returned with volunteers to rebuild the walls and gates and repair the temple in a miraculously short time. This gives me hope that the Lord might act similarly again and that He is always looking for a Nehemiah who values the things of God, even above his own welfare.

I'm writing to Grey Eagles in this chapter. I know those characteristics describe some of you. If the Spirit leads you to reengage with God's community of faith to rebuild or strengthen the kingdom of God, give it some thought and take heart in what you might do. Make it your holy ambition.

"For **the eyes of the Lord move to and fro throughout the earth that He may strongly support those whose heart is completely His**" (2 Chronicles 16:9a).

"When I saw their fear, I rose and spoke to the nobles, the officials and the rest of the people: **'Do not be afraid of them; remember the Lord who is great and awesome, and fight for your brothers, your sons, your daughters, your wives and your houses'**" (Nehemiah 4:14). The people listened, obeyed, and we learn: "So the wall was completed on the twenty-fifth of the month Elul, in fifty-two days" (Nehemiah 6:15).

Thoughts on Death and Dying

I was on my first big flying adventure outside the local area in 2016 to Oshkosh, Wisconsin, when my dad died. Dad had been in a nursing home for a few months because it became apparent that my siblings and I, with the caregiver who came to his home, couldn't provide all the attention he needed. He was about to turn ninety-three.

My brother, sister, and two of their friends were with him, laughing and telling stories while Dad peacefully slept off and on. Then they heard him take a big deep breath, and he was gone. When they called to tell me, I said that I would be right home. But they said I needn't come because all the arrangements had been made long ago, and if anything came up, they could handle it. They said, "Dad would want you to stay."

I have great siblings. Dad was proud of each of us for our accomplishments. He loved that I was a pilot, and his way of telling me to be careful and fly safely when I departed was: "Son, don't buy any of that cheap gas." He was quite an adventurer and risk-taker; I guess that's where we all got it.

He was humble about it, but Dad had shown a lot of courage in dealing with criminals during his long life, and a lot of character in every area of life. An accomplished outdoorsman and dentist from Harrison, AR, one of seven commissioners overseeing the Arkansas Game and Fish Commission, once told me, "Your dad is a man among boys."

But we all succumb to age and diminished power as we journey past our prime toward death. We'd act more wisely if we often thought of that reality. None of us are going to get out of this alive. Solomon addressed this issue with verses like: "**It is better to go to a house of mourning than to go to a house of feasting**, because that is the end of every man, and the living takes it to heart" (Ecclesiastes 7:2). And: "**A good name is better than a good ointment**, and **the day of one's death is better than the day of one's birth**" (Ecclesiastes 7:1).

Obviously God sees things differently than most of us do. Dad used to say, "I'm not afraid to die; I just don't want to be on the next train." If we spend more time with God, we will come to see that His perspective is the best and trust in Him more. Verses like these come to mind: "**Precious in the sight of the Lord is the death of His godly ones**" (Psalm 116:15). "For **a day in Your courts is better than a thousand outside**" (Psalm 84:10). "**Weeping may last for the night, but a shout of joy comes in the morning**" (Psalm 30:5b).

The New Testament echos this sentiment: "**For to me, to live is Christ and to die is gain**" (Philippians 1:21). "Therefore if you have been raised up with Christ, keep seeking the things above, where Christ is, seated at the right hand of God. **Set your mind on the things above, not on the things that are on earth**" (Colossians 3:1-2).

I once noticed there is no record of Jesus preaching at a funeral. However, He presided over a few resurrections. He said that Lazarus and Jairus' daughter were only asleep. So God doesn't see death like most of us do. But He knew apparent death was germane to the human condition and was moved to tears by the torn hearts of Lazarus' grieving friends. Maybe that's why Jesus seemed so happy when He often retorted, "**And I give eternal life to them, and they will never perish; and no one will snatch them out of My**

hand" (John 10:28). (Also note: Matthew 19:29, Mark 10:30, John 3:16, John 3:36, John 4:36, John 5:24 and others.)

If you read the Word daily you live in awareness of the blessed hope of our faith—the resurrection from the dead and eternal life with Jesus Who loved us, died for us, and is coming back for us soon. "**For the Lord Himself will descend from heaven with a shout, with the voice of the archangel and with the trumpet of God, and the dead in Christ will rise first. Then we who are alive and remain will be caught up together with them in the clouds to meet the Lord in the air, and so we shall always be with the Lord. Therefore comfort one another with these words**" (1 Thessalonians 4:16-18).

Thoughts on Living

*"Time has a wonderful way of showing
us what really matters."*
—Margret Peters

What are the best things about being seventy or sixty-five to ninety-five? You have time to listen and speak with the Holy One. People typically don't expect that much from you or request your services. Unhurried time is yours again, like when you were a child, hopefully with a little more wisdom on how to use that gift—grace.

We prioritize being part of a faith community, serving, teaching, loving, enjoying, mentoring, and telling the next generation about God's goodness and faithfulness. It's more blessed to give than receive. But there must be boundaries because many of our fleshy communities are built around human strength and activities, not resting and joining the flow of the Spirit with His power and direction (See Isaiah 30:15).

I tell many of our community's younger elders and leaders, "We can know a little bit about where you are because we've been there. We're giving you grace for your generation because this one has unique challenges and struggles, but you can't know where we are. We are experiencing grace for our moment, freedom, and opportunity for joy that we don't want to give up randomly or without a calculated decision." We are aware that the vineyard is the Lord's, and maybe He doesn't expect of us all that we've been conditioned or led to believe. It gets back to your ideas about God.

Switching Gears

Let me recommend a useful and funny book to you. *Younger Next Year: A Guide to Living Like 50 Until You're 80 and Beyond* by Crowley and Lodge.

The authors are probably not believers, but they are truth speakers and seekers.

The M.D. is a little hard to take when he trails off into evolution tirades occasionally, but you're forewarned and can skip those if you wish. He's well-credentialed, and his science is well-researched. In layman's terms, he says it's been shown that if you exercise six days a week in certain fashions, your body sends messages to itself at a cellular level calling for the production of regenerating tissue and substances to keep the body going. Like the plastic mind, the adaptive body can tell its parts, "Hey, he's not through yet! Send help in the form of this and that substance to this or that organ or joint." There is a version written for women too. My wife read it and said it was good.

The older author, a septuagenarian lawyer, and the doctor's patient is as funny as funny can be—also very convincing and motivational. Remember how important the mind is in setting your course. We need motivation and convincing to form our habits, and then our habits form us.

Here are a couple more critical and credible reviews of the book:

"One of our highest recommendations so far on growing old gracefully . . . Dr. Lodge, a prominent M.D., focuses on developments in cellular and evolutionary biology. Crowley, his guinea pig, is a firm believer in Dr. Lodge's science and very good at convincing the reader that, if you're a fifty-year-old man, you'd be an idiot not to start following the rules as soon as possible. . . . Should be read avidly by anyone growing older as well as forward-thinking youngsters."
— Kirkus Reports

"An extraordinary book . . . it is easy to read, the science is right, and if one follows Henry Lodge's and Chris Crowley's recommendations, both mental and physical aging can be delayed. I wish my patients would follow their advice."
— K. Craig Kent, M.D., chief of vascular surgery, New York–Presbyterian Hospital
(The New York Times)

I was going to give you some funny quotes, but I've given my book away or loaned it. I will order another to motivate me and hone what I've learned and want to practice. One statement that Chris Crowley makes that really sold me on their credibility and motivation for writing went like this: "Spirituality: That's something we both agree is the most important element in not aging or aging well, but neither of us feels qualified to speak to that, so we won't."

On the note of exercise, I want to tout the value of walking and the habit of walking as a spiritual discipline, habit, or rhythm. It's not often listed among spiritual disciplines, but it has the value of being alone, quiet, and healthy for your body and soul. There is an unpressured, unhurried time to think, to dwell on those thoughts, which is meditation, and to listen for thoughts that may come to you. Your body feels refreshed and rejuvenated, too.

My wife and I walk about an hour or three miles around our neighborhood's lake and streets every morning. It was my wife's idea initially, but I knew it couldn't hurt me either, and I wanted to encourage her as much as I could. She has over 807 consecutive days of walking more than 10,000 steps per day—five miles. She's a little OCD, and I jokingly tell her they call it a disorder for a reason, but she's healthy and in shape. You have to be a little bit compulsive and determined to exercise regularly. Our bodies don't want to do it naturally, at least initially.

I'm sure it does even more for our mental well-being, sense of living, and value of life. Everyone wants to stay as healthy as possible, so start doing something about it.

"Walking is a man's best medicine."
— Hippocrates

"All truly great thoughts are conceived while walking."
— Friedrich Nietzsche

"If you are seeking creative ideas, go out walking. Angels whisper to a man when he goes for a walk."
— Raymond Inmon

"After a day's walk, everything has twice its usual value."
— G.M. Trevelyan

"Walking is the ultimate travel adventure. You never know where your feet will take you."
— Richard A. Schmidt

I'll also tout the value of rising early to do it. I'm not an early-morning person. I like to sleep. But by habitually rolling out of bed around 6 AM every morning, my body now wakes up about that time, and usually, it is ready to slip on tennis shoes and gym shorts and head out the door. We witness amazing sunrises that are soothing to the soul in some peaceful, mystical fashion. After I get back and shower, I'm ready to grab a cup of coffee, read, and journal, energized and excited to start the day.

"An early morning walk is a blessing for the whole day."
— Henry David Thoreau

As you age, soul care is more essential and joyful than ever. So, as you reflect on these thoughts and stories, I hope you're motivated to spend time with God daily by reading the Bible, praying, meditating, walking, and reading—quiet time with your thoughts and with God. May the Holy Spirit give you the understanding you need and the help you desire. In your graying years, you can live free and above the fray. You can "mount up on wings like eagles" (Isaiah 40:28-31).

> "Grow old along with me! The best is yet to be,
> the last of life, for which the first was made.
> Our times are in his hand who saith,
> 'A whole I planned, youth shows but half;
> Trust God: See all, nor be afraid!"
> — Robert Browning

> "The woods are lovely, dark and deep,
> But I have promises to keep,
> And miles to go before I sleep,
> And miles to go before I sleep."
> — Robert Frost

****

> *"I will lift up my eyes to the mountains;*
> *From where shall my help come?*
> *My help comes from the Lord,*
> *Who made heaven and earth.*
> *He will not allow your foot to slip;*
> *He who keeps you will not slumber.*
> *Behold, He who keeps Israel*

Will neither slumber nor sleep.
The Lord is your keeper;
The Lord is your shade on your right hand.
The sun will not smite you by day,
Nor the moon by night.
The Lord will protect you from all evil;
He will keep your soul.
The Lord will guard your going out and your coming
in from this time forth and forever."
(Psalm 121)

"Get yourself up on a high mountain,
O Zion, bearer of good news,
Lift up your voice mightily,
O Jerusalem, bearer of good news;
Lift it up, do not fear.
Say to the cities of Judah,
'Here is your God!'"
(Isaiah 40:9)

"Those from among you will rebuild the ancient ruins;
You will raise up the age-old foundations;
And you will be called the repairer of the breach,
The restorer of the streets in which to dwell."
(Isaiah 58:12)

"Therefore we do not lose heart. Though outwardly we are wasting away, yet inwardly we are being renewed day by day. For our light and momentary troubles are achieving for us an eternal glory that far outweighs them all. So we fix our eyes not on what is seen,

*but on what is unseen, since what is seen is
temporary, but what is unseen is eternal."*
(2 Corinthians 4:16-18)

*"There is nothing better for a man than to eat and
drink and tell himself that his labor is good.
This also I have seen that it is from the hand of God.
For who can eat and who can have enjoyment
without Him?"*
(Ecclesiastes 2:24-25)

*"He has made everything beautiful in its time.
He has also set eternity in the human heart;
yet no one can fathom what God has done
from beginning to end."*
(Ecclesiastes 3:11 NIV)

CHAPTER 10

Prepare For War

---

*"A time to love, and a time to hate;
a time of war, and a time of peace."*
(Ecclesiastes 3:8)

*"Come, you children, listen to me;
I will teach you the fear of the Lord."*
(Psalm 34:11)

Generations & The Fear of the LORD

Soul-care practices are your best plan and wisest activity in times of war and times of relative peace. Upon reading Exodus 30, I'm taken with the awareness of the soul-care disciplines or rhythms the Lord lays out for his people. The text speaks of a relationship ordered and made possible by the God of creation with His people, beginning with one person, Abraham, and extending to his descendants and descendants in faith, walking through a world at war.

How and why did God prepare Abraham's descendants for war? We find part of the answer here: "Now when Pharaoh had let the people go, God did not lead them by the way of the land of the Philistines, even though it was near; for God said, 'The people might change their minds when they see war, and return to Egypt'" (Exodus 13:17). Also He knew the warfare that awaited them in Caanan, the land He promised to Abraham and his descendants forever. The children of Israel would learn that the Lord would fight for them, but they would have to exercise courage, faith, risk, and show up for the battles. How would He prepare them for war? And how does He prepare us?

Tabernacle

The biblical meaning of the word "tabernacle" is "dwelling." God took them out into the desert, where they would learn He was their source, protection, and life. He would dwell with them, and they would dwell with Him in a special relationship that would come to mean more than life to them. In dwelling, abiding, staying near, they would come to see Him for who He is, One worthy of worship and devoted to their welfare—One who would lead them with the cloud of His presence by day and fire by night. The people would get to know the God of Abraham, Isaac, and Jacob for themselves. They would also come to know themselves as God came near to love and know them.

Let's look at what this tabernacle God instructed Moses to build for the children of Israel in the desert might mean for us, in our day, a day we may be preparing for war.

I see an invitation to prayer, communication, and communion with the most powerful Being in the universe. I see order, boundaries, and continual awareness of who He is and the objects of His affections. I see a commitment to honor the covenant of relationship. Then I see the living it out by demonstrating obedience daily "throughout your generations."

I see prayer in the burning of incense morning and evening as close as one can stand to the presence of God behind the veil, which was a curtain separating the holy place from the Most Holy Place and the Ark of the Covenant. In that place, the Lord said He would speak to the priest, who came near to minister.

The golden lampstand with seven lights fueled by the oil of beaten olives was just behind the worshiping priest to his left. These flames shed light on the table of bread directly across from it and behind the priest to his right, who was praying and listening. The New Testament tells us that believers are a kingdom of priests by his blood and design (1 Peter 2:9). Seven is the number of completion and perfection in the Bible, and the menorah or lampstand has become the symbol of the nation of Israel (Exodus 19:6), and also of the Holy Spirit with His power to illuminate the human spirit.

The bread was to be placed before the Lord every Sabbath to demonstrate that we know where our provision, food, and strength come from, then eaten at a prescribed time to enjoy the very real benefits of that bread—the Word of God.

The light from the lampstand illuminated the furnishings of the holy place and facilitated the actions of worship and communion, of relationship, and of dwelling with our Father, Creator, the Holy One.

Some 1500 years later, Jesus would say and demonstrate, "I am the bread of life." And, "I am the light of the world" (John 9:5). Also, "I am the way, and the truth, and the life; no one comes to the Father but through Me" (John 14:6). He also said, "If anyone walks in the day, he does not stumble, because he sees the light of this world" (John 11:10). A prophet said of Him, "The people who walk in darkness will see a great light" (Isaiah 9:2).

I see bread for life, strength, and living. I see light for sight, enabling walking and functioning in the dark world. I see light for seeing the spirit of revelation and our relationship with God, Who humbly dwells with men a short distance away.

I see prayer, a pleasing aroma to God, being spoken and offered by His obedient, humble children who desire relationship, closeness, and intimacy with Him—to know Him better each day and year of our sojourn and enjoy the journey in a winsome and compelling way fueled and inspired by His mysterious presence, learning to hear and flow with His Spirit. He is Spirit (John 4:24).

I see confession as daily asking for forgiveness for where we miss the mark—sin as defined by Him, the only wise Father and God, the only One who can forgive sins (Mark

2:7, Luke 5:21). We are chosen by Him and have chosen to walk with Him, according to His way, just like the priests. But they had to wash their hands and feet daily before coming to the holy place to minister before the Lord on behalf of the people—lest they die.

I can hear soft, deluded 21st-century Christians saying, "That seems harsh—I don't know if I could love a God like that or trust Him." I can hear the Spirit say, "Come, I will teach you the difference between the holy and the profane" (Ezekiel 44:23, Leviticus 10:10). Or the shepherd king of Israel saying, "Come, you children, listen to me; I will teach you the fear of the Lord"(Psalm 34:11).

If you practice soul care, reading, and hiding the Word in your heart by meditation, the Spirit will teach you "The fear of the LORD." You'll get it, and that awareness is the beginning of wisdom. It leads to understanding and keeping the commandments with His help. Soul care is daily communion with the Spirit of the Lord. It's washing yourself with the water of the Word. It's walking in light so you don't stumble. It's righteousness, peace, and joy in the Holy Spirit.

The Spirit's job is to convict us concerning sin, righteousness, and judgment—sin is "missing the mark," an archery term in the original language. I pray that He continues to convict you and me when we miss the mark. It's a sign we're His children and that He is near. What does it show if we've grown cold to confessing our sin, or don't feel the need, and have forsaken the practice? It shows that we are deceived and deluded and need His light to find our way back to Him.

Peter in the New Testament teaches us the same truth the priest in Exodus 30 teaches: Confession is necessary and real. Forgiveness is central to the King and to life in His kingdom. Do you recall what happened with Peter on the night of Jesus' last Passover? It was the Lord's supper, communion with his disciples. Jesus took the place and role of a servant and washed the disciple's feet. When He got to Peter, he refused, perhaps thinking he wasn't worthy for the Master to wash his feet. But Jesus told him if I don't wash your feet, you have no part in Me. Peter did a complete about-face and exclaimed, "Wash me all over then."

Jesus told him, "You already have had a bath and are clean. Only your feet need to be cleaned daily by Me because they pick up contamination from walking a dusty road." The Lord loves dependence. It is His design, and we're only affirming that truth. We depend on Him for breath, life, and all that life promises.

He doesn't want codependence. He won't have it and never practices it. If you're in that kind of relationship, it's with a familiar spirit or another person controlled by dark spirits. The Lord loves truth. The truth sets us free to become living, loving sons and daughters of the King—happily dependent on Him and each other, but not codependent. If you're codependent, you've made someone in your life an idol, or they have made you one, and you allow it.

He lifts us from the dark morass of low living if we accept His gracious gift of salvation and commit to Him as Lord, to walk in His way, with His help—the definition of grace—nurtured and kept vibrant by soul care practices. Read, meditate, and pray in a holy (set apart) place. Meet regularly with the community of faith. Walk in the light, aware of the light. Eat the bread, drink the cup, and remember the Lord's death until He comes. Do this with thanksgiving. Godspeed.

"Transgression speaks to the ungodly within his
heart; there is no fear of God before his eyes."
(Psalm 36:1)

"For with You is the fountain of life;
In Your light we see light."
(Psalm 36:9)

"For this is the covenant that I will make with the
house of Israel
After those days, says the Lord:
I will put My laws into their minds,
And I will write them on their hearts.
And I will be their God,
And they shall be My people.
"And they shall not teach everyone his fellow citizen,
And everyone his brother, saying, 'Know the Lord,'
For all will know Me,
From the least to the greatest of them.
"For I will be merciful to their iniquities,
And I will remember their sins no more."
(Hebrews 8:10-12)

I was in Israel with a college group near Jericho once when we visited a full-scale replica of the Tabernacle God told Moses to build. It was humble and beautiful simultaneously, giving one a sense of what happened there, where God's presence dwelled with His people as they sojourned from 1500 BC until Solomon built the temple in Jerusalem around 1000 BC.

The attendant mentioned that two other full-scale replicas in the world were better than this one. He said one was near Arad in the Negev north of Beersheba. The other, he said, was in the United States. "Where?" I asked. "In Arkansas, near the town of Eureka Springs." You should take the opportunity to go if you're near. It will help you visualize what I've described above and sense what God had in mind when He invites us to draw near.

"Know Thyself"

> *"Now it came about when Joshua was by Jericho, that he lifted up his eyes and looked, and behold, a man was standing opposite him with his sword drawn in his hand, and Joshua went to him and said to him, "Are you for us or for our adversaries?"*
> (Joshua 5:13)

Hopefully, by the end of this chapter, you will see and agree that practicing the spiritual disciplines, habits, and rhythms is the best thing you can do for yourself in a time of peace, but especially in times of war. Charles Simpson, one of my favorite mentors, said, "You are born into a world at war. You will need a vacation from time to time, and God will give you one. But you are born into a world at war." So, what is the connection between knowing yourself and suffering or prospering in times of war?

You can Google "Know Thyself" and see what turns up. I did. I always try to discover who said important quotes first and what they meant by it. Is it seminal truth? If so, who else with cunning intellect and an intrigued interest will pick up on it and try to mine that philosophical truth?

Truth seekers try to ferret out the meaning as it pertains to the deeper meaning of life, or the Father of life, also known as the Father of lights. "Every good thing given and every perfect gift is from above, coming down from the Father of lights, with whom there is no variation or shifting shadow" (James 1:17).

The origin of this quote is often attributed to Aristotle. I'm still researching that. I found many wise men from different cultures and times who saw this truth and the light it promised and subsequently tried to pry deeper and see further. Sun Tzu, author of the brilliant and timeless book *The Art of War*, was one of the most amazing and unexpected minds to grasp this truth and exploit or see its universal value. Here's a quote from it:

> "Know thyself, know thy enemy.
> A thousand battles,
> A thousand victories."
> —Sun Tzu

Here is the broader version expounding on the meaning and its spiritual truth:

> "If you know the enemy and know yourself,
> you need not fear the result of a hundred battles.
> If you know yourself but not the enemy, for every victory gained you will also suffer a defeat.
> If you know neither the enemy nor yourself, you will succumb in every battle."
> — Sun Tzu, The Art of War

This is from the widely acclaimed, widely acknowledged master of warfare or the art of war. His writings are revered and studied by all the armies of the world. His book was required reading when I completed Air Command and Staff College as an Air Force major.

Could his insights and genius apply to personal and spiritual warfare too? He certainly thought so. It reverberates with the writings of ancient Jewish kings about 1000 BC. "He that is slow to anger is better than the mighty; and he that ruleth his spirit than he that taketh a city" (Proverbs 16:32 KJV). "He that hath no rule over his own spirit is like a city that is broken down, and without walls" (Proverbs 25:28).

Let's see what other great minds have thought this is important. Then we'll move on to the New Testament and the Bible to see what insights the apostles and prophets give us in embracing the truth with our lives so that it works for us and in us.

Pythagoras said, "Man know thyself; then thou shalt know the universe and God." He was a Greek who lived from 570 BC to 495 BC. He contributed to the fields of mathematics and philosophy and influenced the thought of Plato and Aristotle.

Socrates says, "Know thyself, and thou shalt know the universe." Aristotle says: "Knowing yourself is the beginning of all wisdom."

Immediately you see a collision between Greek wisdom and Hebrew philosophy and theology. The Scriptures teach in many places that "The fear of the Lord is the beginning of wisdom, and the knowledge of the Holy One is understanding" (Proverbs 9:10). Maybe Aristotle and Socrates didn't have the ancient Jewish writings that predated them by 700 years, or maybe they did.

I see these thoughts not as conflicting but complementary. If you know yourself or attempt to in any meaningful fashion, that will drive you to God. Because you will see both the beauty of your human soul and body, enabling you to experience and enjoy a beautiful, mysterious creation filled with other creatures to enjoy, study, and share the experience. But along the way, as you contemplate your purpose, destiny, and the meaning of life—and we all do—you'll look at the world, or you'll look in the mirror and see dysfunction, brokenness, pain, suffering, etc. You realize something is missing—or Someone. You sense more power or insight is needed to live a happy, healthy, whole life. We stretch for a whole life that makes sense of the joy and pain we experience while continually reaching for the stars or peering into the heavens.

An ancient Jewish king and poet peered into the heavens. He wrote most of the Book of Psalms in the Bible. His reply to this quandary in life or his discovery might read like this:

"The Lord is my shepherd,
I shall not want.
He makes me lie down in green pastures;
He leads me beside quiet waters.
He restores my soul;
He guides me in the paths of righteousness
For His name's sake.
Even though I walk through the valley
of the shadow of death,
I fear no evil, for You are with me;
Your rod and Your staff, they comfort me.

> You prepare a table before me in the
> presence of my enemies;
> You have anointed my head with oil;
> My cup overflows.
> Surely goodness and lovingkindness
> will follow me all the days of my life,
> And I will dwell in the house of the Lord forever."
> (Psalm 23)

Or:

> "I will lift up my eyes to the mountains;
> From where shall my help come?
> My help comes from the Lord,
> Who made heaven and earth.
> He will not allow your foot to slip;
> …
> The Lord is your keeper;
> The Lord is your shade on your right hand.
> The sun will not smite you by day,
> Nor the moon by night.
> The Lord will protect you from all evil;
> He will keep your soul…."
> (Psalm 121)

Or this one known as the soldier's Psalm:

> "He who dwells in the shelter of the Most High
> Will abide in the shadow of the Almighty.
> I will say to the Lord, 'My refuge and my fortress,
> My God, in whom I trust!'

For it is He who delivers you from
the snare of the trapper
And from the deadly pestilence.
He will cover you with His pinions,
And under His wings you may seek refuge;
His faithfulness is a shield and bulwark.
You will not be afraid of the terror by night,
Or of the arrow that flies by day;
Of the pestilence that stalks in darkness,
Or of the destruction that lays waste at noon.
A thousand may fall at your side
And ten thousand at your right hand,
But it shall not approach you.
...
For He will give His angels charge concerning you,
To guard you in all your ways.
....
'Because he has loved Me,
therefore I will deliver him;
I will set him securely on high,
because he has known My name.
He will call upon Me, and I will answer him;
I will be with him in trouble;
I will rescue him and honor him.
With a long life I will satisfy him
And let him see My salvation.'"
(Psalm 91)

"He trains my hands for battle,
So that my arms can bend a bow of bronze.
You have also given me the shield of Your salvation,

> And Your right hand upholds me;
> And Your gentleness makes me great.
> You enlarge my steps under me,
> And my feet have not slipped."
> (Psalm 18:34-36)

> "Blessed be the Lord, my rock,
> Who trains my hands for war,
> And my fingers for battle;
> My lovingkindness and my fortress,
> My stronghold and my deliverer,
> My shield and He in whom I take refuge,
> Who subdues my people under me."
> (Psalm 144:1-2)

This warrior king, David, seemed to trust in a relationship rather than in his strength or methods of prevailing in war—warfare he had known up close and personal most of his life. People have read his songs for three millennia, been encouraged and comforted by them, and felt a kindred spirit with David. He gave pen and voice to what people feel who come to know themselves, warfare, and the Creator God, the Father of us all (Ephesians 3:14-21).

It is mysterious but experiential. Do you completely understand it with your mind? No, but then, do you understand how you got here? How or why do your lungs breathe oxygen, or how and why your heart pumps blood? Do you even pause to note both go on many repetitions per day? No, for the most part, you just live, move, and have your being.

Whether you attend high school, college, or medical school, you may be more aware of how the human body or psyche works. But you don't think about it, and you don't really know. You're just on a journey to live your life, enjoy the journey, and discover its meaning and your destiny.

I suggest this is to know your Creator and Father. Blaise Pascal, a French mathematician and physicist, said this: "There is a God-shaped vacuum in the heart of every [person] which cannot be filled by any created thing, but only by God the Creator, made known through Jesus Christ." The process has always been as mysterious and mystical as spirits are to us. We don't apprehend them with our body's five physical senses or our soul's tripartite composition of mind, will, and emotion.

Two scriptures come to mind. The first is: "**As to this salvation, the prophets who prophesied of the grace that would come to you made careful searches and inquiries,- seeking to know what person or time the Spirit of Christ within them was indicating**" as He predicted the sufferings of Christ and the glories to follow. It was revealed to them that they were not serving themselves, but you, in these things which now have been announced to you through those who preached the gospel to you by **the Holy Spirit sent from heaven—things into which angels long to look**" (1 Peter 1:10-12). And, "**Now we have received**, not the spirit of the world, but **the Spirit who is from God, so that we may know the things freely given to us by God**" (1 Corinthians 2:12). Meditating on the second chapter of Paul's first letter to the Corinthians will give insight into this whole affair. But I'm getting ahead of myself. Everything changed with Jesus.

God Visits Earth

Everything changed when Jesus came to Earth! That's an understatement. I want to focus on soul care, spiritual warfare, and the additional revelation and understanding He gave us of how the spirit, soul, and body work together. Not that knowing how it works is necessary for the process of it working. It isn't, any more than knowing the basics of how your lungs work is to living. But knowing will help you adopt some practices of lung care like exercise, and avoid some hurtful habits damaging your lungs like smoking.

Watching what Jesus did will help us prioritize and focus on what's important. He motivates us and shows us some practices to help us keep the main thing the main thing. This has always been important—but perhaps more so in our age of distraction. Just as weeds can soak up nutrients and compete for light with plants in the garden, idols can distract and suffocate a soul. Soul care becomes critical to knowing real life and enjoying that life.

Where do we get insight and power to survive and thrive? How do we find answers to the meaning of life and our destiny? What did Jesus come to tell us? And what did He practice as an earthling? Both are instructive and insightful—life giving.

Read Jesus' parables told in the Gospels for their truth and light. Meditate on the timeless spiritual insights He taught us in the Sermon on the Mount (Matthew 5-7) and the Sermon on the Plain (Luke 6). Be with his disciples searching for Him early in the morning after a day of many miracles, only to find He had been up early in a remote place praying and listening to His Father (Mark 1:35). And note when He tells them to come aside and do the same thing (Mark 6:31).

If you would go deeper into Jesus' spiritual life and soul care, read the Gospel of John, "The disciple Jesus loved"(John 13:23, 21:24). John didn't record as many miracles or parables as the other Gospel writers but instead focused on Jesus' motive and purpose. This was namely to "show us the Father" (John 15:9, John 14:8) and to model and describe for us His dependence on the Holy Spirit (John 5:30, 14:26, 8:28).

Soul care is life care. It's how we come to know God and demonstrate that we do. Our spirits are made perfect when we believe and are born from above. But our souls and bodies need a little work. That's the joy in the journey of soul care. That's experiencing God and His grace like your life depends upon it. It does. Godspeed. (Romans 12:1–2).

If Your Enemy Is Hungry

"If your enemy is hungry, give him food to eat; and if he is thirsty, give him water to drink."
(Proverbs 25:21)

I'm trying to share something insightful and helpful about soul care and spiritual warfare with you. I promise I will get to that quickly because it is imperative to be aware of the warfare around you and know your enemy. You simply must wage a good battle to suffer less harm for yourself, your family, and your friends.

I just returned from our Sunday morning church service, where I heard an amazing sermon about The Good Samaritan. Now, I wonder if I'm asking the right questions about spiritual warfare.

An expert in the law came and asked Jesus a question to find out what kind of rabbi He was, and if He was leading the people astray. Jesus answered by asking him a question. You can read the beautiful, insightful dialogue in Luke chapter 10.

Part of it went like this: "One day an expert in religious law stood up to test Jesus by asking him this question: 'Teacher, what should I do to inherit eternal life?' Jesus replied, 'What does the law of Moses say? How do you read it?' The man answered, '**You must love the Lord your God with all your heart, all your soul, all your strength, and all your mind.**' And, '**Love your neighbor as yourself.**' 'Right!' Jesus told him. 'Do this and you will live!'" (Luke 10:25-28 NLT). The Lord of Creation and the lawyer agreed that this is humankind's most important issue and its most lofty goal.

Did you notice Jesus' last word to the lawyer? "Do this, and you will live!" The lawyer tries to exalt himself, and then there follows a most insightful discussion of love and what it looks like as Jesus paints a beautiful picture for all humanity and eternity.

Love! Is it possible to experience and practice love in this day and age? People want it! We read in Scripture that it's the secret desire of man's heart: "**What a person desires is unfailing love**" (Proverbs 19:22a NIV). Many applaud love. Many fake it. Have you watched much TV lately? The hate spewing out in debates and pundits talking over each other is nauseating. They ruthlessly put people down and exalt themselves or their causes, routinely being less than kind. This kind of behavior, along with the nightly news of bloodshed and violence, is causing many souls to become calloused and unfeeling. The Bible says, "**Because lawlessness is increased, most people's love will grow cold**" (Matthew 24:12).

The Holy Bible is the most authoritative book on life and conduct in human history. It says our highest good, goal, and aim is to love God and love our neighbor.

Why is this important and pertinent to the subject of spiritual warfare? If you can experience and practice love, it is a deterrent to warfare. Sacrificial love and its close cousin, sacrificial forgiveness, are the most potent offensive weapons in spiritual battles. If they don't bring peace to the battlefield, they will bring peace to the heart of the combatant who practices them. And in most cases, they will bring peace to the battlefield in time.

Living close to the Holy Spirit, being available to Him with habits, rhythms, and disciplines that amount to T-I-M-E daily spent with God, will keep your heart soft, pliable, compassionate, and available to others, just like the story of a good Samaritan (Luke 10). It makes for a life well-lived and full of peace.

The Advanced Course First

You may realize I have given you the advanced course in tactics and spiritual warfare techniques first. It's to have a relationship with the Rider of the white horse, the Lamb that was slain (Revelation 19:11-16).

Before teaching you to fly, strafe, dogfight, or drop bombs, I've given you the tenets and secrets of the advanced course. Before learning the basics of holding a rifle, cleaning it, and marching and fighting as a squad, I have discussed what gives you nuclear advantages in spiritual warfare. That is a covenant relationship with the King, the Lord of heaven's armies—the Lord of hosts. He will teach you what you need to know, and His forces are available to you when the need arises or the enemy comes near.

We took the Lord's supper this morning as a community. I thought of what I had just heard. There was a man, beaten and robbed—left half dead beside the road. It was a road between the highest city on earth, spiritually speaking, Jerusalem, the City of the Great King, and the lowest city, Jericho. We don't know anything about that man, but maybe you do. Someone with love in his heart and spiritual sensitivity went to him and poured oil and wine on his wounds to stop infection and start the healing process. He bandaged and covered these wounds and carried the man to where he could rest, heal, and recover, paying the whole price himself. During the Eucharist (which means "thanksgiving"), I recalled that wine represents Jesus' blood, which cleanses us and takes away our sins. The oil represents the Holy Spirit, which administers God's healing, restorative, and recuperating power. God with us—Immanuel.

Landing the Plane

When I spoke at the Hunters banquet, I told the audience I had been all over the sky with my stories of faith and flight. So I will ask the church pastor to land the plane. He can give some summary remarks, encourage you to make a decision or a commitment, or invite you to a community where you can get to know and experience God—and also experience love, fellowship, and friendship.

I need to land the spiritual warfare airplane now. I'm not out of gas, but my editor is about to travel to Korea for a few weeks. And it's time. If you take my advice and spend habitual, daily time with God, it will be like my flight to Idaho and the Rockies. You'll have your instructor pilot, your mechanic, and some friends with you. You'll enjoy the journey, and the help is there when you need it.

Beans, Bullets, and Bandages

"Beans and Bullets" is a logistical term for ammo and food, along with all the natural weapons of warfare. "Bandages" symbolize field hospitals, medics, and soldier care. Together, they symbolize the basics of conducting warfare within and between nations.

In Ephesians, chapter 6, the best-known Bible passage about spiritual warfare, Paul, an apostle of Jesus Christ, tells us that the weapons of our warfare are not natural but spiritual. "For **our struggle is** not against flesh and blood, but against the rulers, **against the powers, against the world forces of this darkness, against the spiritual forces of wickedness in the heavenly places**" (Ephesians 6:12).

In fact we need to read that whole passage slowly and meditate on it for the many insights it contains. May the Holy Spirit point out to you what is important for you to know at this time or recall in the future. It reads:

"**Finally, be strong in the Lord and in the strength of His might. Put on the full armor of God, so that you will be able to stand firm against the schemes of the devil.** For our struggle is not against flesh and blood, but against the rulers, against the powers, against the world forces of this darkness, against the spiritual forces of wickedness in the heavenly places. Therefore, **take up the full armor of God, so that you will be able to resist in the evil day, and having done everything, to stand firm. Stand firm** therefore, having girded your loins with truth, and having put on the breastplate of righteousness, and having shod your feet with the preparation of the gospel of peace; in addition to all, **taking up the shield of faith with which you will be able to extinguish all the flaming arrows of the evil one. And take the helmet of salvation, and the sword of the Spirit, which is the word of God.** With all prayer and petition **pray at all times in the Spirit, and with this in view, be on the alert with all perseverance and petition for all the saints**" (Ephesians 6:10-18).

I couldn't help but bold some of the soul care items and issues popping up in my mind. I hope my emphasis didn't distract you from what the Spirit might emphasize. You can read it in an unmarked Bible, meditate on it, and listen for guidance or insight. How much of the battle is God's stands out to me. Also, "stand" and let God fight for you is a theme. Two things always stand out about the sword: (1) Whose it is? It's the Spirit's not yours, and (2) How powerful it is: "For **the weapons of our warfare are not of the flesh, but divinely powerful for the destruction of fortresses**" (2 Corinthians 10:4). "For **the word of God is living and active and sharper than any two-edged sword, and piercing as far as the division of soul and spirit, of both joints and marrow, and able to judge the thoughts and intentions of the heart**" (Hebrews 4:12).

Conquer Sin?

Have you seen *The Chosen* film series, produced and made free by crowdfunding and other means, available on YouTube and its own Chosen App? I hope you have. According to the *Atlanta Journal-Constitution*, the show had 200 million viewers and 770 million episode views as of January 2024. One of the most popular episodes was the Nicodemus (John 3:16) clip, which I encourage you to watch. It's accurate, moving, and insightful on life's biggest question. You can hear the words of "A Teacher sent from God" and "The Teacher of Israel" discuss it. Jesus tells Nicodemus that He didn't come to conquer Rome but sin.

Sin is the enemy of our souls, but more so, it's used by an evil, angry enemy against us to destroy our souls and bodies and keep them from knowing and practicing truth and knowing the Truth. Sin can make you an enemy of God, but He graciously forgives sin for the asking and then will help you in your battle with sin and the devil, the enemy of your soul.

Many theologians would say from the little written about dark spirits in the Bible that Satan had been a powerful angel in God's realm, an archangel like Michael and Gabriel who stood in the presence of God. But he deceived himself and one-third of the angels in heaven to rebel against God, claiming God wasn't good and just. There ensued a battle, but it wasn't much of a battle. Satan was defeated and thrown to earth with his rebellious followers, who were given some authority and access to humans for some purpose and some time. That's my version, and it's admittedly sketchy but as brief and true as I can tell it.

If one-third of heaven's angels were cast to earth and

became the dark enemy of humankind, two-thirds of heaven's angels still serve God's purposes daily by supporting and helping His children—those who know Him by revelation and faith and spend time with Him. This is worth remembering and an incentive to pray and stay sensitive to the spiritual realm.

Let me offer a couple of Scriptures and observations about the realm and purpose of demons or dark spirits, and we'll move on. There isn't much said about them, probably for a reason, but their effects and presence are widely felt and written about in history.

As an international airline pilot, I had the opportunity to spend many days in Paris, London, and Madrid. I would frequent the Louvre, the National Gallery, and the Prado art museums. The number of paintings of angels and demons in conflict from the early Middle Ages to the Enlightenment in these world-famous art repositories is staggering. I used to think, "Wow, these people were superstitious!" But now I think they were more in touch with reality and the spiritual realm than modern humans.

Scripture tells us that God is the same yesterday, today, and forever, and for the most part, people are the same, too. Under inspiration by the Spirit, Solomon wrote, **"That which has been is that which will be, and that which has been done is that which will be done. So there is nothing new under the sun"** (Ecclesiastes 1:9). The Dead Sea Scrolls include several exorcism incantations directed against disease-causing demons. Josephus recounts incidents of possession and exorcism in his Antiquities of the Jews (2, 5, 8, 45-48).

The New Testament reports Jesus performed numerous exorcisms of demonic spirits in first-century Israel (Matthew

12; Mark 5, 6, 13; Luke 8) and gave his followers the authority to do the same. Jesus' reaction was interesting when His disciples came back to Him, as we learn: "The seventy returned with joy, saying, '**Lord, even the demons are subject to us in Your name.' And He said to them, 'I was watching Satan fall from heaven like lightning**'" (Luke 10:17-18).

To Give Life — To Kill and Destroy

The situation is most succinctly stated in the Bible like this: "**The thief comes only to steal and kill and destroy; I came that they may have life, and have it abundantly**" (John 10:10). And: "**Why do you not understand what I am saying? It is because you cannot hear My word**. You are of your father the devil, and you want to do the desires of your father. He was a murderer from the beginning, and does not stand in the truth because there is no truth in him. Whenever he speaks a lie, he speaks from his own nature, for **he is a liar and the father of lies**" (John 8:43-44).

So, there you have it. Know yourself and know your enemy, and you can successfully fight against his lies. You can be constantly reminded, instructed, refreshed, and helped in this warfare in real-time as you spend habitual, daily time with God. Don't listen to lies. Take thoughts captive and reject those that exalt themselves against the knowledge of God and His Word. Resist the devil, and he will flee from you. Limit your exposure to lies, advertising, propaganda, and such that promote the lust of the flesh, the lust of the eyes, and the boastful pride of life. Think about things above and eternal. Put no worthless thing before your eyes—your eyes are the window to your heart. When you do think about things on earth, consider this admonition from the Bible: **"Finally, brethren, whatever is true, whatever is honorable, whatever is right, whatever is pure, whatever is lovely, whatever is of good repute, if there is any excellence and if anything worthy of praise, dwell on these things"** (Philippians 4:8). Keep your eyes from looking on violence and your ears from hearing about bloodshed, and you will dwell securely under the wings of the Almighty and the shadow of the Most High.

> "Know thyself, know thy enemy.
> A thousand battles,
> A thousand victories."
> —Sun Tzu

****

> *"We are destroying speculations and every lofty thing raised up against the knowledge of God, and we are taking every thought captive to the obedience of Christ."*
> (2 Corinthians 10:5)

> *"Submit therefore to God. Resist the devil and he will flee from you."*
> (James 4:7)

> *"But He turned and said to Peter, "Get behind Me, Satan! You are a stumbling block to Me; for you are not setting your mind on God's interests, but man's."*
> (Matthew 16:23)

*"Set your mind on the things above, not
on the things that are on earth."*
(Colossians 3:2)

*"He who walks righteously and speaks with sincerity,
He who rejects unjust gain
And shakes his hands so that they hold no bribe;
He who stops his ears from hearing about bloodshed
And shuts his eyes from looking upon evil;
He will dwell on the heights,
His refuge will be the impregnable rock;
His bread will be given him,
His water will be sure.
Your eyes will see the King in His beauty;
They will behold a far-distant land."*
(Isaiah 33:15-17)

*"Then those who feared the Lord spoke to one another,
and the Lord gave attention and heard it, and a book
of remembrance was written before Him for those
who fear the Lord and who esteem His name.
'They will be Mine,' says the Lord of hosts,
'on the day that I prepare My own possession,
and I will spare them as a man spares his own
son who serves him.' So you will again distinguish
between the righteous and the wicked, between one
who serves God and one who does not serve Him."*
(Malachi 3:16-18)

*"The Lord is the portion of my inheritance
and my cup; You support my lot.*

The lines have fallen to me in pleasant places;
Indeed, my heritage is beautiful to me.
I will bless the Lord who has counseled me;
Indeed, my mind instructs me in the night.
I have set the Lord continually before me;
Because He is at my right hand, I will not be shaken.
Therefore my heart is glad and my glory rejoices;
My flesh also will dwell securely.
For You will not abandon my soul to Sheol;
Nor will You allow Your Holy One to undergo decay.
You will make known to me the path of life;
In Your presence is fullness of joy;
In Your right hand there are pleasures forever."
(Psalm 16:5-11)

"The Lord will fight for you; you need only to be still."
(Exodus 14:14NIV)

CHAPTER ELEVEN
ISRAEL - A TIME FOR WAR

Jeremiah & Ecclesiastes

I was reading Ecclesiastes and Jeremiah at the same time Israel is embroiled in a war against a bloody, evil enemy gunning down innocent women and children and committing even more grotesque atrocities.

As bad as it was, it's child's play compared to what happened to Israel in 722 BC, 586 BC, and 70 AD. If you read the Bible and history, you know this is not that unusual and is predictable—just not the time, place, or scope. The Biblical narrative is the only explanation that makes sense as to the why of it all.

This morning, my eyes fell on Ecclesiastes 7:14. It brought to mind Ecclesiastes 3:1-8, in which Solomon speaks philosophically about life on the planet before God. He mentions, "There is a time for war."

Israel — A Time for War

It seems the church in the West is woefully ignorant about Israel, her place in the Bible and history, and how God sees her—which is the most important part. How God sees things is how they are! See Isaiah 46:9-10 and Psalm 2. Israel, God's chosen image bearer nation, has been historically important for four thousand years. And she will be until the end, and especially at the end of time, according to prophecy and the word of the Lord. That's why I address Israel in this book. So you can know what to think about her among the family of nations, pray for her and the peace of Jerusalem, and experience peace for yourself.

How are we to view Israel? How are Christians, all nations, and all people to view Israel? First, we should honor and bless Israel! God made Abraham a promise, then extended it to Isaac and Jacob and their descendants forever: **"I will bless those who bless you, and curse those who curse you, and in you all the nations of the earth will be blessed"** (Genesis 12:3). Secondly, we are to **"Pray for the peace of Jerusalem"** (Psalm 122:6). Thirdly we are to **realize the miracle that is Israel** (Isaiah 66:8), and visit Israel if we can. That will bless them, and you will be blessed beyond your expectations! Fourthly, **Israel is the apple of God's eye, and He gave them**

the land forever (Genesis 35:10-12 and others). Even if they don't keep their covenant with Him, He will honor His word to them because that's who He is—a God that is faithful and keeps His word forever (2 Timothy 2:13, Isaiah 40:8). Lastly, He will punish or correct his children as any good father would, for their good. Throughout history, God has used other nations to do this or has allowed it—then He has crushed those people and nations because they raised their hand against God's anointed and often went beyond their boundaries in doing so. (See Isaiah, Jeremiah, Habakkuk, Hebrews 12:6-7). God's judgments are true and righteous (Ps 19:9, Rev 19:2). He can make the punishment fit the crime, and He sees into every human heart's very thoughts and intent.

I wrote a chapter about Israel as God's chosen nation and God's timepiece in human history in *Puzzling 2020*. The best short history of Israel with an accurate Biblical perspective I've read recently is *Miracle of Israel* (Frazier & Fletcher). The most insightful book I've read on Islam is in the past few years is *The Mystery of Islam* (Little).

Enjoy Your Life — Sow Seed — Let God Be God

As the world focused on Israel again, I found myself reading: "In the day of prosperity be happy, but in the day of adversity consider—God has made the one as well as the other so that man will not discover anything that will be after him" (Ecclesiastes 7:14).

The secular humanist and Christian humanist (which should be an oxymoron), will focus on Israel or other hot spots of war in the world, wring their hands, watch the news to constantly be in the know, be fearful, and feel that humans must fix this situation!

People with an accurate view of God and an ongoing relationship with Him will leave that up to Him, pray, and do what they can or feel led to do. But they go about their lives obeying the impressions of the Spirit and doing what their hands find to do—usually to love and serve others and grow their relationship with God by spending time with Him daily. And they will enjoy their lives—a beautiful gift! Psalm 46:10, Isaiah 30:15, Psalm 121, Ecclesiastes 2:24, Hebrews 4:11-13, I Thessalonians 4:11, Matthew 11:27-30 and many other Scriptures speak to this.

This year I've found myself actively involved in our multigenerational, collegiate community of believers, mentoring and being mentored, helping churches in Honduras, Uganda, and Malaysia, and being involved in men's groups and with young parents. And I've gone with my wife and friends on a Rhine cruise. I think you get the idea. Read through Ecclesiastes and Jeremiah this month if it isn't clear. Pray for the peace of Jerusalem as you go about doing good (Ephesians 2:10) and spending time with God daily in His Word and prayer. Shalom and Godspeed as you journey.

****

"A time to tear apart and a time to sew together;
A time to be silent and a time to speak.
A time to love and a time to hate;
A time for war and a time for peace.
What profit is there to the worker from that in

which he toils? I have seen the task which God has
given the sons of men with which to
occupy themselves.
He has made everything appropriate in its time.
He has also set eternity in their heart, yet so that
man will not find out the work which God has
done from the beginning even to the end.
I know that there is nothing better for them than to
rejoice and to do good in one's lifetime;moreover,
that every man who eats and drinks sees good
in all his labor—it is the gift of God. I know
that everything God does will remain forever;
there is nothing to add to it and there is
nothing to take from it, for God has so worked
that men should fear Him."
(Ecclesiastes 3:8-14)

"In the day of prosperity be happy,
But in the day of adversity consider—
God has made the one as well as the other
So that man will not discover anything
that will be after him."
(Ecclesiastes 7:14)

A Time for War — Daily War

Those who know me know I don't watch the news much—that is an understatement. I speak to that and why in my last book, *Puzzling 2020*. It's something along the lines of these verses and what they convey:

> "Who stops his ears from hearing of bloodshed and shuts his eyes from looking on evil, he will dwell on the heights; his place of defense will be the fortresses of rocks; his bread will be given him; his water will be sure. Your eyes will behold the king in his beauty; they will see a land that stretches afar."
> (Isaiah 33: 15b-17a ESV)

It's also so I can be still and quiet in my spirit and hear better the impressions from the Holy Spirit when they come. I'm a fighter pilot and a warrior at heart, so I can get as stirred up as anyone. But I try not to do so. It aids in my joy and effectiveness in living the kingdom life God has gifted and planned for me. The following verses speak to this aspect of living:

> "Be still, and know that I am God.
> I will be exalted among the nations,
> I will be exalted in the earth!"
> (Psalm 46:10)

Who's Reporting to Trust

All the above said, I can quickly tell you who's reporting to trust, or at least that I trust—Amir Tsarfati, a Jew living in Israel. He has a historical, Biblical, and God-fearing perspective. He also has served in the IDF and has military insights and battlefield awareness. I would call it finger-on-the-pulse awareness of how the Israeli defense forces and intelligence community are thinking about the defense of Israel and her people. Also, what's really going on there on the ground?

Objective, truthful, no hype, to the point—that's how I see his messages and briefings. If you want to know the man and hear some of his reporting, you can find him on YouTube and Telegram social media platforms. He recently gave an interview in which he shared his own life story and Biblical/historical perspective on the nation of Israel entitled "Who is Amir Tsarfati?" That would be a good place to start.

Love What God Loves

As barbaric and evil as the October 7, 2023, attack on Israel by its Palestinian neighbors in Gaza was, the anti-Semitism that has come to light around the world since then is more troubling. People are marching, rioting, burning flags around the world, and threatening violence against Jewish people who probably don't know a Jew or who have never met a Jewish person. How do you explain that? Outside of dark, evil spirits?

People are jumping up and down around the world, protesting for media attention, burning Israeli and US flags, waving Palestinian flags, and defacing and destroying property. At the same time, they chant, "Free Palestine" or "From the river to the sea, Palestine will be free."

In a recent survey, college students were asked about the chant "From the River to the Sea, Palestine will be free." They were asked which river and which sea. An overwhelming majority of them did not know. Their guesses were as preposterous and humorous as they are sad and telling—telling that college-educated adults in the US have so little grasp of the history, religion, geography, and politics of the region, as well as the Bible.

My experience asking three college students in our church wasn't all that different, which is also telling. The referenced sea and river are the Mediterranean Sea and the Jordan River. The PLO popularized the phrase in the 1960s, calling for them to have a state that encompasses all of Israel and for Israel to have no country or state at all.

Those familiar with the Bible will recall that God gave Abraham, Isaac, Jacob, and their descendants forever the land from the Mediterranean Sea to the Euphrates River, a much larger part of the Middle East. Israel's boundaries under King Solomon about 1000 BC—1700 years before Islam—were as large as they have ever been, but the whole possession hasn't been under Israeli control yet. All the while, for 4000 years since Abraham, Jews have lived in the land. They didn't have an officially recognized nation since the Romans destroyed and dispersed them 70-73 AD, that is, until the miraculous return to the land after WWII and the rebirth of their nation on May 14, 1948.

"Your territory will extend from the desert to Lebanon, and from the great river, the Euphrates—all the Hittite country—to the Mediterranean Sea in the west" (Joshua 1:4—also see Genesis 15:18-20, Genesis 26:3, Genesis 28:13).

That is a short history, geography, and theology lesson. Grab your Bible and some history books, or do some valid research on the web. This will be a critical issue in the future until the end of time. You should know what you believe and why it's important. You should know what is right, historical, just, and true—the facts.

Jesus said, "You shall know them [people] by their fruit,"

by what they do, not what they say. Consider what both sides in the conflict have said and done throughout history, especially since 1948. Then, draw your conclusions.

In the meantime, you can dwell on the Bible-stated truth that God hates violence and loves Israel. You will always do well to love what God loves and hate what God hates. And **God loves Israel, declaring, "I have loved you with an everlasting love; therefore I have drawn you with lovingkindness**" (Jeremiah 31:3b). "The LORD examines the righteous, but the wicked, **those who love violence, he hates with a passion**" (Psalms 11:5 NIV).

Those who do not love what God loves and hate what God hates,—those who passionately support violence and hate Israel—are shaking their angry fists at God. This never ends well for them, their political organization, or those who support them.

This is how to make sense of it, even with the smoke and media haze—misguided secular-humanist deception. Be aware of these verses: "**They perish because they refused to love the truth and so be saved. For this reason God sends them a powerful delusion so that they will believe the lie**" (2 Thessalonians 2:10b-11).

Fear God and keep His commandments. Or if that seems out-of-date or too draconian for you, "Love What God loves, and hate what God hates." You'll be fine and fare well. Shalom and Godspeed on your journey to truth—also righteousness, peace, and joy. "For **the kingdom of God is not eating and drinking, but righteousness and peace and joy in the Holy Spirit**" (Romans 14:17).

"From the river to the sea, Palestine will be free." Indeed, that's what Israel is in the process of doing right now—in their second year! They are freeing Israel (the same place the Romans changed to Palestine for hate of the Jews) from a people who love violence, oppress their own, practice lawlessness and injustice, hate Israel their neighbors, and fire rockets and missiles at them incessantly. You reap what you sow. There is One who sees to it.

May our gracious Creator and King exercise justice and judgment mixed with mercy. It's His to do. And He is the only One who can. "To Him who sits on the throne, and to the Lamb, be blessing and honor and glory and dominion forever and ever" (Revelation 5:13).

Passover

Passover marks the deliverance from slavery to freedom by the death of a firstborn and the death of an innocent lamb. It's also an act of judgment and mercy born in the heart of the gracious, loving, and just Most High God. Amen.

Sin and death seem linked, as do innocent blood and forgiveness—forever.

On Earth at the moment, the scope of anti-Semitism and humanistic rebellion against this magnificent God is noteworthy. Similar situations have had their moments in history but have not swelled to the proportions seen in the past century and at this moment. Nor has it been seen to this extent in people professing faith in God. What does this portend for us as human beings? A time for war!

Angels, demons, and the people they influence worldwide are players in this cosmic and cataclysmic scenario. The most important part and factor is the judgment of the Almighty—

how and when He will choose to act, but act He will, out of justice and love.

There will be deliverance and protection for his own, those who fear him and draw near in fidelity and obedience. And there will be judgment on the evil and the unjust—a removal of cancer, if you will, for the healing of the nations and His creation.

Remember Passover each year and the gracious, merciful Holy One who initiated this deliverance—the Passover of the death angel who judged a rebellious, idol-ridden world power bent on destroying God's chosen people. Worship the Lamb and celebrate the victory He gives and makes possible over sin and death—also over sin and slavery.

> "'O death, where is your victory?
> O death, where is your sting?'
> For sin is the sting that results in death, and the law
> gives sin its power. But thank God! He gives
> us victory over sin and death through our
> Lord Jesus Christ."
> (1 Corinthians 15:55-57 NLT)

Presently Jewish people are coming to faith in Jesus as Messiah in historically unprecedented numbers. A friend in Israel told me a few years ago there are Messianic communities in every village in Israel and every neighborhood in Jerusalem. That this is happening in our times is significant and worth monitoring. One good resource is oneforisrael.org.

Shabbat or Sabbath

"So there remains a Sabbath rest
for the people of God."
(Hebrews 4:9)

"More than Israel has kept the Sabbath,
the Sabbath has kept Israel."
— Ahad Ha'am

Israel was an ancient nation and people even to the Romans at the time of Christ. Josephus, roughly a contemporary of Jesus, was hired by the Roman emperor Domitian to write a history of the Jewish people. He entitled it *Antiquities of the Jews.*

Israel gave the world the Law, the Prophets, and a King to restore and set things right—Jesus of Nazareth, King of the Jews, whose kingdom has no beginning and will know no end (Micah 5).

God planned and foretold Jesus' entrance and exit in Earth's history. In His Earth time, King Jesus came personally to start a new chapter of His reign with his Holy Spirit poured out and operating in His family of faith. They would then do His bidding with angels at His command until His second coming or advent.

He gave us hints about the timing of this event but left it nebulous for a reason, with a strong admonition to "keep watch" and not forget that He is coming with His angels in the clouds. Everyone on the planet will know it at once: **"Then they will see the Son of Man coming in clouds with great power and glory"** (Mark 13:26).

Israel is the key to all this knowledge. They received and kept the oracles of God for mankind from early in mankind's history on earth until the appearance of the King and since. It seems I can't make sense of a book, understand history, or discuss current events without mentioning and understanding what the Bible says about Israel's place in the world.

I don't want to! I love them for what they have faithfully kept and left for mankind. And when they were unfaithful or astray, I love them for what they showed us about a faithful God Who keeps His word to Abraham, Isaac, and Jacob (Israel) and their descendants to "**a thousand generations**" (Deuteronomy 7:9). This is our God. We who believe in Him and are known by Him, the King of the universe. His name be praised.

Keeping the Sabbath is a part of the covenant known as The Ten Commandments outlined in Exodus chapter 20 of the Holy Bible. God gave these commandments to the people for their good, and they agreed to keep them. **The fourth commandment says: "Remember the sabbath to keep it holy.**" Then a few chapters later, we read: "**The Israelites are to observe the Sabbath, celebrating it for the generations to come as a lasting covenant. 'It will be a sign between me and the Israelites forever,** for in six days the Lord made the heavens and the earth, and **on the seventh day he rested and was refreshed**'"(Exodus 31:16-17 NIV).

A sign, between the God of Creation and the Jews, forever. It reminded them weekly He was the mighty Creator of all. He took time off to contemplate creation and be refreshed. He wanted them to enjoy the identical rest and refreshing as a part of their rhythm of life—to keep a life of work balanced with knowing and worshiping the Holy One, their Father and Creator, and enjoying necessary and beneficial rest for their bodies and souls. In that sense the sabbath is a spiritual discipline and rhythm.

This practice certainly set them apart from the peoples of the earth, which God also wanted to do. To create a people for Himself and to show the peoples of the Earth what that relationship and life with God might look like—and prepare a people to give birth to a righteous King and Messiah.

****

*"**Why are the nations in an uproar and the peoples devising a vain thing? The kings of the earth take their stand and the rulers take counsel together against the Lord and against His Anointed**, saying, 'Let us tear their fetters apart and cast away their cords from us!' **He who sits in the heavens laughs, the Lord scoffs at them.**
Then He will speak to them in His anger and terrify them in His fury, saying, '**But as for Me, I have installed My King upon Zion,
My holy mountain.**' ...
How blessed are all who take refuge in Him!"*
(Psalm 2)

*"'This is what **the Sovereign Lord says: When I gather the people of Israel from the nations where they have been scattered, I will be proved holy through them in the sight of the nations**. Then **they will live in their own land, which I gave to my servant Jacob**. They will live there in safety and will build houses and plant vineyards; **they will live*

in safety when I inflict punishment on all their neighbors who maligned them. Then they will know that I am the Lord their God.'"
(Ezekiel 28:25-26 NIV)

"For I will take you from the nations, gather you from all the lands and bring you into your own land."
(Ezekiel 36:24)

*"**Your eyes will see the King in His beauty**;* They will behold a far-distant land."
(Isaiah 33:17)

CHAPTER TWELVE
AVENUES OF SOUL CARE

*"...Not forsaking our own assembling together,
as is the habit of some, but encouraging
one another; and all the more as you
see the day drawing near."*
(Hebrews 10:25)

Seek and Savor Community and Reading

Community is a spiritual discipline I have not written or spoken about as I should. Soul care is all about relationships—relationships with our Creator and with each other. In the interest of stressing the individual nature and responsibility of soul care and the absolute need for solitude and silence, I have not properly acknowledged the importance of community.

Life Together, as Bonhoeffer aptly named it, is a precious aspect of our earthly journey, regardless of the circumstances. However, its value is particularly pronounced in times of persecution and warfare, when the support of a community is most needed.

Dietrich Bonhoeffer's most famous book, and a Christian classic, is *The Cost of Discipleship*. He wrote it as a Christ follower during the terror of the Nazi regime in the 1930's. *The Cost of Discipleship* is beautiful and powerful, based on Jesus' Sermon on the Mount. It's certainly worth the read, alone or with friends, as is his shorter, simpler *Life Together*, describing their community experiences in the worst and best times.

Elizabeth and I went to see *Sound of Hope: The Story of Possum Trot* with friends Sunday after church. It's a movie well worth seeing alone or with friends—community. It's a story about foster care in our country and what one largely-black community in Texas did to rescue unwanted children or children in need of a home. It's based on a true story, and you'll meet the real, true-life people involved in the heart-touching saga.

While at the movie, we saw previews of an upcoming movie about Bonhoeffer: *Bonhoeffer: Pastor, Spy, Assassin,* hopefully based on Eric Metaxas's excellent biography *Bonhoeffer: Pastor, Martyr, Prophet, Spy*. This book is another must-read to understand what happened in Germany, what's happening again today, and how the Spirit of God moves in all ages and circumstances.

Reading is a spiritual discipline and can be a habit or rhythm. As such, it is an excellent avenue to soul care. When you read, you humble yourself to listen to someone else. You experience solitude and silence, just being with your thoughts, the author, and the Lord.

You can also do it as part of a reading group or a book club and experience the above benefits with the additional community benefit. Read *Bonhoeffer: Pastor, Martyr, Prophet, Spy*, and you'll thank me. Consider making reading good books a part of your rhythm for the rest of your life and the rest of your soul.

> "Books open windows to the world and have the power to transform lives."
>
> — Ralph Lauren

Solitude and Silence

> "The most important thing in your life is not what you do; it's who you become. That's what you will take into eternity."
>
> — Dallas Willard

Dallas Willard's quote is at the core of why you should take care of your soul and want to practice spiritual disciplines, habits, and rhythms. When you spend time with God, looking at his image as described in the Bible and at the person of Jesus of Nazareth, you become like Him. That's a much better version of yourself you want to enjoy on earth and take into eternity. This is the purpose and essence of soul care.

Dallas Willard (September 4, 1935 – May 8, 2013) was an American philosopher known for his writings on Christian spiritual formation. He was a Professor of Philosophy at The University of Southern California in Los Angeles, teaching and serving as the department chair for many years. Twenty years ago, I read his book *The Spirit of the Disciplines: Understanding How God Changes Lives*, which impacted me greatly.

He wasn't in the business of telling us how to practice the spiritual disciplines. He said better people than him had written books about that and mentioned Richard Foster's *The Celebration of Discipline*, another highly recommended source. Willard said I'm here to tell you we should practice the spiritual disciplines. If Jesus and Paul practiced them, why should we not practice them? He went on to say that solitude and silence were the most important spiritual disciplines, and he thought solitude was the hinge of them all.

Getting alone with God and your thoughts is increasingly difficult in our day of speed and distracting technological gadgets. But it's no less important than it's been throughout the centuries and millennia. It's a practice that lets you experience the beauty of the human soul and the human being. It's where you think about the truth you know and why it's important. It's where you evaluate what's happening around you for more truth. It's where you decide what you want to become and how to get there. It's how you listen for the Holy Spirit of God to speak into your life and soul via your spirit.

So, do you see how the world's hurry and din is public enemy number one for your soul? When is there time to think? Where is there a quiet place to reason? Will you find these times and places with intentionality, shut out the world for a while so your soul can breathe, and listen to your spirit and the Holy Spirit for impetus, inspiration, and power to make needed or desired changes? You must do so habitually, or you'll be conformed to the world and cultural forces around you by default. You do not want that to happen, as it would be deforming, if not damning, to your soul. You want to light a candle instead of cursing the darkness. You want God's help to create a clean heart and renew a right spirit within you.

In my last book, *Puzzling 2020, Connecting the Pieces*, I described a Christian worldview and healthy paradigm for living. Several times, I mentioned a verse from Second Thessalonians that perfectly describes our time: "**Let no one deceive you by any means**; for that Day [the coming of the Lord] will not come unless the falling away comes first … Because **they did not receive the love of the truth, that they might be saved. And for this reason God will send them strong delusion, that they should believe the lie**" (2 Thessalonians 2:3a, 10b-11 NKJV). Hurry and technology addiction seem like the tools of a strong delusion. Practicing soul care can keep those two forces at bay, providing a more peaceful life as we are transformed into His image for our good and the greater good of those around us.

> "We don't believe something by merely saying we believe it, or even when we believe that we believe it. We believe something when we act as if it were true."
> — Dallas Willard

"The greatest issue facing the world today, with all its heartbreaking needs, is whether those who, by profession or culture, are identified as 'Christians' will become disciples – students, apprentices, practitioners – of Jesus Christ, steadily learning from him how to live the life of the Kingdom of the Heavens into every corner of human existence."

— Dallas Willard

"The first act of love is always the giving of attention."

— Dallas Willard

"A disciple is a person who has decided that the most important thing in their life is to learn how to do what Jesus said to do."

— Dallas Willard

"Ruthlessly eliminate hurry from your life."

— Dallas Willard

"Spiritual people are not those who engage in certain spiritual practices; they are those who draw their life from a conversational relationship with God."

— Dallas Willard

Other Habits, Rhythms, and Disciplines

I will follow Dallas Willard's lead here and say there are better people than me to tell you how to practice some of these habits. They will get you on the higher and brighter path to a full-orbed day. Richard Foster's *The Celebration of Discipline* is a classic. There is also the gifted communicator John Mark Comer, who seems to speak to the oldest and youngest generations effectively about these truths and practices. Two of his most popular books are *The Ruthless Elimination of Hurry* and *Practicing the Way.*

Foster describes twelve disciplines divided into three categories. The Inward Disciplines comprise meditation, prayer, fasting, and study. The Outward Disciplines comprise simplicity, solitude, submission, and service. The Corporate Disciplines comprise confession, worship, guidance, and celebration. So there is plenty to choose from to develop habits and rhythms that work for you if you want to change and know God better. It's not one size fits all.

In these books you'll be guided and inspired to find a few habits or rhythms that work for you in spending T-I-M-E with God. These may change occasionally. You can experiment with them to see what works for you. But the bottom line is you must continually practice some of these habits to know God better and be transformed into the best version of yourself, or you will conform to something else.

In a YouTube video discussing *Practicing the Way*, John Mark Comer cites a survey that says 71% of Americans say they are Christians, while 4% say they are practicing disciples of Jesus. Why the gap? Where are you? It's worth pondering and doing something about it.

The Bible

The purpose of this book is to give thanks and credit to God for His grace in my life and the lives of my family and friends, the times He has come near, and His gracious faithfulness in staying near all our lives long.

I've come to see that the most important pursuit in life is taking care of our souls. Of course this is so we can know God, enjoy our life on earth to the full, and enjoy life with our Creator forever. *The Westminster Catechism* comes to mind: **"Man's chief end is to glorify God and enjoy Him forever."** This is the most essential and rewarding pursuit in life. Most friends my age speak of it often and wonder why we're discovering it so late in life. Yet, to a person, we're just joyful to find it now with its beauty, peace, and rest.

The habits, disciplines, and rhythms that I've described can be used in part or in whole to care for your soul. Consider them activities in the craft of soul care. They are your part. Then God, by His grace and goodwill, does the more lasting, more complex, more mystical part, as His word and the lives of millions of believers attest. "For God, who said, 'Light shall shine out of darkness,' is **the One who has shone in our hearts to give the Light of the knowledge of the glory of God in the face of Christ. But we have this treasure in earthen vessels, so that the surpassing greatness of the power will be of God and not from ourselves**" (2 Corinthians 4:6-7).

I hope you see the value and are motivated to adopt as many of these habits as you see fit. These habits may change for variety and in different seasons of your life. Remember, you make your habits, and then your habits make you. "Practice makes perfect" may take on a whole new meaning and dimension in your life.

We know it's the Spirit that does the perfecting. **"Can the Ethiopian change his skin or the leopard his spots?**

Then you also can do good who are accustomed to doing evil" (Jeremiah 13:23). The inference is that you can't do this on your own, change your bad habits, but the Holy Spirit can do anything. We read about the Spirit: "'**Not by might nor by power, but by My Spirit,' says the Lord of hosts**" (Zechariah 4:6b). Jesus' words on the matter are the most compelling and clear: "**It is the Spirit who gives life; the flesh profits nothing; the words that I have spoken to you are spirit and are life**" (John 6:63).

But by choosing to seek a relationship with God and exercise your mind, emotions, and will to practice these habits, which amount to T-I-M-E with God, you place yourself under the waterfall of His grace. You will be changed for the better by His love and power into another person and the best version of yourself. It's His pleasure to help you and know you. So do it! Out with the bad habits! And in with the good! You decide, and start showing your decision by your actions today. He will help you.

All the spiritual habits, disciplines, or rhythms benefit your soul. Some will be more to your liking and tailored to your desires and lifestyle. Reading the word of God, the Bible, daily surely tops the list. There's just something arresting, magical, mystical, and decisive about what it does for your soul, and your psyche.

The Scripture says about itself that it is "God-breathed." "**All Scripture is God-breathed and is useful for teaching, rebuking, correcting and training in righteousness,so that the servant of God may be thoroughly equipped for every good work**" (2 Timothy 3:16-17 NIV). You will recall that in the beginning: "…**The Lord God** formed man of the dust of the ground, and **breathed into his nostrils the breath** of life; and man became a living soul" (Genesis 2:7 KJV). There is a connection. He is still breathing life into souls through the revelation of His Word accompanied by spiritual power.

In the arena of spiritual warfare against dark, lying spirits, we're told that the Bible is the sword of the Spirit: "And take the helmet of salvation, and **the sword of the Spirit, which is the word of God**" (Ephesians 6:17). We are told that the Bible can be used for healing and spiritual surgery too: "For **the word of God is living and active and sharper than any two-edged sword**, and **piercing as far as the division of soul and spirit, of both joints and marrow, and able to judge the thoughts and intentions of the heart**" (Hebrews 4:12). This is very valuable in regard to soul care—the soul's health and healing.

Practice the additional habits and rhythms as you like, but start and stay with this one: Read the word of God daily. Get under the refreshing waterfall of His grace often and much. Abide there habitually. It will change your day when you start this way and your direction and destiny in life.

David, a man after God's heart and the king of Israel said: "**Your word is a lamp to my feet and a light to my path**" (Psalm 119:105). He said many other things about the critical nature and importance of the Word to our souls in Psalm 119 and elsewhere: "**How can a young man keep his way pure? By keeping it according to Your word.**" "**Your word I have treasured in my heart, that I may not sin against You.**" "**I will meditate on Your precepts and regard Your ways. I shall delight in Your statutes; I shall not forget Your word**" (Psalm 119: 9,11,15-16). "I will give thanks to You, for I am fearfully and wonderfully made; **wonderful** are Your works, and my soul knows it very well." "**How precious also are Your thoughts to me**, O God! How vast is the sum of them! If I should count them, they would outnumber the sand. **When I awake, I am still with You**" (Psalm 139:14, 17-18).

A Word About the Word from the Cabin

While building the cabin, I wondered if it would be wise to include an alarm system and possibly some cameras on the doors for security since electronics were becoming less expensive and more common. I visited a local audiovisual shop and got to know the owner. I told him my vision for the cabin to be a spiritual retreat, a place for family gatherings, and a place to share the beauty of solitude, silence, and nature with others. He was intrigued and said he would give me a quote. I flew him to the mountaintop with his right-hand man so he could survey the situation and give me that quote, and he offered to do it for us at his cost, an offer I didn't refuse. The Bible teaches that a workman is worthy of his wages. I usually insist upon paying, but I'm also learning to receive and accept grace for the beautiful gift it is.

While standing there and looking out over the view, while his helper measured things and prepared the quote, this brother said something remarkable that was entirely out of the blue—and quite true: "Most of the country's problems would be solved if people just read their Bibles."

I think our country's history and that of Western Civilization bear that out. So, don't curse the darkness—light a candle in your soul today by reading the Word of God regularly and encouraging your friends to do the same. Talk about it over coffee and meals—study books of the Bible or its themes. Go online and find a yearly reading plan that appeals to you. If you miss a day, start where you are the next time you pick it up. You know what to do.

> "**Be diligent to present yourself approved to God as a workman who does not need to be ashamed, accurately handling the word of truth.**"
> (2 Timothy 2:15)

> "**Ezra opened the book in the sight of all the people** for he was standing above all the people; and **when he opened it, all the people stood up**. Then **Ezra blessed the Lord the great God. And all the people answered, 'Amen, Amen!' while lifting up their hands; then they bowed low and worshiped the Lord with their faces to the ground.**"
> (Nehemiah 8:5-6)

Lord of the Sabbath

> "For the Son of Man is Lord of the Sabbath."
> (Matthew 12:8)

The elements of soul care are the practices that keep our spirits attuned to the Holy Spirit. He is the source of help, truth, and life to the full. He's willing to grace us with His presence and help if we demonstrate that we want it by our actions. This is soul care—solitude and silence, reading the Word

Avenues of Soul Care

daily, praying daily, and staying in a community of believers, and other such habits—time spent with God.

Revisiting Sabbath

When I was a young child in America in the 1950s and 1960s, stores were closed on Sundays in almost every community except for one gas station and one pharmacy in case someone needed emergency fuel or medicine. This honored the Biblical institution of the Sabbath, which we celebrated on Sundays in keeping with early Christian traditions.

Now, some 50 years later, in cities of any size, it's not uncommon to see neon signs on 24/7 sex shops! That's a steep dive morally away from God. Commerce and the rush of life are ongoing 24/7/365. That's noteworthy, and it happened in my life span of 70 years—or one generation, depending on how you wish to define a generation. I wonder if keeping the Sabbath might have helped stand against this cultural tide—and do so even now.

Shabat or Sabbath

Of all the Ten Commandments, the command to "Remember the sabbath to keep it holy" may be the hardest to understand by moderns. And that lack of understanding or paying heed demonstrates our betrayal of the truth and our deceived hearts.

Of the seven simple words in the ancient commandment to Israel and mankind, two are ambiguous to moderns—"Sabbath and holy." Sabbath means "stop." "Cease from your work and labor" by your volition and willpower. Decide to risk not working because God chose to rest and tells you to do the same every seventh day. In doing so, you reflect and come to know that He can keep everything as it should be, and you can rest. That thought and act is holy, "set apart." Because God is holy—"set apart" from His creation. He invites you to join him in rest in deference to Him, His example, and His command. I'm coming to see it as a gift.

I saw my friend Tim at church Sunday and asked for his thoughts about the Sabbath since I was researching it and meditating on it. Tim is an electrical engineer who lived with his family in China for five years. He is the leader of our missions leadership team, and he has considerable Quaker influence in his spiritual DNA. Off the cuff, he said: "Well, it set Israel apart from the other nations. I guess you would ask yourself what your motive for observing the Sabbath is and what the benefit is. It was to be rest for yourself, from your work and efforts. It shows that you trust in God's care and that if you rest, He will take care of you." I think that's well said and true.

You can hear echoes of Jesus' sermon on the mount. "Therefore I say unto you, **Be not anxious for your life**, what ye shall eat, or what ye shall drink; nor yet for your body, what ye shall put on. Is not the life more than the food, and the body than the raiment? **Behold the birds of the heaven**, that they sow not, neither do they reap, nor gather into barns; and **your heavenly Father feedeth them. Are not ye of much more value than they?**" (Matthew 6:25-26). You can read the entire, powerful, short sermon in Matthew 6:25-34 and Luke 12:22-32. In a brief meditation, I saw: "Your Father sees, your Father knows, your Father cares for the lilies of the fields and the birds of the air—see and believe, see and receive, the grace and blessing and peace of the Lord." The Sabbath is meant to be peaceful—to give your soul space to breathe, meditate, contemplate spiritual matters and the deeper issues of life. It provides silence to hear from God if He speaks, or rest from thinking altogether with some downtime to refresh.

Tim texted me some more thoughts about the Sabbath from John chapter 9 a few days later. Jesus healed a blind man on the Sabbath, and the religious concluded that He couldn't be from God, that He must be a sinner. Blindness and sightedness are connected here and in much of the New Testament to the practice of the Sabbath. As it was then, it may still be today. Maybe we should practice keeping the Sabbath and see if our spiritual sight improves.

Christians benefit from The Law but are also free from The Law. We have a new and better way, a living way: "Therefore, brethren, since **we have confidence to enter the holy place by the blood of Jesus, by a new and living way** which He inaugurated for us through the veil, that is, His flesh" (Hebrews 10:19-20). Christians aren't bound to keep the Sabbath; we'll hear the Apostle Paul speak to that later. But should we keep it in some shape, form, or fashion anyway?

Three Words

Three words of the command stick out. "Remember" may be the operative word. Jesus remembered and observed it. He was sinless. But He did some things that didn't meet the religious standards of the day—traditions of men, man-made requirements some had added to God's Word.

"Sabbath" is the point and action required in the command. Its primitive root is a verb. The BDB Hebrew English Lexicon defines it: 1. To cease 2. To rest, desist (from labor). Strong's Lexicon adds "intermission."

"Holy" means to be set apart and consecrated. BDB defines it: "1. to be set apart, consecrated 2. to be hollowed 3. consecrated, tabooed." God Himself set it apart and explained His thoughts in 98 words: "**Remember the sabbath day, to keep it holy. Six days you shall labor and do all your work**, but **the seventh day is a sabbath of the Lord your God; in it you shall not do any work, you or your son or your daughter**, your male or your female servant or your cattle or your sojourner who stays with you. For **in six days the Lord made the heavens and the earth, the sea and all that is in them, and rested on the seventh day**; therefore **the Lord blessed the sabbath day** and made it holy" (Exodus 20:8-11).

Later in Exodus, God adds confirmation of His intent and expands slightly on His thoughts about the Sabbath: "**The Israelites are to observe the Sabbath, celebrating it for the generations to come as a lasting covenant. 'It will be a sign between me and the Israelites forever,** for in six days the Lord made the heavens and the earth, and **on the seventh day he rested** and **was refreshed**'"(Exodus 31:16-17 NIV).

In these passages, it's clear that the **Sabbath observance is tied to creation**, using your God-given authority **to teach about creation and God's role and place in creation and the universe to those near you, rest**, and **being refreshed**.

Paul and the early Jewish Christians almost certainly kept the Sabbath. Jesus did. In their minds, they were still Jews—God's covenant people. Only they had seen the Messiah come to fulfill a promise, a covenant, and to initiate a new one.

They met, at least sometimes, on the first day of the week. And that would end up setting them apart (being holy) from the common—Greeks, pagans, Romans, and non-believing Jews. But the reason was the same—to remember the Creator weekly, to rest their bodies and souls, to commune with God, and to honor His example and wishes.

I think the Saturday vs Sunday day of Sabbath isn't the main discussion. I'll give you some historical and theological thoughts on it, but the main issue isn't the day—it's whether to practice or not to practice Sabbath. For millennia, Jews and Christians have practiced Sabbath, but today, relatively few Christians do.

The Bible reports instances of the first Christians meeting on Sundays (Acts 20:7, 1 Corinthians 16:2). Sunday was called the Lord's Day by John (Revelation 1:10). Jesus was resurrected on Sunday. The Holy Spirit came into the upper room to the Disciples on a Sunday. Probably the most critical evidence that the earliest disciples adopted Sunday worship was the meeting in Jerusalem where the Apostles and church's elders decided what to require of the large numbers of Gentiles coming to faith in Christ and receiving His Holy Spirit. They didn't mention keeping the Jewish Sabbath, and they certainly would have if they thought it imperative to the new covenant. "Therefore **it is my judgment that we do not trouble those who are turning to God from among the Gentiles, but that we write to them that they abstain from things contaminated by idols and from fornication and from what is strangled and from blood**" (Acts 15:19-20).

Paul elsewhere wrote: "<u>Therefore</u> **no one is to act as your judge in regard to** food or drink or in respect to a festival or a new moon or **a Sabbath day**—things which are a mere shadow of what is to come; but **the substance belongs to Christ**" (Colossians 2:16-17). And: "**One person regards one day above another, another regards every day alike. Each person must be fully convinced in his own mind. He who observes the day, observes it for the Lord... So then each one of us will give an account of himself to God.**" (Romans 14:5-6a,12).

The Holy Spirit seems to have made it about motivation and what's in your heart, and doing it as worship to the Lord, honor, and rest. The words still hang in the air and the heavens as they have for 3500 years when God instructed Moses to write them in stone. It is incredible how much turmoil and peace the practice has precipitated since then. Peace if you keep it. Turmoil and fatigue of body, soul, and spirit if you don't.

A profound quote from A.W. Tozer comes to mind: "What you believe about God is the most important thing about you." What do you think God thinks about the Sabbath? It is essentially about:

1. Rest
2. Separation (the holy from the profane)
3. Honoring and Loving God
4. Trusting God
5. Teaching that God is the Creator (to the next generation and all in your realm, remembering)
6. Doing this weekly (you make your habits, and then they make you)
7. Restoration of body and soul (weekly, rhythmically).

When reading Colossians 2:16 above, I wanted to know what the "Therefore" was there for. So I read Colossians 2 in the Amplified Bible, and it's my new favorite chapter, along with John 3 and Psalm 23. It's for such a time and purpose as this and such a Savior and King as Jesus. I encourage you to read it slowly and repeatedly and meditate on the profound, insightful truth shared therein.

The Finger of God

"**Remember the sabbath day, to keep it holy.**" This injunction was first written by the finger of God in stone on Mount Horeb for the family of Israel and, through them, the peoples of the Earth. Some would see it or hear and believe in the one true God among all the idols of the Earth, which are contrived by dark spirits and the imaginations of mankind. Due to the spiritual sensitivity Sabbath fosters, many would recognize the coming of Christ, the Messiah.

The command is located right there with: "Thou shall not murder," "Thou shall not commit adultery," and "Honor your father and mother." In ten brief commandments, we were given the most succinct and impactful moral code mankind has known.

Sabbath doesn't seem to fit with prohibitions about destroying life without cause, destroying families, and destroying others possessions or material living. But it's given in this context, so you know it fits and it's there for a reason. Like the top button on a shirt, if it's in the wrong hole, all the others are also. So, it deserves investigation, consideration, and getting it right.

When reading the Bible, it's important to read the context

of verses, and also the context of chapters, that is, the chapters just before and after the one that caught your interest. Before Exodus 20, the Ten Commandments, we read in Exodus 19: **"You yourselves have seen what I did to the Egyptians, and how I bore you on eagles' wings, and brought you to Myself"** (Exodus 19:4). That chapter is full of passion and pathos, for the past, present, and future. Words like slavery, deliverance, covenant, mountaintop, quaking violently, "on the third day" numerous times, burning, holy, and fire are all woven into what's transpiring just before Moses receives the Law in the presence of the Lord God. It sets the stage for the solemn assembly and convocation and forever gives it its proper place in the lives of the people and their generations. It's T-I-M-E with a God jealous for a relationship with a people jealous for Him.

Sabbath as a Discipline

Sabbath isn't usually listed as a spiritual discipline, but it may be the first and most important. John Mark Comer is the former pastor of a megachurch in Oregon. He resigned and moved to Southern California to write and live like a disciple of Jesus. I'm told that practicing the Sabbath is the first rule he advocates in following Jesus. A friend just gave me his new book, *Practicing the Way*. I have yet to start reading it, but I intend to lead our young community group of seekers to give it a look. We all need to be motivated to practice the habits, rhythms, and disciplines of our ancient-future Faith—to know God, and continually experience His life with Him.

Practicing the Sabbath makes sense. Not only did it come from God's heart, mouth, and finger to us and for us—it provides the solitude, silence, space, rest, and peace that our souls crave and need. We fill our souls with continuous noise and activity, effectively shutting off spiritual hearing, seeing, and being. It's not by coincidence that Sabbath is in the same context as idol worship and dishonoring God—the Creator and Life-giver.

Sabbath may be the top button of the disciplines, habits, and rhythms of our Faith. I'm ready to give it a try. It could be the top button of our shirts, and the rest of our habits will follow and be in the correct place. Then, we will be appropriately dressed and ready to go out into the world to experience life and relationships with power underneath our hoods for living and loving.

"So **if the Son makes you free, you will be free indeed**" (John 8:36). "You blind Pharisee, **first clean the inside of the cup and of the dish, so that the outside of it may become clean also**" (Matthew 23:26). "But **we have this treasure in earthen vessels, so that the surpassing greatness of the power will be of God and not from ourselves**" (2 Corinthians 4:7). Practice the way.

****

"Thus says the Lord,
"Stand by the ways and see and
ask for the ancient paths,
Where the good way is, and walk in it;
And you will find rest for your souls.
But they said, 'We will not walk in it.'"
(Jeremiah 6:16)

> "Then he said to them, **"The Sabbath was made for man, not man for the Sabbath."**
> (Mark 2:27 NIV)

> "Now **the day** on which **Jesus had made the mud and opened the man's eyes was a Sabbath.**"
> (John 9:14 NIV)

> "...Envying, drunkenness, carousing, and things like these, of which I forewarn you, just as I have forewarned you, that **those who practice such things will not inherit the kingdom of God**."
> (Galatians 5:21)

> "The things you have learned and received and heard and seen in me, **practice these things, and the God of peace will be with you**."
> (Philippians 4:9)

> "Therefore, brethren, be all the more diligent to make certain about His calling and choosing you; for as long **as you practice these things, you will never stumble**."
> (2 Peter 1:10)

> "Therefore **everyone who hears these words of Mine and acts on them**, may be compared to a wise man who built his house on the rock. And the rain fell, and the floods came, and the winds blew and

slammed against that house; and yet it did not fall, for it had been founded on the rock."
(Matthew 7:24-25)

"Grace and peace be yours in abundance through the knowledge of God and of Jesus our Lord."
(2 Peter 1:2)

"The household of God, *which* **is the church of the living God, the pillar and support of the truth."**
(1 Timothy 3:15b)

"By common confession, great is the mystery of godliness."
(1 Timothy 3:16a)

"Discipline yourself *for the purpose of godliness."*
(1 Timothy 4:7b)

CHAPTER THIRTEEN

Community and Soul Care

"But you will receive power when the Holy Spirit has
come upon you, and you will be my witnesses in Jerusalem and in all Judea and Samaria,
and to the end of the earth."
(Acts 1:8)

"For the kingdom of God does not
consist in talk but in power."
(1 Corinthians 4:20)

Beware of the Church

Jesus told us that. It's recorded in Matthew 12 and other places. He was telling His disciples about an issue and problem with religion—leadership that has stopped listening to God's Spirit, trusting in themselves and their knowledge of the Way, and teaching others to do the same. They rely on their strength apart from God. They probably don't even know it. If you're deceived, you don't know it.

> "But when the Pharisees saw this, they said to Him, 'Look, Your disciples do what is not lawful to do on a Sabbath.' … [Jesus responded] Have you not read in the Law, that on the Sabbath the priests in the temple break the Sabbath and are innocent? But I say to you that something greater than the temple is here. But **if you had known what this means, 'I desire compassion, and not a sacrifice,' you would not have condemned the innocent. For the Son of Man is Lord of the Sabbath**"
> (Matthew 12:2-8).

That's why we need community, truth-seeking and truth-speaking friends, and the mirror of the Holy Scriptures. These are elements of soul care—practices that keep our spirits attuned to the Holy Spirit. He is the source of help, truth, and life to the full. He's willing to grace us with His presence and help if we demonstrate that we want it by our actions. This is soul care—solitude and silence, reading the Bible daily, praying daily, staying in a community of believers, and other such habits—time spent with God.

A life spent memorizing and learning rules to exalt oneself or one's community is not winsome or compelling, and it's not life in the Spirit. It's blinding, actually—to the way, the truth, and the life. So make it your practice to be in a lively community of believers who are humble learners and care for your soul.

Be Aware of the Church

You probably won't meet anyone more critical and supportive of the church than me. I'm critical of the church because of what I see and what Jesus taught in the parable above. Churches and church leaders often lead people astray into trusting in their own strength and ways instead of the true teaching of the Bible, as demonstrated by a living relationship with the Holy Spirit.

It's like a false hope in tradition or an institution when the Spirit has left the building. One of my favorite spiritual mentors, Charles Simpson, said it this way, "The church in the West is like a bunch of men playing cards in a hotel that's on fire." And a pastor I recently met in Malaysia told me: "Our Baptists are not like many of yours. If something is on the menu, it should be in the kitchen."

Love the Church

On the other hand, **Christ loved the church and gave Himself for her** (Ephesians 5:2)! So I love the church too. The true church is a community of believers who seek to know God as revealed in the Holy Bible, conform to His ways, obey His precepts, and seek to be led and empowered by His

Spirit. It's a mysterious but observable living relationship. It's a romance, a commitment, a blessing, and a joy. It leads to lives that are winsome, joyful, and compelling.

Like most romances, it's something to be experienced and enjoyed more than analyzed. It's a living and feeling thing—not something you only talk about, describe, and say you have when you don't. I think you understand what I'm saying and perhaps have experienced it.

Be aware of the church's proper place in Christ's affections, and find a group or community that seeks to teach the whole Bible and be led by the Holy Spirit. If it's not perfect—and it won't be—**seek to be light and salt there, and in humility, work to reform her while you "work out your salvation with fear and trembling**" (Philippians 2:12b).

It's not an option if you call Jesus Lord and want to know Him better for your good, welfare, joy, power in living and for the immense pleasure of His company. The Scripture says it like this: "**Not giving up meeting together, as some are in the habit of doing, but encouraging one another—and all the more as you see the Day approaching**" (Hebrews 10:25 NIV). And: "**Why do you call Me, 'Lord, Lord,' and do not do what I say? Everyone who comes to Me and hears My words and acts on them**, I will show you whom he is like: **he is like a man building a house, who dug deep and laid a foundation on the rock; and when a flood occurred, the torrent burst against that house and could not shake it, because it had been well built**" (Luke 6:46-48). Habitually, rhythmically, and continually meeting with other believers is an essential element and a reward of soul care.

It's the way of peace and life—and a good deal of joy!

Godspeed as you journey and live in community with like-minded believers.

****

"But Jesus answered them, 'You are wrong, because you know neither the Scriptures nor the power of God.'"
(Matthew 22:29)

"For I decided to know nothing among you except Jesus Christ and Him crucified. And I was with you in weakness and in fear and much trembling, and my speech and my message were not in plausible words of wisdom, but in demonstration of the Spirit and of power, so that your faith might not rest in the wisdom of men but in the power of God."
(1 Corinthians 2:2-5)

"Once God has spoken; twice have I heard this: that power belongs to God, and that to you, O Lord, belongs steadfast love. For you will render to a man according to his work."
(Psalm 62:10-11)

CHAPTER FOURTEEN
Self Control

KNOW THYSELF
CONTROL THYSELF
BE WHO YOU WANT TO BE

That's what I was hearing as I awakened recently.

Self-control (http://selfctrl.com) is a ministry my young friend Ian founded with his wife Hayley. It's so needed and crucial to happiness and long-term joy. It means repeatedly making decisions that make you who you are and who you want to be—who you choose to be. If you get to know Jesus, that's who you'll choose to imitate. He's the best!

Ian is my mentee, or so he calls himself. I call him a friend. We have a lot in common, even though he's younger than my son, at about half my age. What we hold most in common is a love for Jesus and His ways.

Ian's ministry is mainly about self-control in the area of screen time and technology addiction, as opposed to its appropriate use—also awareness of its hidden (and not so hidden) dangers. The overuse or unwise use of technology is very unhealthy for your soul. Thus, there is a need to see the danger and exercise self-control.

I know Ian well. We went on a mission to Africa last year and were roommates. The young church we went to support in Uganda was permeated by a loving atmosphere. However, the surrounding culture was a hostile spiritual atmosphere; meeting the challenge of spiritual warfare for the first time with a friend like Ian was a bonding experience. We've also spent more than a few hours sharing lives, struggles, and choices in the Old Pine coffee shop or my living room. I consider our friendship a treasure and look forward to knowing Ian even better as we encourage each other, pray for each other, and fight more spiritual battles—increasingly about self-control.

We live in a culture, country, and time where people are out of control. They have cast off restraint. They no longer believe or know that the person who exercises the most self-control enjoys God's favor, long-term happiness, and a character worth having.

Self-control and these character traits can be experienced, won, and achieved by *Practicing the Way*. That's the name of the new book by John Mark Comer. It's also the practice of

Jesus' followers throughout the centuries—our ancient-future faith's habits, rhythms, and disciplines. It's a way of living life above the fray. It's spending time with the Master daily so you can focus on the most important issues—those of character—and experience the power of His Spirit to help you as you go.

Want to Go It Alone?

Self-discipline or self-restraint in a runaway world will benefit its adherents and speak loudly to those around them. Can you do it by yourself, or is it a fruit of the Spirit? "Yes" might be the answer, I'm not sure. But even if you can master willpower and habits to prove your strength or superiority over the rank and file of humans, what is the benefit? A better-than-average life with some health benefits and some peace, but a lonely and restless soul still not knowing its loving Creator, Father, and Friend.

You may prove yourself stronger than he who conquers the city (Proverbs 16:32) . But as Jesus said, "**What does it profit a man to gain the whole world, and forfeit his soul**?" (Mark 8:36). Or, "**What will a man give in exchange for his soul?**" (Mark 8:37). It's often said in our materialistic culture, "He who dies with the most toys wins." Some seer has countered, "He who dies with the most toys wins—nothing."

The fact that it's even possible to live a life of self-control without God's help is a testimony to the power God invested in human souls when He breathed life into them. It's a powerful testimony to the power and presence of choice He has granted them in their lifetime journey in a world of dark spirits seeking to destroy them.

In the end, they can say, with the poet author of *Invictus*, "I am the master of my fate and the captain of my soul." Or they can sing with Frank Sinatra, "I did it my way." Both beautifully express pride in a human soul, wanting to go it alone with the gift of life and take credit for their successes and failures. Our gracious, magnanimous Creator allows it. Knowing all the outcomes, He gave this gift and permitted the choices. Powerful, loving, and generous is He. The scripture comes to mind: "**The Most High … is kind to those who are unthankful and wicked**" (Luke 6:35b NLT).

But at the end of such a life, with all the sweat, blood, and tears expended, are two sad realities. The battles and journey could have been much easier with God's help, which He proffers from the abiding of His Spirit. And in the end, your soul would have the pleasure of knowing its Creator and enjoying His presence in times of warfare and peace. Like the Lord told Abraham after a battle: "**I am your shield, your very great reward**" (Genesis 15:1b NIV).

To know God is your best destiny, and to be known by Him is the greatest treasure imaginable—not the pleasure of "doing it my way." Seek to do it His way! With habits of solitude and silence, read His word and get to know Him. Make it your lifelong practice and see the pleasure of His ways for the rest of your life and the rest of your soul.

Summary

You can fight the battles of self-control on your own your whole life. But that's super tiring, and many wear out trying or don't even attempt to control themselves—their bodies, impulses, and passions. But you must control them, or they will control you! They are not all necessarily bad. They are a part of you that is given to you for a purpose. But they must be controlled to have a good character and a life worth living—peaceful, joyful, and free. It's been said that following Jesus is not a do-it-yourself project. You will need His help through His Holy Spirit, which is proffered to you. Self-control is described in the Bible as a fruit of the Spirit.

I'm going to pour a cup of coffee and read my Bible. I'll spend some T-I-M-E with God and give some care to my soul. In doing so, His Spirit helps me with self-control. Godspeed as you journey on the road to self-control.

****

*"If you are wise, you are wise for yourself,
and if you scoff, you alone will bear it."*
(Proverbs 9:12)

*"He who is slow to anger is better than the mighty,
and he who rules his spirit, than
he who captures a city."*
(Proverbs 16:32)

*"As the deer pants for streams of water,
so my soul pants for you, my God."*
(Psalm 42:1 NIV)

*"Take my yoke upon you and learn from me,
for I am gentle and humble in heart,
and you will find rest for your souls."*
(Matthew 11:29)

*"For what shall it profit a man, if he shall gain
the whole world, and lose his own soul?"*
(Mark 8:36 KJV)

*"But the fruit of the Spirit is love, joy, peace, patience,
kindness, goodness, faithfulness, gentleness, self-control."*
(Galatians 5:22-23a)

CHAPTER FIFTEEN
Vignettes of Flight and Faith

My Brother's Hayfield

One of my main motivations for having a light airplane was to fly to visit my brother, who lives in a remote and knock-dead-beautiful place in northern Arkansas. It was a four-hour drive from where we lived but only a forty-five minute flight. The Cessna-172 that Ivan sold me could land on grass strips with no concerns, but it was not overpowered and not well suited to landing on relatively short grass strips that might also be a bit rough, like my bother's hay fields.

I trained and experimented with the plane on asphalt and smooth grass strips until I could land it on a picked spot every time, and I walked my brother's hay fields to learn which ones had acceptable surfaces and suitable lengths. There was one that would work: a quarter mile in length and a slope where I could land uphill for shorter stopping distances and take off downhill for shorter takeoff rolls. But with 50-foot trees at the south end at the fence line, this would be a one-way-in and one-way-out approach and landing. Everything had to be just right. Light winds would aid in better take-off performance, preferably out of the south. A light plane with a minimum fuel load and colder temperatures would be necessary for more lift and better engine performance. I landed there once in these conditions to prove I could and say that I had, but I also demonstrated to myself that there wasn't much margin for error and that I needed similar conditions to do it in the future. This largely influenced my decision to switch to a plane designed for the backcountry with short takeoff and landing (STOL) characteristics. I was all in when my friend Ken suggested it a few months later.

After obtaining a Maule MX7-235 in 2014 and practicing for a couple of years, I became proficient and familiar enough with the plane's capabilities that I routinely landed in the field mentioned above and an even shorter football-length field right beside my brother's house, where I could park and walk a hundred steps to his front porch. I enjoyed these experiences and the utility and flexibility this plane afforded.

Just Visiting My Dad

The first night my dad spent in the nursing home in our hometown of Jasper, Arkansas, I decided to call to see if he had a roommate and if it might be permissible for me to come and spend the night with him in his room. They responded, "Your father doesn't have a roommate yet, and that is a beautiful idea. You are welcome to do so." I knew the longest hayfield within walking distance was just behind the Jasper Baptist Church nearby, so I looked on Google Earth to see how long it was diagonally. It was a quarter of a mile. Perfect! I landed there before dark, taxied up to the fence behind the church, and tied the airplane down for the night. Then I walked over to the parsonage beside the church, knocked on the door, and asked the pastor if he knew who owned that field because the guy who owned it when I was growing up had passed away. Looking with a wild gaze at an airplane parked next to the church and at me, he said, "No, it belongs to someone out of town. They are hardly ever here." "Do you think leaving my airplane there overnight will be OK? I'm going to the nursing home to spend Dad's first night with him." "I think so. No one will see it from the highway, and I don't mind." He knew who I was, but we didn't know each other well, and of course, he knew my family—everyone in the small town did. Dad was a legend in the county, where he had been a game warden or wildlife officer, and civic leader for over forty years. So I said goodbye, picked up my overnight bag, and walked to the nursing home and into Dad's room.

He smiled and asked, "What are you doing here?" "I came to spend the night with you. I thought you might like a little company, and I wanted to check out the beds in this place." He grinned and nodded his head in pleased agreement. Dad was still very with it mentally, lion-like in his character and demeanor, but gentle and kind. Only his strength had begun to diminish, as happens to us all.

The staff had yet to learn how I had traveled there. A few weeks later, I returned for a visit and decided to land in the hay field next to the nursing home. It was a little shorter but had the right slope, and walking to spend the night with Dad had allowed me to check out the surface. I landed between Highway 7 and the Newton County Nursing Home, touching down just at the edge of their parking lot, east to west. I rolled a short distance, turned around, taxied back to a spot adjacent to the facility, and shut the engine off. Several employees and nurses came running to the plane, exclaiming, "Are you all right? Are you all right?" "Yes, I just came to visit my dad." "Well! Call us next time, for heaven's sake!"

They were alarmed, thinking someone had made a forced or crash landing, having never seen a plane in the unlikely spot. It was a fair request, and I did call them the next couple of times, but no one seemed to notice or care after the first big event. So, I kept landing there when desired and suspended the calls. The best part was more frequent visits with Dad and his friends. But it was also like a dream to land by the highway where I rode my horse into town as a boy and turn around a few feet from what once was VJ's Barber Shop, where I received many boyhood haircuts. Then I began my takeoff roll to the east, clearing the tall trees that lined Carlton Branch, and flew along the Little Buffalo River, where I had spent many hours swimming and fishing as a kid. It was surreal, like a dream to revisit this fairytale land of memories from my distant past. My soul smiled, and I was deeply grateful, feeling the goodness and grace of God in the land of the living.

Faith and Spirit — How Does Faith Come?

> *"And no one can say, 'Jesus is Lord,'*
> *except by the Holy Spirit."*
> (1 Corinthians 12:3b NIV)

Let's switch to vignettes of faith for a bit. How does one come to faith? It's a good question to ponder, especially since this book is largely about flight and faith—you might even say "flights of faith."

It's admittedly mysterious with agents or an Agent at work that we do not see or perceive until it's time or in the fullness of time. But we observe it happening to people and witness its long-term effects.

I recently saw a video where John Mark Comer and Tyler Stanton took a rabbit trail to discuss the difference between the "Gifts of the Spirit" and the "Fruits of the Spirit." We usually look immediately at gifts versus fruits and compare those items. What they have in common seems much more significant—"of the Spirit." They are gifts and fruits "of the Spirit." That's where they come from. He is their origin, genesis, and power. They are His gifts to us—grace and life-long gifts for living.

I continually tout the practices of making yourself available to the Spirit so you can be changed into His image and a better version of yourself. The time spent in His presence produces the fruits (Galatians 5:22-23) and energizes the gifts

(1 Corinthians 12:4-11) that help us and others. But I am getting ahead of myself. I am emphasizing the Spirit and the vital, instrumental, essential part He plays, communicating with our spirits once they are made alive so they can communicate with our hearts and minds (our souls) to help transform us if we choose. But it seems the Holy Spirit is also mystically and necessarily involved in how and when we come to faith, resulting in our spirits being made alive or born again in the first place. John chapter three is the clearest discussion of this in the Bible, and still mystical. Jesus ends the explanation to Nicodemus: "As Moses lifted up the serpent in the wilderness, even so must **the Son of Man be lifted up; so that whoever believes will in Him have eternal life**" (John 3:14-15). These words precede the most familiar and famous verse in the Holy Bible, John 3:16. I will offer two beautiful and insightful examples of how faith comes and let you draw your conclusions.

A Very Young Girl Comes to Faith

Thankfully, I wrote this entire account on the inside flap of my Bible shortly after it happened.

Nov 14, 1986. I picked up Amanda from school, ran errands, and had lunch at Mazzio's Pizza. It's the third day she's mentioned she wants to be baptized. She is five years old now. We leave the pizza place and discuss it in the van. I want to record excerpts from our conversation before my memory of the happy occasion dims. "Why do you want to be baptized?" "Cause." "Well, why?" "Just cause." Amanda isn't a very talkative child, but quite deep, I'm learning. "Has Joshua told you something about heaven or hell that scares you?" "No." "Well, why do you want to be baptized now and not before?" "I just do." "Well, being baptized is very important, but something more important must happen first. Do you know what that is?" "Yes. Be saved." "Do you know how to be saved?" "You ask Jesus into your heart." "Well, that's right," I say, smiling and amazed at the calm, serious way she is talking and looking into my eyes. I continued, "There is a Scripture that says: 'Behold I stand at the door and knock, if anyone hears My voice and opens their heart, I'll come in and live with them, and they with Me.'" Her quick reply was, "I think He's knocking!" "I think so too, Mandy," is my reply. The Spirit confirms in my spirit that she is sincere, knowledgeable, and being drawn to the Father via the Son. I ask her if she knows she needs Jesus to be right (eous) in God's sight. "Yes." "Why do you want to ask Jesus into your heart?" "Cause He's God." "Any other reason?" "Because He loves me," she replies with the sweetest little voice. I share a few simple scriptures about salvation. She knows them and heard them five months earlier as she sat in front of the house with the whole family, and her older brother, who is seven years old, asked Jesus into his heart. But now is her time. We pray a simple prayer, knowing that God looks on the heart and she must really mean what she says. She repeats after me and lights up in her countenance as joy comes while we pray and afterward. "Thank You, Father," from Mandy's father. "Jesus and Holy Spirit, You are so good."

The Spirit

"**It is the Spirit who gives life; the flesh profits nothing**" (John 6:63a). That should get our attention if we believe the words of Jesus are authoritative and that "the Spirit gives life" (2 Corinthians 3:6b). Somehow we've overlooked or minimized the power and place of the Holy Spirit in following Jesus, and knowing Him—even in coming to know Him. I'll show another example or observation.

But first, let me say we have forgotten or have been taught incomplete information about the Holy Spirit. He is not 1/3 God. He is 100% God. And **"The wind blows where it wants to"** (John 3:8). Jesus said it many times, sometimes cryptically, sometimes plainly. John recorded many of these conversations and truths about the power and purpose of the Holy Spirit in the believer's life. I won't recount them here. You can read them for yourself, study the subject, or be alert whenever and wherever you see Bible references to the Holy Spirit. Especially note the Gospels, the Acts of the Apostles, and the Epistles (letters) to the early church. But there are references scattered throughout the Old Testament, too. It's one Bible and one story about one God and how He relates to mankind recorded in sixty-six books written by forty authors over 1,500 years. It's what He intended to say and the revelation He intended us to have, breathed and empowered by His Holy Spirit, who gave it. The same Holy Spirit still breathes revelation and life into the words of the Bible about its subjects and objects—humankind, us, you, and me.

A Fighter Pilot Finds Jesus

As I write the title of this section, I chuckle inwardly and muse at the statement. I'm unsure if anyone finds Jesus or if it's Jesus who finds them. And I don't think anyone else is either.

The fact they found each other can be known, after the fact, by a person's testimony (Romans 10:9) and the fruit in their lives (Matthew 7:15-20). The book of Romans tells us: "That **if you confess with your mouth Jesus as Lord, and believe in your heart that God raised Him from the dead, you will be saved**" (Romans 10:9). And Jesus tells us an important insight about the fruit in people's lives as it applies to all people, especially those who claim to be believers: "**A good tree cannot produce bad fruit, nor can a bad tree produce good fruit.** Every tree that does not bear good fruit is cut down and thrown into the fire. So then, **you will know them by their fruits**" (Matthew 7:18-20).

Paul, in the letter to the Galatians, tells us what the fruits of the Spirit are: "… The **fruit of the Spirit is love, joy, peace, patience, kindness, goodness, faithfulness, gentleness, self-control**" (Galatians 5:22-23). So if a person has found Jesus and the Holy Spirit now dwells with that person, this fruit should be present in an ever-increasing quantity and remain over time.

Again, Jesus tells us, "It's impossible for a good tree to produce bad fruit, and a bad tree to produce good fruit" (Matthew 7:15-20). Hopefully that little rabbit trail was helpful. This vignette is about how one fighter pilot came to know Jesus, as well as I can describe it. I think you'll see the Spirit of God was the vital operative.

Our fighter squadron of F-4 Phantoms was ordered to participate in an Army exercise in Yakima, Washington. The purpose was to test the viability of infantry and special forces using light, mobile vehicles like four-wheelers and dirt bikes against tanks and heavy armor forces on the battlefield. It became a realistic and valuable exercise for the Army, proving new technology. The Air Force, represented by our fighter squadron, attacked armor and command post targets during the day while C-130 Spectre gunships flying night missions over the high desert battlefield killed tanks hidden under camouflage in the dark with heat-seeking missiles. They also proved and improved targeting tactics and evaluated new targeting sensors.

I wanted to go to Whidbey Island Naval Air Station, where our squadron would be based, and launch all its sorties. It was a dream for a fighter pilot to operate out of such a beautiful and desirable location and experience it with his squadron mates, then interact with each other and navy fighter pilots socially at the officer's club in the evenings. But our commander had promised the Army he would send one F-4 pilot to be with the Army on the ground as an evaluator, which ended up being me. The colonel told me, "You don't have to wear chemical warfare gear like the other participants. You can wear your flight suit and a white armband. You'll have a helicopter assigned to you and a pilot to take you to the target area for the air strikes so you can evaluate our effectiveness and the army's effectiveness in defending against airstrikes." "With all due respect, Sir, I don't want to do it. But I know you can order me to do it anyway, and for some strange reason, I feel like I'm supposed to, so I'll go." It was a spiritual time of solitude for me, even with long hours of activity and in the middle of war games. I was separated from my squadron mates and anyone else I knew. That was the backdrop for this spiritual event and several others I won't take the time to tell. It was right after a pastor friend had prayed for me to receive a baptism of the Holy Spirit.

I flew to Seattle, where I was ordered to pick up a rental

car and wait for an A-10 pilot to arrive. Then, I was to drive us to Yakima, Washington, for the military exercise. In an unusual turn of events, they had no Ford Pinto or similar rental car the military usually rents and gave me a Lincoln Continental to drive. Looking back on it now, I see it was a harbinger of the Spirit going before me and the grace I would experience during this adventure. I drove to the curb and saw my new fighter pilot friend standing in his flight suit beside his suitcase. I got out and shook his hand. He looked at the car, smiled, and said, "Wow, you Guard guys really know how to live!" I smiled and said, "Yeah, whatever, get in."

We had the whole day to travel and get to our duty station, and I had never seen Mount Rainier, so I decided to drive as close as possible to the top and down the backside. It was a beautiful, pristine day in the Pacific Northwest, and we could see it from the airport. About halfway there, we stopped to fill up with gas, and my new friend picked up a *Playboy* magazine. I thought, "We probably don't have that much in common at this point in our lives." In the afternoon, as we drove down the backside of the mountain toward our destination, he droned on about all the problems in the country and how in the world are we going to solve them. My mind was elsewhere on the new spiritual world I was experiencing, so I was disinterested, and it probably showed even though I tried not to appear rude or unkind. Then, finally, a bit exasperated he said, "I've been talking about all the problems our country is facing for thirty minutes, and you haven't said a thing! Are you going to tell me what you think?" Almost without thinking, I responded with the thoughts coming to me, "I don't think it matters what two hundred million Americans do, but probably what two million Christians do, because there is a verse in the Bible that says: '[If] My people who are called by My name humble themselves and pray and seek My face and turn from their wicked ways, then I will hear from heaven, will forgive their sin and will heal their land'" (2 Chronicles 7:14). I turned to look him in the eyes for a moment, paused to guage what he might be thinking, then turned my eyes back to the road. He seemed expressionless, but I'll never forget his reply a few moments later, "You can witness to me if you want to."

I think I was more shocked or taken aback by his statement than he was by mine. For most of my life, I would welcome an invitation to share my faith. But I wasn't feeling it, and instead, I said to him the first thing that came to mind again: "OK, if I want to, I will." Then I continued driving, looking straight ahead in silence, amazed at what I had just said and wondering what it must have sounded like to him.

Honestly, I can't remember any of our conversations for the next few hours until we arrived in Yakima and I dropped him off. We must've had some spiritual conversation because of what happened the last day we were together. The only time we were together after that drive was driving from the hotel where we stayed to the division headquarters, where the war games started each day at 4 AM. The rental car company had caught up with us and reclaimed the Lincoln Town Car, replacing it with a Ford Pinto. So after I backed into its small parking space and turned off the key, still half asleep, I opened my door, and the dome light came on. At that very instant, he yelled, "Wait!"

"What!? You scared me half to death!" "You said you'd pray with me." I closed the car door, the dome light went off, and I started to remember in my groggy mind that we had briefly talked about how someone comes to faith. And I told him I would pray with him if he wanted me to. "Well, just repeat after me." And he did so. But I couldn't remember John 3:16 or any other related Scriptures. It was the most pathetic little prayer imaginable. Finally, I just told him what I had told Amanda, "Man looks at the outward appearance, but the Lord looks at the heart" (1 Samuel 16:7b). "So, if you sincerely mean it, God knows, and you are accepted into the family of God." His countenance lit up, and he thanked me. We both opened our doors and headed to our respective assembly points for the games to begin.

I never expected to hear from him again. However, six months later, I received a handwritten letter saying that his wife had come to faith, they were putting their marriage back together, and they had found a church where they could grow in community with other believers. I was pleased and humbled by the news—ecstatic. I thought, "You can't make this stuff up." Leading someone to faith doesn't depend on flowery presentations or even logically arranged thoughts. But on the Spirit of God. This lesson gave me peace, rest, and more faith in God. It was a lesson I never forgot and still enjoy recounting.

Baptism of the Spirit

I mentioned the Baptism of the Holy Spirit, and I shouldn't leave you wondering what that is. It's an experience that goes by several different names. People are often conflicted about it, and most have probably never heard of it. "Of the Spirit" is the operative thought here, too. I'll tell you briefly what happened to me because it shaped my spiritual formation and life in ways I'm still coming to realize and continually experience.

I came to faith when I was twelve years old. I heard the way of salvation and an invitation to come to faith in Christ as we did at almost every service in the Baptist Church where I grew up. But somehow, when I heard it this Wednesday night, I was aware of its truth and validity. I knew somehow that Jesus did die on the cross as a sacrifice for my sin. I was aware of the enormity of that sacrifice. I saw two paths before me. One path led off in a direction where I would be my boss and determine my own way. I even thought that it could be more fun. The other path led in a direction where Jesus would be the Lord of my life and determine my direction and experiences. The overwhelming awareness of His love and sacrifice caused me to choose the second path, to follow wherever He would lead me. He would be the Lord of my life. When we got home that night, I asked my parents to pray with me after telling them what I had experienced. They did so in the basement of our home, where my brother and I slept.

After that, I lived a fairly normal Christian life in the South during my high school and college years. I attended church regularly, read my Bible some, prayed some, and sought out Christian friends for community. All the while, the culture was becoming more godless and rebellious than in my childhood and certainly in my parent's generation. It was the 60s and 70s in America. Looking back, I would say most churches became more embattled, withdrawn, and introverted. I found my own heart straying some with all the temptations at university. I'm very thankful for the college church I frequented with my friends and their leading edge, seemingly Spirit-filled pastor H.D. McCarty, who was so infatuated with Jesus he was inspiring and compelling. He was a stabilizing influence in my life that might have gone otherwise astray.

After college, while in the Air Force, my wife and I would visit and join Baptist churches off-base, where we were stationed. We got involved in their communities and experienced a stable, normal Christian walk, which was rewarding and good. But what I had known as normal began to change after four years when we departed the Air Force for civilian life and Air Force Reserve life in Fort Smith, Arkansas. We attended the First Baptist Church, even after being alerted by some friends to be careful because "Some funny things are going on there."

The first Sunday night we attended, we had to sit in the balcony because the large auditorium was filled to the brim with people. As I peered over the balcony during their worship time, I saw several people with their hands raised. I remember thinking, "I wonder what those people are doing?" I'd never seen it before, but I felt something in my spirit and a tingling on my forearms that I hadn't experienced since I prayed to receive Christ when I was twelve. I immediately thought, "I don't know what these people are doing, but I know it's right."

Soon, we joined the church amid spiritual warfare, and experienced community and the power of the Spirit in ways we never had before. Our two-year-old daughter became critically ill during this time. People in that fellowship, known for their power in prayer and sensitivity to hearing God, prayed for her and told us she would be healed. I remember thinking, "Who are these people who pray to God and receive an answer?" But she was healed of an incurable disease. I tell the event's details in an earlier book, *God Came Near*. Nothing was the same for us after the Spirit's healing and kindness in our daughter's life. Our faith grew, as did our desire to know the Holy Spirit.

I hesitate to write about these spiritual experiences because they are so personal and intimate. And they could sound like bragging or pride—something I hate and wish to avoid. But then, there's nothing to be proud about. It's something He did. I was only seeking Him.

As I came from the Nehemiah group this morning, I was aware that it may be the very thing I'm supposed to write about and encourage you to do—get in the presence of God and abide there routinely and habitually. Sometimes the Spirit will show up in a powerful way you can sense. So I will share these stories as examples of what God does to heal and empower people on their journey. He helps us live lives winsome and compelling as He, the Great Physician, heals our emotional pains and helps us walk in freedom. He breaks the chains holding us back and gives us the power to soar in our spirits, souls, and lives.

Jesus had such spiritual encounters during his sojourn on earth, some of which are recorded for us. The mount of transfiguration is one, and when seventy of his disciples returned, telling of demons being subject to them in His name was another. In this instance, the original language says that Jesus "jumped with joy." On this note, Jesus' time of temptation in the wilderness by the devil himself, and immediately afterward when angels came and ministered to Him, had to be a high spiritual experience.

The wedding in Cana of Galilee was a spiritual experience

of joy and power. He was with people He loved, celebrating the life and relationships our Father planned and provided for us. He heard the Spirit say, "Fill those stone jars with water to the brim, then take it to the headwaiter." The term "new wine" took on a new meaning as Jesus felt the pleasure and power of His Father's Spirit work through Him to meet the needs of a poor young couple, their friends and family, His mother, and the community of faith. It also gave His disciples a glimpse of what lay in store for them. It must have brought Jesus much joy, as He heard the voice, obeyed what He heard, and felt the power of the Spirit do something special for all present. Some knew what had happened, and some didn't. Such is the nature of spiritual sensitivity. John says, "**This beginning of His signs Jesus did in Cana of Galilee, and manifested His glory, and His disciples believed in Him**" (John 2:11). In this vein and for this purpose, I'll share flights of faith or some spiritual experiences in my life.

My experience of more of the Holy Spirit started when some of my friends and I noticed a difference in the life of one of our pastors. We asked him individually and together, "What has happened to you? You seem different." He told us a teenager in the youth group who had also changed a great deal had prayed for him to receive "a second anointing or a baptism of the Holy Spirit." My friends and I, who I would categorize as seekers, went into his office one at a time, almost secretly, and asked if he would pray for us. He shared a few scriptures about the subject and related his experience, then prayed for us as requested.

David ate what the priest ate when he was fleeing Saul. He was in uncharted territory and engaged in spiritual warfare, near and close at hand. We are in uncharted territory.

We must risk doing the same—being led by the same Spirit.

My peers have their stories, but I will only relate mine. I bowed on my knees, and Tom Newton, Ph.D., placed his hands on my shoulders and began praying. I have only a fuzzy recollection of what he prayed. It was something like: "Please give Dwayne what his heart desires and what You desire for him to have." I began to experience a great amount of light seemingly in my whole being. My eyes were closed, and it was like my soul and spirit were listening, or reaching out, or trying to sense what was happening or would happen. Extreme light in volume and intensity is the only way I can describe it. It wasn't painful, but I began to feel like I was going to cease to exist if the light didn't stop or stop increasing. I was silent during all of this—just listening and trying to sense what He might say or in some way communicate to me. The only thought I uttered in silence was, "Father, this is amazing, but if You don't stop, I think I may die." I was in silent awe of what was happening to me and wondered if any communication might occur. Oddly, Tom got called from his office for a few minutes during this time. I scarcely heard what he said or cared that he was gone. He said something like, "Just remain here with the Lord."

Shortly thereafter, I heard the first of two phrases that came to my mind, "**To them gave He the power to become the sons of God, even to those who believe in His name**." There was a little silent time to meditate on this; then it came again. Then, a pause, and the second thing I heard was, "**I am not ashamed to call you My son**." This undid me because I felt unworthy to be experiencing anything like this and be in His presence. But I knew it was real, and He was saying it. I had to accept it and let it go deep in my spirit and produce anything it would. It was His word, and His to do with it what He wished. It was only mine to believe that He was speaking, and how could I not believe it in this setting and moment? At some point, the light and presence started lifting or decreasing. I don't have any recollection of the time involved. Time did not matter. Tom returned and later told me, "You were there a while."

The experience was so personal, private, and sacred that I have told only a handful of people about it, not even my children nor my wife, in this much detail. As I recount it and relive the moment etched in my memory, I can hardly believe I'm writing it in a book for the first time after all these years. After debating whether I should, I picked up my Bible to read my selection for today: John chapter one. John the Baptist, who was filled with the Holy Spirit in the womb and knew a few things about hearing from the Spirit, recounts: "**I have seen the Spirit descending as a dove out of heaven, and He remained upon Him. I did not recognize Him, but He who sent me to baptize in water said to me, 'He upon whom you see the Spirit descending and remaining upon Him, this is the One who baptizes in the Holy Spirit**" (John 1:32-33). I've come to recognize this kind of synchronicity as the Spirit's way of telling me something is from Him. I almost decided not to share my experience, but only that of Dwight L. Moody.

Years after my experience, I read D.L. Moody's experience, which described almost precisely what happened to me that day. R.A. Torrey tells of Moody's experience and thoughts in his book, *Why God Used D.L. Moody*. Torrey was the first superintendent of Moody's Bible Institute in Chicago. He gives seven reasons the Lord used Moody, and the last is:

"He was definitely endued with power from on high." He then explains clearly what "power from on high is" and how Moody received and valued it. Torrey describes what happened to Moody walking up Wall Street in New York City.

Excerpts follow:

"In the midst of the bustle and hurry of that city his prayer was answered; the power of God fell upon him as he walked up the street and he had to hurry off to the house of a friend and ask that he might have a room by himself, and in that room he stayed alone for hours; and the Holy Ghost came upon him, filling his soul with such joy that at last he had to ask God to withhold his hand, lest he die on the spot from very joy. He went out from that place with the power of the Holy Ghost upon him. [p32]

Moody notes that the effects of his preaching after this encounter were significantly enhanced, that hundreds now began to be saved. He also said that this experience he had was beyond description, and that it was so sacred to him that he rarely spoke of it.

I think it is clearly taught in the Scripture that every believer has the Holy Ghost dwelling in him. He may be quenching the Spirit of God, and he may not glorify God as he should, but if he is a believer on the Lord Jesus Christ, the Holy Ghost dwells in him. But I want to call your attention to another fact. I believe today, that though Christian men and women have the Holy Spirit dwelling in them, yet He is not dwelling within them in power; in other words, God has a great many sons and daughters without power. [p34]

In this same work, Moody contends powerfully for ministers and the church to recognize and receive the Holy Spirit in His fullness."

In Moody's own words recorded in a book written by his son, *The Life of D.L. Moody:*

"My heart was not in the work of begging," he said. "I could not appeal. I was crying all the time that God would fill me with His Spirit. Well, one day, in the city of New York—oh, what a day!—I cannot describe it, I seldom refer to it; it is almost too sacred an experience to name. Paul had an experience of which he never spoke for fourteen years. I can only say that God revealed Himself to me, and I had such an experience of His love that I had to ask Him to stay His hand. I went to preaching again. The sermons were not different; I did not present any new truths, and yet hundreds were converted. I would not now be placed back where I was before that blessed experience if you should give me all the world—it would be as the small dust of the balance" (pages 146, 147, and 149).

Slain in the Spirit

First, let me say I don't care for the term. It sounds a bit dramatic, but that's what most folks call it when one falls in the presence of the Holy Spirit moving in some measure of power in a meeting or among individuals. In a sense, it is dramatic to feel God's presence. I wasn't necessarily seeking or looking for it when it happened to me.

One Sunday night before the Spirit encounter recounted above, I was sitting with three young couples, awaiting the service at First Baptist Church, which was about to begin. We were seated on the right side of the auditorium near the front. Tom Newton came by to greet us. He was our spiritual leader and mentor in many ways. After some small talk and hugs, he said that Emmett Spencer was conducting a meeting a few blocks away. We knew that Emmett was a local nondenominational pastor with Pentecostal roots, and it was widely circulated that the Holy Spirit moved in many of his meetings. Even though we were curious about the validity of the Holy Spirit moving in people's lives, it seemed like a stretch to go there and investigate. What was Tom suggesting? Finally, he just said, "If I were you guys, I'd leave before the meeting starts here and go there." "Why don't you go?" "Remember, I work here." "Oh, yeah." We all slipped away and went to the meeting about twelve blocks east.

I don't recall a lot about the meeting. I do recall thinking he wasn't the best teacher or preacher I'd heard, but he wasn't teaching anything that wasn't in the Bible. When he gave an invitation to be prayed for at the front altar, I felt compelled and shot up there, along with about twenty others who stood in a line. I couldn't tell you who, if anyone from our group, went up with me, although I would hear an interesting story about it years later. All I know is that when he came to me and started to pray without touching me, I fell backward to the floor. As I fell, I recall having the momentary thought, "This could hurt." But it didn't, and I just lay there for some time with absolute peace flooding over me. That's all I recall.

For twenty-five years or more, I canoed every spring on the Buffalo River with friends from several different churches and a few pagans. It was a beautiful adventure with a great bunch of men, and we savored every trip with lots of war stories from previous trips shared around the campfire at night. One night just a few years ago, the conversation turned to spiritual experiences, and someone mentioned Emmett Spencer and his meetings years before. I told the story I just related, and Terry Layne, a good friend and long-time canoeing buddy, spoke up. "I was there with you guys at that meeting. I only went up front because you did, Dwayne. I saw you fall. When Emmett came to me, he started to pray and then stopped and said, 'You've never prayed to receive Jesus as Lord, have you?'" "No, Sir, I haven't." "Would you like to?" "Yes, Sir, I would." He led me in a short prayer of salvation. That's how and when I came to faith. "That's amazing. Why did you never tell me this before?" "It never came up, and I thought you knew."

Looking back on such mysterious serendipity, I think of John 3:8: "The wind blows where it wishes and you hear the sound of it, but do not know where it comes from and where it is going; so is everyone who is born of the Spirit." This describes the life of believers born and led by the Spirit. I think it also speaks of the Spirit Himself. He acts in these understated ways because of His humility and His winsome and compelling nature. And so no one can boast in pride and take credit for things wholly and solely wrought by the Spirit. As Paul told the church in Ephesus and the church of all time: "For by grace you have been saved through faith; and that not of yourselves, it is the gift of God; not as a result of works, so that no one may boast" (Ephesians 2:8-9).

1994 — Israel ישראל — Aunt Mary

I will always be grateful to my high school friend Randy Russell, M. D., who invited me to join a group he led from Lake Village, Arkansas, to Israel. You are always going to have an encounter with God's Spirit if you're a seeker and you visit Israel. Your knowledge and awareness of the Holy One will increase severalfold, as well as your faith. I had many encounters related to the people of Israel, the land, and the Bible—also near encounters with the Holy Spirit, I could sense and feel. But the experience I want to relate is not necessarily connected to the land. It was an unexpected spiritual encounter at the home of Aunt Mary in Jerusalem.

My good friend Ralph Irwin, the artist who did the artwork on the cover of this book and my first book, *A Friend of the King*, learned I was going to Israel and exclaimed, "You have to go visit my aunt Mary!" I remember thinking, "I have no idea what we will be doing there. This is my first time. But it is intriguing and a nice coincidence that a spiritual adventurer and close friend of mine has an aunt in Jerusalem. And he wants me to meet her for relational and spiritual reasons."

The trip was beautiful in every way imaginable and beyond description. Three couples from Fort Smith bonded with the larger group from Southeast Arkansas like a happy, close-knit family. We had a free day in Jerusalem to explore, revisit any site, or rest. Our wives wanted to shop on Ben Yehuda Street, so we three men who knew Ralph decided we'd visit Aunt Mary as he had passionately suggested. We called her, and she seemed delighted at the prospect, "I'll send my son to pick you up!"

She was a widow; her husband had been an inventor and scientist. She had emigrated (made aliyah) to Israel from Southern California shortly after Israel miraculously became a nation again in 1948, after a 2000-year diaspora. We knew Ralph loved her dearly. He also considered her a holy woman—very in tune with God.

Her apartment was warm and cheery. We immediately noticed a box of Post Corn Flakes on the table with only Hebrew print but graphics like ours. She greeted us with hugs like we were sons and answered all our questions about life in Jerusalem. We eventually asked, "Are you Jewish or Christian?" "Yes," she replied with a warm, peaceful smile.

We asked if she would pray for us when we were ready to leave. She did, and as she prayed, she prophesied over each of us in turn, beginning with Clyde, then Rodger, and then me. I don't remember what I did yesterday many times. But I recall vividly what she spoke over me: "You are like one of the priests carrying the Ark of the Covenant, the presence of God, opposite Jericho, into the promised land. Wade into the water and stay there until all the people have crossed."

God came and stayed near in the 1980s and was coming near again in the 1990s in beautiful, meaningful ways. I have seen this word come true many days and in many ways. It seems now that it is still coming true as I reflect and meditate upon it. It has been a guiding star pointing to the path the Spirit has for me and is a part of my purpose and spiritual destiny.

The Blessing — Toronto, Canada — 1994

"Who has ascended into heaven, or descended?
Who has gathered the wind in His fists?
Who has bound the waters in a garment?
Who has established all the ends of the earth?
What is His name, and what is His Son's name,
If you know?"
(Proverbs 30:4 NKJV)

First, let me tell Toronto's who, what, when, and where because it was a few days ago. Then I will tell the how—how I got there and how it impacted me. It's a story of how God came near, how He stays near, what He showed me, and what He deposited in my spirit and soul for the journey ahead.

What came to be known as the Toronto Blessing began on January 20, 1994, at the Toronto Airport Vineyard Church, Canada. If you research it online, you'll find it still debated, with some Christians criticizing it and others arguing it was a genuine manifestation of the Holy Spirit. That's often the case where the Holy Spirit is moving. Note what happened to Jesus when the Holy Spirit descended on Him like a dove at His baptism in His day's religious setting and culture.

Over two million people came during the next five years and well beyond. I went four times myself, partially enabled by the airline job, allowing me to easily fly to the meeting place. I met two groups from our Fort Smith community who drove the two-day journey on different occasions. I went once with a friend, Randy Russell, M.D., who I asked on a spiritual leading. And I went once by myself.

I called Randy, not expecting that I would get him by

phone or that he would possibly be able to go. He's a very busy physician. But he answered his phone, "Hey Dwayne, what a pleasant surprise. What's up?" "Well, I'm calling from the pilot's lounge in DFW, about to leave on a three-day trip. When I return, I will fly to Toronto, Canada, where they are experiencing a move of the Holy Spirit. I had the impression to ask you if you wanted to go with me." "I'll go." "What? You will go?" "Yes, I'll go." "But I haven't even told you about it yet." "It doesn't matter. I trust you. And my wife told me this morning, 'You are so burned out! You have got to get out of town!'" So we went together, procured a hotel room nearby, and rented a car. I had gone twice before, so I knew the ropes and could plan our time. But every time was a little bit different. This was a relaxed and healing time for both of us. We attended most meetings but took a day off and drove to Niagara Falls to catch up on our friendship, adventure, and rest.

The first time I went, I finished flying a trip for American Airlines in DFW, flew into Toronto Pearson Field, and was met by one of our church members, Vanessa, who led me to the others and the seat they had saved for me amid a cavernous room with a few thousand people. The service was underway. People were standing, singing, and worshipping, and you could feel the presence of the Spirit in the room. It felt like home, comfortable, like being in your living room, with unity, peace, and joy. I recall thinking, "I just got here, walked inside, and feel all this already!"

Looking down the row at the ten people who had driven two days from our church of about two hundred in Fort Smith, Arkansas, I felt the Spirit speak to me in a thought that wasn't my thought: "I can accomplish what I want to do with these people." I had been pondering for weeks what it would take to get our community to where we were spiritually mature enough to do kingdom work and serve the Lord in a fashion He deserved and was worthy of Him. So I was taken aback by the thought and the conversation of thoughts that ensued.

"With these people?" I loved our little community of believers, but we were all over the spectrum regarding maturity and spiritual gifts. I thought we had a long way to go before we could accurately reflect our Lord and effectively do His kingdom's work—making disciples, serving each other, and the community. "Yes, these people," I heard in reply.

There was a pause as I pondered what I was hearing, and then another thought came: "You have a problem with the fact that I would create something with imperfection, don't you?" "Yes, sort of." "Well, I do, so it will take my Spirit's oil to function well. This results in relationships." I only partially understood what I was hearing then, but I heard it and never forgot it. Now that I'm past seventy, I see it more clearly—the truth and the beauty.

I will share two other experiences there that shaped or formed me spiritually. The second time I came, I met eight different people from our community who drove while I flew to join them. "Thank God for the airline job," I often say and think. The giant warehouse-type room was full of people worshiping and praising God in boisterous and sometimes quiet ways with a hush over the crowd. There was a station in the center of the room where several translators sat at any given service, with colored headsets for different languages. There might be yellow for German, blue for Korean, red for Japanese, etc. You could slip a headset on for your language and hear the message translated in real time. Did I mention that between two million and two and one-half million people came here to experience God over ten years?

One night, on my second visit, a messianic Jewish rabbi from Orlando, Florida, spoke and announced his talk loudly at the beginning: "There Is a Whore in the Pharisee's House!" The large audience seemed to take a deep, collective gasp. I know I did. There was a lot of spiritual freedom there. You could feel it. But I immediately wondered, "Can you say that in a church meeting?" Then he announced his text would be Luke chapter seven—the story of Simon the Pharisee (see Luke 7:36-50).

With the fervor and passion only a Jewish religious leader, familiar with the ways of his ancient people could feel, he painted a word picture of what happened there. Jesus was wildly popular and attracted big crowds of people wherever He went due to the miracles performed and His wise words about God and living the good life. So the house was full, with people milling around outside to hear what they could when Jesus accepted Simons's invitation to a meal. But when a prostitute from the city entered the house, the news spread like lightning, and the whole town rushed there to see the sparks fly!

"Simon, I have something to say to you." "Speak, teacher, what's on your mind." You know the story or can read it for revelation. Like all of Jesus' masterful, powerful stories, they speak to everyone in every age. They can divide the bone from the marrow and show the thoughts and intentions of the heart. Jesus only spoke the kind, obvious truth to Simon, showing him his heart and allowing him to consider his ways and change directions with God and man—"Repent" is the biblical word; do a 180 degree turn in one's thinking and actions.

We can only hope he did, as it appears Joseph of Arimathea and Nicodemus of the council, and the disciples did. We tend to forget that the early church was almost completely Jewish—sons and daughters of the Covenant.

The unlikely and unintentional heroine of the story is the prostitute. She was so touched by Jesus' love and forgiveness that she risked humiliation, rejection, and possible violence by entering a Pharisee's house to show her deep love, appreciation, and worship of Jesus. Her sins, which were many, were forgiven by the only One who could. As Jesus told Simon, "The one who is forgiven much loves much."

Jesus dined with sinners, tax collectors (traitors), and religious people. In one meal, probably in one hour, He showed us all that we are or have been, both the prideful religious person and the whore. He leaves it for us to decide what we will do about it. If we see him healing our spiritual blindness and forgiving our sins, we will love Him very much.

Whenever I hear Luke 7, Simon, whore, or Pharisee, I think of this story and the timeless, personal truth of it all. It's etched in my heart by the Spirit of revelation and I feel love for the matchless One who forgives my sin and became the necessary sacrifice for that to happen. I become still, eternally grateful, and worship. Even though I've heard thousands of sermons and Bible expositions, this one sits elevated in a special place in my conscience. It happened in Toronto.

The last Toronto experience I'll share occurred on my final trip and involved "expectations." I've never forgotten it. This was a solitary experience for me. I was looking to encounter or experience God in any way He wished. I learned to have anticipations but not expectations.

Typically, after the service or teaching, people lined up in rows to be prayed over while the worship team and others continued to worship. Most folks being prayed for at Toronto would fall under the power of the Spirit. This phenomenon is known as "being slain in the Spirit" in some circles. I was familiar with it, having witnessed it in a few meetings where I sought more of God. I experienced it myself once, as I have shared. The short version for those unfamiliar is that a small team of praying people or an individual minister walks in front of a person, extends their hand toward the forehead or the heart, and prays a blessing or whatever comes to them. Probably 90% of those prayed for at Toronto would stiffen and fall backward. The person prayed for often falls to the ground, lying there for some time, conscious but in a somewhat euphoric state under the influence or power of the Spirit. Most don't report any big revelations or thoughts during that time, only deep peace and a general feeling of well-being. It's commonly thought the Spirit does some healing of the heart or soul. Often, people suddenly fall very hard to the floor, but no one gets hurt or injured.

With falling so common, the Toronto leaders enlisted the use of catchers. These volunteers stood a short distance behind those receiving prayer to catch them or ease their fall to the ground. Occasionally, a person would fall forward, but the person praying could catch them and ease them to the ground before going to the next person. The people who fell were left on the floor to spend time with God.

I was there to receive something very personal from God on my fourth and last trip to Toronto. Someone approached me as I was getting in line to be prayed for, tapped me on the shoulder, and said, "Would you please volunteer to be a catcher tonight? We have a lot of people in lines and not that many catchers." "Of course, I'll help." I thought, "Surely, there will be an opportunity for me to get in line and be prayed over at some point. And observing could be interesting."

There was never an opportunity, as people prayed and fell for about half an hour. The worship band stopped playing to signal the end of the prayer time. They put on soft, recorded worship music as people lingered and talked softly, and hundreds lay on the floor. I smiled and mused, "It looks like a war zone." Thinking back on it now, it was a peace zone. But I hadn't been prayed over, and the opportunity had passed. I sat on the floor with my back against the wall near the little snack bar open until midnight or whenever they turned off the lights. I was happy to be there, and God's Spirit was certainly there in ways you could observe and feel. But I felt left out and neglected.

Then the familiar thought exchange began with a thought that wasn't mine, "Were you expecting something you didn't receive?" "Yes, I was." "So, do you think your plans for you are better than My plans for you?" "Well, now that you say it that way, 'No,' I feel Your plans for me are the best." I was now content. I knew He could have manifested Himself to me if He wanted to, but He hadn't. I was now okay with it. Besides, He had just spoken to me in my thoughts.

At that moment, two guys from Iceland approached me and asked, "Has anyone prayed for you?" "No." "Can we pray for you?" "Of course." No sooner had they begun, I fell to the floor, forward actually, but my involuntary or uninitiated fall was somewhat cushioned by a giant beanbag nearby. It was like a surrender to whatever God wanted to do with me. They prayed over me for some time as I lay face down on the floor in a wave of deep peace. Their fingertips on my back felt hot as if they had put them on a hot stove top and then applied them to my back. I could feel every digit, but I felt no pain. I remember thinking, "I wonder what this feels like to them?" They continued to pray over me aloud in tongues or Icelandic. I didn't know which or care, and I never got to ask them or thank them as they wandered away when they were finished praying, leaving me to bask in the presence of the Spirit.

I certainly now felt that Father saw me and cared about me. He noticed and gave me a desire of my heart. There is no other feeling like that in the world.

I have shared this experience very few times. It was very intimate and personal. Also, it can be very controversial for those who haven't experienced such things. They typically say things like, "That's not in the Bible or described in the Bible." I regard the Bible in the highest light and consider it the highest authority we have in speaking about God and his dealings with mankind. I compare everything spiritual and natural with the Bible for validity, accuracy, and staying on the path God has for us. Yet God does many things outside the Biblical record and does whatever He pleases in heaven and earth. I would also judge Him to give good gifts to His children, sons and daughters who seek Him and want to know Him more fully. Also, it's an advantage of getting older that you don't care so much about what people think. You feel more obligated to be truthful, transparent and humbly share your personal experiences. I also recall Charles Simpson's encouragement: "A person with an experience is never at the mercy of a person with an argument."

A more significant danger than seeking to know God better and experientially is settling. If we settle on our theology, doctrine, and denominational beliefs and then worship them as the truth, we may have missed God entirely. We may be worshiping and trusting an idol of our own making. A.W. Tozer says, "The essence of idolatry is the entertainment of thoughts about God that are unworthy of Him." In the first book of our Bible, we are told, "**Abraham believed God, and it was credited to him as righteousness**" (Romans 4:3, Genesis 15:6). The father of the faith trusted God, not what he believed about God. We should do the same without laying aside theology, our collection of facts about God. They are compatible. Jesus came to earth partly for this purpose, to set this situation straight—what most religious teachers were teaching versus the truth about God and a relationship with Him.

He told his followers to be aware of the yeast of the religious (Pharisees) and the pride that puffs them up like bread rising. When confronted by the Truth and His Holy Spirit, their teaching and actions betrayed them. But left to themselves, they were happy and content in their appearances and deceived state. Jesus tells his followers about them, how to identify them by their fruit, and to be on guard against their deceived and deceiving ways. The book of Jude comes to mind. The half brother of Jesus starts his short book of the Bible by saying he intended to write about our common salvation. But the Spirit compelled him to warn instead about false teachers in the church (Jude 3-4).

Controversy and the Spirit of God

At my age, I've come to see that controversy almost always surrounds a move of the Spirit as a shield or barrier to keep people away with the wrong motives, those not hot or cold but lukewarm, and trusting themselves. And to keep those who would take measured risks to know Him invited to His table. The ten lepers come to mind, as does the Syrophoenician woman with the demonized daughter, the woman with the issue of blood, the man with the demonized son the disciples could not help, Jairus with a very sick little girl, and others. It must be noted that controversies surrounded Jesus and His ministry from the beginning to the end. It goes with living, knowing, and proclaiming the truth in a deceived and deceiving world in the clutches of the father of lies—Satan and his minions, and wherever light and dark spirits clash.

Jesus said, "**Do not think that I came to bring peace on the earth; I did not come to bring peace, but a sword. For I came to set a man against his father, and a daughter against her mother, and a daughter-in-law against her mother-in-law**" (Matthew 10:34-35). As important as family and relationships are to God, the truth is even more critical. Without it, nobody prospers. And if you put people or relationships above the truth, you are in a codependent relationship, which is destructive for both of you.

Paul said, "**Indeed, all who desire to live godly in Christ Jesus will be persecuted**" (2 Timothy 3:12). If you haven't suffered any persecution because of your faith, you might need to look more deeply into it and consider what to do. The Proverbs tell us, "**Every word of God is tested; He is a** shield to those who take refuge in Him" (Proverbs 30:5). This is the language of warfare.

Don't fight naked! The apostle Paul describes the essential armor of our spiritual warfare well in Ephesians 6:10-17. It's worth meditating on the purpose and importance of each piece. You will notice that Paul ends with the only offensive weapon of the battle apparel, "The sword of the Spirit." "And **take the helmet of salvation, and the sword of the Spirit, which is the word of God**" (Ephesians 6:17).

Don't fight alone! It's an axiom in aerial combat from World War I and has proven true to the present day that you don't fly and fight alone. Don't go to the fight alone, and if you end up in the battle alone, escape as swiftly as you can to safety. In the fighter pilot world, we always fly in formations of two, three, or four planes. We do this to check each other's 6 o'clock from where unobserved and lethal enemy missiles are usually fired. A single fighter in an aerial battle usually doesn't come home.

Did you notice in the last Scripture who owns the sword? The Spirit! It is his sword. He knows how and when to use it, and He is strong. There's no need to fight alone. He will fight for you if you are in a relationship with Him and will help you know what to do. The warrior king, David, tells us, "**He who dwells in the shelter of the Most High will abide in the shadow of the Almighty**" (Psalm 91:1). The Son of David tells us He came to bring a sword. And that He would send His Spirit to help in the fight: "**But the Helper, the Holy Spirit, whom the Father will send in My name, He will teach you all things, and bring to your remembrance all that I said to you**" (John 14:26).

Paul found twelve believers outside Ephesus and asked

them if they had received the Holy Spirit. They replied, "**No, we have not even heard whether there is a Holy Spirit**" (Acts 19:2b). That seems descriptive of the church in America and the West today. My point is not lament but action: "**Seek the Lord while He may be found; call upon Him while He is near**" (Isaiah 55:6). "**You will seek Me and find Me when you search for Me with all your heart**" (Jeremiah 29:13). Make the space and form the habit. Spend time with God. He will show Himself to you and make Himself available to help you in times of peace and warfare.

After the "sword of the spirit" revelation, you may notice Paul continues: "**With all prayer and petition pray at all times in the Spirit, and with this in view, be on the alert with all perseverance and petition for all the saints**" (Ephesians 6:18). The context and language are still about warfare, and he adds prayer to the mix as an offensive weapon for each other.

If you are still trying to figure out the power and importance of the Holy Spirit in being a follower of Christ Jesus and want to look into it further, let me recommend three excellent books. Francis Chan released *Forgotten God* in 2009. Mark Batterson published *Wild Goose Chase* in 2008. You might also try *They Speak with Other Tongues* by John L. Sherrill for a deeper, historic dive by a high churchman. He published it in 1964, and there are half a million copies in print.

One last thing about the Toronto experience should be shared. There were some unusual manifestations in some people. Most experienced joy, lightheartedness, laughter, and such when the Spirit came near. I've mentioned people falling under the Spirit's power. There were also some instances of people making animal sounds accompanied by laughter. I choose not to judge this and feel no need to do so. A few solid believers in our community experienced it there and occasionally for a short time afterward. This prompted my 17-year-old son, a critical thinker, very spiritually sensitive, and very discerning, to say, "Dad, I don't know about the animal sounds and all that, but you've been different ever since you came back in a good way." That's an interesting observation and conclusion to my Toronto spiritual experiences.

Over the Long Haul

In the next two decades, there were no more unusual or powerful encounters with the Spirt that I can recall, but just the steady plodding of life. That's more the norm of how God works in our lives anyway—slowly over time. We choose to form our habits, and then our habits form us. The mystical part is when these habits are spiritual, like reading the Bible, praying, staying in community with believers, and being obedient to what you hear. The Holy Spirit transforms us into His likeness and a better version of ourselves—a win-win situation.

Come to think of it; there were some times of intense spiritual warfare during these decades and times of pain and suffering. These aren't spiritual disciplines but significant factors in our spiritual formation. They serve as trailheads on a journey with God that grows our faith and heals our souls, causing us to walk in more freedom and less fear. The times above can be thought of as "green pastures and still waters." The times of warfare and suffering are like "walking through the valley of the shadow of death," to use David's imagery from Psalm 23, the most famous chapter in the Bible. To grow healthily, spend time with God daily so you know Him better, learn to hear His voice, and watch for His activity around you.

A few more recent spiritual experiences come to mind. I'll share those briefly before returning to some final flight vignettes.

Ordination

About five years ago, I received a call from friends in northern Louisiana who I had been with on mission trips to Honduras more than ten times. They invited me to their church, where they wanted to ordain me as a minister of the gospel. I told them, "I really don't see the purpose of that. I'm in my late 60s, and what the Lord has led me to do, He has empowered me to do, and I don't see that would add anything or is necessary." "Well, we want to do it; we've served with you over the last ten years, and we just want to acknowledge what we see the Lord doing." "I want to be humble and listen to what you guys think because I respect your spiritual sensitivity and kingdom service, but I still don't see that it accomplishes anything, and I'm not keen on doing it." They responded, "We want you to do it. We want to honor you, and you would honor us."

I love these brothers and their community. I've seen them serve the church internationally in Honduras and other countries. I've seen their hearts, and them move in the power of the Holy Spirit, praying for the sick who recovered and praying against demonic powers with success. I started to see that I didn't have a better option and that it was something

I should submit to do, even though I didn't want to do it. Then I asked, "Is Charles Simpson going to be there? Do you think he might lay hands on me and pray for me?" "Yes, and that can likely be arranged."

I invited one of my good college friends to go with me to Monroe for the weekend. We mounted up with wings in the Maule and went to their annual conference, where Charles Simpson was to minister. It was a beautiful friendship time and a time of spiritual adventure. My friend Bill enjoyed being with Charles, and the feeling was mutual, as Charles invited Bill to sit by him at every meal. On the last night of the meetings, Charles Simpson, with the other church elders, laid hands on me, prayed over me, and ordained me as a minister of the Gospel of Jesus Christ. It was more of a spiritual and solemn time than I anticipated.

And I must say that since then, I've been much more active in the ministry than ever before, with more people seeking me out for prayer and counsel. I've felt more urgency and an unction to be more direct with people, speaking the truth in love. I've experienced many more synchronicities and divine appointments. I've felt more peace, kindness, and joy in spending time alone with God. In short, something mystical happened there that I can't put my finger on, but the effects can be seen and are ongoing. It's exciting and fulfilling, and I'm grateful. It's like experiencing Psalm 23 and Isaiah 40 at the same time. "But **those who wait on the Lord shall renew their strength; they shall mount up with wings like eagles, they shall run and not be weary, they shall walk and not faint**" (Isaiah 40:31 NKJV).

Unite Arkansas

The September 19, 2024, UNITE in Bud Walton Arena at the University of Arkansas in Fayetteville was awesome! Ten thousand college students gathered and heard a blistering word about sexual purity and the gospel of grace—the Gospel of Jesus Christ. There was a call to holy (set apart) living, and Jesus was worshiped until after 10:30 PM. The meeting was about to end, so my wife and I left to walk a friend driving in from another city an hour away to her car. We learned later that the meeting continued until 2:00 AM, moving across the street to an outdoor setting where many students were baptized.

We were there from 5:15 PM with people from our faith community who set up a tent for food and fellowship before the event. Some of us had been asked to go into the venue a few minutes early to walk and pray. I heard that the Spirit moved in similar events at Auburn, the University of Alabama, the University of Georgia, and Ohio State, but I didn't know what to expect. The straight talk about sexual issues, sexual purity, and sexual healing was shocking to me. But judging by the response of thousands of students—it was very needed and refreshing, accompanied by the gospel of grace for forgiveness and the promise of the Holy Spirit for healing and transforming lives to live on a higher plain.

In the previous month, I heard similar messages in the Spirit and blogged about sexual freedom and the self-control available as a fruit of the Spirit. But to hear this forceful message delivered to ten thousand college kids and see their reaction to embracing it in their lives was mind-blowing.

The musical group Elevation Rhythm led the crowd in

vibrant worship, which at times was loud and powerful, blasting with the college kids dancing and singing after rushing the stage area, then quiet and still—so melodic and calm you thought you might touch heaven or be touched by the same, with a hush over the crowd.

Speaking of the crowd, one of my college friends just called me. He and his wife were there doing the same thing we were. He told his wife earlier in the day, "They have only issued four thousand advance tickets for the event and are secretly hoping and praying for ten thousand attendees—that's just too big a gap and not going to happen." During our phone call, he said, "I'm going to have to stop underestimating God."

A phrase repeated in one of the songs was: "There is no waste at the altar." I don't recall that phrase in the Scriptures and wondered what it could mean. Maybe it speaks to all the sexual sins and addictions being brought to the altar last night? That's no waste, as they are accepted and burned up—forgotten by the One Who matters as an act of mercy and grace. You can come as you are with your idols to the altar and leave as a son or daughter for the courts of the King, ruined by His love, ravished by His magnanimous generosity and goodwill.

What you lay at the altar, you get back if it was a promise from God, only with the unhealthy attachment burned away—a bit like Abraham offering up his son Isaac and getting him back, both of them now realizing that "God will provide the Lamb."

So there we were, a few grey eagles who had attended the same university fifty years ago, watching lots of young eagles experience God in similar ways we did under H.D. McCarty, with the promise of change and soaring through life and into old age with adventures galore and relationships to make, mend, and restore.

"Time has a wonderful way of showing us what really matters."

— Margaret Peters

Military Flying Experiences

Once I transitioned from the Air Force to the Air Force Reserves, I knew there wouldn't be many travel opportunities like there are in the Air Force. But I also knew I wouldn't be required to spend a year away from my family twice in a twenty-year career like most Air Force fighter pilots. And I would still get to fly some of the fastest, most maneuverable aircraft in the world routinely while practicing air-to-air combat (dogfighting), and dropping bombs and strafing after flying low-level routes at 600-700 miles per hour 100 feet to 500 feet above the ground, training to avoid enemy air defenses—an ultimate flying experience, as well as a patriotic opportunity to serve.

That said, we did travel a few times and adventure with these amazing airplanes in other countries and environments. We flew to Panama, practicing aerial refueling en route, and air defense of the Panama Canal Zone once we arrived flying against A-7s from Puerto Rico. We also fished in the beautiful, dark, clear waters of the Panama Canal catching a lot of peacock bass for a squadron fish fry.

We flew to Cold Lake, Canada, near Edmonton for a joint forces exercise with Canadians and Brits. Our F-4 flyers became quite fond and attached to the British Harrier pilots, playing snooker and hanging out after hours. We were shocked to find they had disappeared overnight during the exercise and learned later they took their airplanes to fight in the war with Argentina over the Falkland Islands. Our Canadian hosts drove us out onto a nearby frozen lake with pickup trucks one weekend! We drilled holes in the ice with a post-hole auger and fished through the ice with success. On one occasion, an airplane on skis circled and landed nearby on the lake. It was a game warden. He walked over and gazed at the sizable number of fish we had thrown in the back of the truck. He noted we were military guys, reminded us there was a limit, but that he didn't have time to count our fish at the moment, turned around, and left. So did we.

There was a trip to Denmark flying our F-16s over the North Atlantic, refueling several times south of Iceland. We flew with all sorts of European fighters in a NATO exercise to targets in Germany and England. On the weekends we rented cars and drove around the enchanting countryside, looking at castles and experiencing the culture and cuisine. On one such jaunt, we ended up in Jelling at the Viking burial mounds of the last great Viking chief, Gorm the Old, and his son, Harold Bluetooth, the first king of Denmark, about 1000 AD. We discovered that Denmark ruled the Viking world. A plaque on Harold's mound read, "I, Harold Bluetooth, have united all of Denmark and made Christians of all the Danes." And, you may have guessed, Bluetooth wireless technology is named for him. Who knew?

But if I can tell only one story in some detail, it would be flying F-4s to Turkey in the 1980s due to its adventure, challenges, and the camaraderie we experienced and enjoyed as military pilots. Several flights of four F-4s took off in the early morning before daylight, heading toward the east coast of the USA where we were to meet up with KC-135 tankers and follow them being refueled multiple times to a rest stop about halfway, the Azores Islands, belonging to Portugal.

All was going well in our flight just south of the Great Lakes when my wingman had a generator warning light come on and a subsequent generator failure, requiring us to leave the formation and divert to a base on the east coast for repairs, and then await another tanker from the 2nd Air Delivery Group to escort us to Turkey. That ended up taking a few days. We made the best of it, borrowed a pickup truck from the motor pool at Pease AFB, New Hampshire, and drove up and down the coast of Maine, sightseeing and eating lobster while we waited. Once a day we checked in with our commander back home, our guys in Turkey, and the tanker guys, awaiting their availability to ferry us eastward.

One evening Majors Bunch and Bielo, went to the bar to drink. Major Hahn was tired and went to his VOQ (Visiting Officer's Quarters) room to retire early. I decided to take an evening two-mile run. I was running around the perimeter of a softball field near a high chainlink fence with barbed wire on top. On the other side were FB-111 tails sticking up out of sand-bagged revetments. There were guards brandishing M-16s. All these were telltale signs these planes were likely sitting on nuclear alert—loaded with actual nuclear weapons, gassed, and ready to go at a moment's notice as and where directed. I was on a softball field, so I thought it safe and prudent to ask one of the guards through the fence, "Is it okay if I run through here?" He immediately pointed his loaded

M-16 at me and barked, "Lay face down on the ground with your legs spread, and don't move."

Well, that settled that. I was in the process of being arrested. Soon four police cars with blue lights flashing came to take me into custody. They were armed too, of course, but seemed more civil. They asked for my ID, but I had none—only my room key tied in the laces of my running shoes. "Who are you, and what are you doing here?" "I'm an F-4 pilot who flew here on one of those two planes you see sitting over there because we had a problem on our way to Turkey." "Do you have anyone who can vouch for you and your identity?" "Yes, Majors Bunch and Bielo, who are in the Officer's Club drinking, but if you tell them it's me, and I've been arrested, they will likely say they don't know me. If that happens, call Major Hahn in the VOQ, he will vouch for me."

They put me in a patrol car and drove me to the security police headquarters, where I was asked to fill out a form stating who I was and what had happened while they confirmed my identity and story. I was finishing my report when I heard the voices of Majors Bunch and Bielo as they came through the door, "Billy Bell, red hair, six foot two, yeah, we know him." "Great!" I thought, "It's already started." They brought tire chains from the pickup and a camera. Major Bielo, my back-seater, piped up, "This is Billy Bell, one of our Christians. Where were we? In the club, drinking where we should be. Where was he? Out causing trouble!"

The officer in charge handed them an official "Release of Prisoner" form filled out and dated. They put the chains around my shoulders, had me hold the form, and took a photo before I knew what was happening. That photo beat me to Turkey and was nailed to the plywood message board in the camp center, where I saw it a week later.

Thankfully, the 2nd Air Delivery Group met with us the next day for a briefing. They had procured a single tanker to escort us to the Azores and Turkey. They briefed us on the forecast weather and alternates we could use in case of problems, and we departed early the next morning. But our problems or challenges continued. One showed itself during the first air-to-air refueling.

Aerial refueling is really quite fun. It's also a bit like practicing bleeding. The tanker maintains 310 knots airspeed (356 MPH), and then the fighters, in turn, fly behind and below the tanker, careful to stay out of wake turbulence from his wings and jet blast from his engines. The fighter creeps up to a close trail formation position and stops in a predefined spot. The boom operator in the tanker lies on his stomach manipulating controls to two little wings on the end of the boom (a flexible hose with a fuel nozzle) and flies it to the fighter's refueling receptacle, which the pilot has opened so the nozzle can be inserted. When a positive hookup is made, the fuel flows to the fighter's fuel bladders in the wings and fuselage. This calls for precise formation flying for five to ten minutes, depending on how much fuel is offloaded.

Fairly soon, over the Atlantic, we made our first hookups. We needed to ensure everything was working correctly and be full of fuel in the event we had to fly to an alternate. Airports are few and far between over the Atlantic. I discovered my external wing tanks would not receive fuel, but I could burn fuel from them. I suggested I refuel more often than the others to keep my tanks full and not use the fuel in my wing tanks except to fly to an alternate. The mission commander agreed this was a reasonable decision and we continued to the Azores, where we went into a crew rest period. I told the maintenance guys what was going on with the airplane, and told them not to touch it or try to repair it. It worked fine. I would fly it to Turkey the next day, and our guys could fix it there.

During the night, some F-4 crew chief thought he could fix it, tried, and broke it, so we were stranded. The other F-4 went on to Turkey the next day, but we could not. That night, at the Officer's Club, I met a C-141 crew who heard about my dilemma. They said, "We can get you to Turkey. You can fly tomorrow with us to Frankfurt, Germany, Rhine-Main AFB, and spend the night as we will. The next day, we will be on crew rest. They will try to put you on a C-5, which will keep breaking all day, and finally cancel the flight. You'll go back to the hotel, and the next day you can fly again with us to Turkey. We only go to Adana, but from there, you can catch a ride on a C-130. They fly routes around Turkey to US and allied bases with supplies. We call those routes the Turkey Trots." I smiled and thought, "You have to be kidding me." But they were serious and believable, so I called back to Fort Smith the following day to talk to Col. Harris about my dilemma and options.

"Dwayne, I think you should just stay there in the Azores until the guys come back through, and you can fly an F-4 home." "With all due respect, Sir, I had to take off from a new and demanding job to do this. If I can't go to Turkey, I just want to come home." "How can you get to Turkey?" I told him the proposal the C-141 crew proffered the night before. "So, you want to hitchhike to Turkey?!" "Yes, Sir." "Do you think you can do it?" "Yes, Sir." "Well then, try it, and keep me posted." That was music to my ears, and I met the guys on the flight line the following day with my duffle bag from the F-4 travel pod. The plan worked out beautifully, just as they described it. There was a beautiful sunrise over the Alps, and I saw Turkey through the eyes of transport pilots who flew there often, with camaraderie, sharing lives and adventures, and helping friends.

Oddly, my squadron mates were mad at me or feigned it when I arrived. "We've been over here roughing it while you guys have been driving up and down the East Coast eating seafood!" Many of them had been sick from the food or water, and I was needed to fly two or three times a day. We did most of our flying in four days so those who wanted could take long weekend trips. We rode the local buses all around Turkey. The people were friendly and liked us. The seven churches of Revelation, or the Apocalypse of Jesus Christ, are in Turkey. So, we set out to visit as many of them as possible. The ruins at Ephesus were particularly impressive—Izmir (Smyrna), too, and Pergamon became my favorite.

Flying Highs And Lows—A Snowy Crash

From my journal January 27, 2023: 2:45 AM, I awakened thirsty and sad, so I decided to get up and sit by the fire with my journal in hand. I then recorded the following:

> "The backcountry flying and flying-freedom part of our lives may be over.
> "I wrecked the airplane yesterday, landing in wet snow—something I didn't see coming and can hardly believe happened.

"Neither Elizabeth nor I was hurt, and that's the main thing. We have much to be thankful for. It's insured, and we'll probably break even on our investment. But something treasured is gone—something that brought joy and beauty to our lives, seeing the earth often from above and visiting inaccessible places. It's about the loss of that ability and freedom. It's about the death of a vision and the change that it brings.

"Something that brought joy, beauty, and adventure to life is gone, with no clear path to getting it back. I know it shouldn't be, but it feels almost like a death in the family—something to be mourned. Our daughter was very sympathetic and kind when we talked to the kids last night. She said, 'It's OK to mourn the loss, Dad—we all feel it.'

"It's not about the metal, although I can't help but feel I've lost an old, trusted friend. It's taken me to Alaska, Idaho, Honduras, and untold places in the Ozarks and around the USA with friends. It's been faithful, trustworthy, strong, and true.

"It's about a way of life that's gone and likely not coming back. That's the way I feel lately about America and the church. Only the grace of God can bring good out of this, and it may take a crash to experience what we've lost. Why wouldn't my heart be sad?

"My hope and trust are in the Lord. That I can say with hope and honesty. Even now, His nearness brings warmth and joy to my soul. I'll put more wood on the fire and read from the Psalms. I'll await more of Your thoughts and any truth You would share. Thank you, Lord.

"The YouVersion verse of the day may apply to the loss and life in the USA in the future: 'No temptation has overtaken you but such as is common to man; and God is faithful, who will not allow you to be tempted beyond what you are able, but with the temptation [to be overly sad, hopeless, have a bad attitude, be negative or worry] will provide the way of escape also, so that you will be able to endure it' (1 Corinthians 10:13).

"It's 3:48 in the morning, and I just sent that verse to a friend with this message: 'I had an airplane crash yesterday. We are OK. Are you OK?' Then I prayed for him. I think self-pity is behind many of our troubles, and I didn't have that revelation until recently.

"As far as the crash goes, I think I heard, 'Don't make more of it than you should or less of it than you should.' Then I heard a twist on an old saying, 'You can take the dog out of the fight, but you can't take the fight out of the dog.'

"Don't be ashamed that you're a man and adventurer who enjoyed exploring every corner of the airplane's capabilities. Yes, what you don't know or see can hurt you. But there is also *The Man in the Arena*.

> *"It is not the critic who counts; not the man who points out how the strong man stumbles, or where the doer of deeds could have done them better. The credit belongs to the man who is actually in the arena, whose face is marred by dust and sweat and blood; who strives valiantly; who errs, who comes short again and again, because there is no effort without error and shortcoming; but who does actually strive to do the deeds; who knows great enthusiasms, the great devotions; who spends himself in a worthy cause; who at the best knows in the end the triumph of high achievement, and who at the worst, if he fails, at least fails*

while daring greatly, so that his place shall never be with those cold and timid souls who neither know victory nor defeat."
— Theodore Roosevelt

"Which is more important? To be totally safe—if there is such a thing? Or to be unafraid of taking a measured risk? What brings you joy and satisfaction? What portals have opened the vastest horizons for you or led out onto the highest peaks and broadest plains?

"I think I hear, 'Don't quit being a man' in all this. Take the hit to your pride; that's a good thing. Honor and tell the truth, then get up and get going again.

"I don't disregard safety. No rational pilot does. But I don't worship it, either. We all learn from our mistakes; what doesn't kill you should make you stronger—unless you cower in fear. Then you're in for a slow death—by degrees.

"I'm not happy this object lesson came my way. I'm very sad about it. It hurts a lot for the reasons I have journaled in the early morning. But there is a flying saying as old as it is true, 'Any landing you walk away from is a good one.' So, I made a good landing on top of the snow-covered mountain yesterday. I got the Jeep from the hangar and drove a short distance to a warm, beautiful cabin to spend the night with my best friend, my lovely wife. Life is good—even with a few bumps, falls, and stings.

"Just before sunset, a friend on the other side of the mountain called to say hello, unaware of the accident. He offered and came with his four-wheel-drive tractor and front-end loader. We flipped the plane back over, then towed it to the hangar for the night. It didn't change things. But it made my heart feel better to see her in a dry hanger on her feet instead of on her back in the snow.

"After writing what I heard and thought in the beautiful stillness of the early morning, I feel better. Circumstances haven't changed. But the Spirit has warmed my heart, let it cry, and pointed me again toward courage, endurance, and soaring in life. Thank You, holy Father. You are Jehovah Shalom, my Lord and my God."

Addendum:

"To those of you I've promised an airplane ride, I'm genuinely sorry. You know I meant it. I've never refused a free flight to anyone who asked. I've given scores of flights and enjoyed each one immensely, watching others experience the wonder and beauty of flight. Don't give up hope. We'll see what happens.

"This speaks to the emotional and spiritual situation surrounding the accident and where our hearts are. In the coming days, for my pilot friends and those interested, I'll speak about what happened and how it happened, as best I understand it, in more detail to add to our corporate body of knowledge and experience. A quick summary might be: 'Wet, dense snow will stop you a lot faster than you can imagine, and if you must try it, have an aft center of gravity—a lot of weight in the rear of the plane.'"

To Fly or Not to Fly Becomes a Question

A friend named Barry wrote a blog about my accident and interviewed me for it:

"There are times in each of our lives when God presents us with an opportunity to consider the current direction of our own life and what is truly important to us. For me, this happened a little more than five years ago, following an auto accident where I was T-boned, causing my vehicle to roll over 1-1/2 times, ending upside down. My head banged against the window, and I was unconscious for quite some time. Two people who attempted to communicate with me during that time thought that I was no longer alive. However, I finally revived, and a trip to the ER showed that I had no broken bones and no internal injuries. The only thing I had was a few cuts and a lot of bruises.

This incident caused me to spend much time contemplating why my life was spared. I bring this up because one of the men in our group had a similar but even more dramatic experience on January 26th. Fortunately, God spared Dwayne Bell and his wife from any serious injuries.

I mentioned to Dwayne some of the questions that I asked myself after my accident:

Does God have something to say through this incident?
Is God taking away something to replace it with something else?
Does God have a new direction and role for my life from this point?
Does God want me to reevaluate my priorities?"

Here are some of the comments Dwayne made regarding this incident and these questions:

"When anything happens like this, you become very spiritually sensitive, especially if you have a high view of God and how intimate and involved He is in our lives. I've experienced more grace or been more aware of it than ever in this chapter of my life. And I have more reason to believe and more conviction that: 'His plans for me are better than mine.' So, I've mainly emphasized hearing Him better by practicing solitude and silence, reading the Word and prayer, and staying in the community of faith.

"This signals something, and in the coming days, I'm sure He'll make it known if I want to learn and will listen. Listening with brothers is a crucial part of that, so feel free to speak into my life in any way you feel led.

"In Psalms 119: 34-37 David says, 'Give me understanding so that I might observe your law, and keep it with all my heart. Guide me in the path of your commands, for I delight to walk in it. Give me a desire for your rules rather than for wealth gained unjustly. Turn my eyes away from what is worthless! Revive me with your word!'

"May our Lord make known to each of us the path He has for our lives, and may we follow Him closely and obediently all the days of our lives.'"

Wager with the Wind—What Just Happened!?
(From my journal and blog)

Well, the time has come. I've dreaded this moment for some reason. It's not hard to tell what happened, as best I understand it. That's straightforward. It's because I don't want to relive the feeling of what we lost.

My wife and I took a 3-mile walk this morning around our frozen neighborhood in the 19°F (which felt like 10°F), frozen, winter wonderland covered with 2-3 inches of sleet from the previous 24 hours. The silence and solitude were beautiful, as were our brief conversations and prayers. I couldn't help but look at the hard, sleet-covered surface of the road and think, "I could have landed the Maule on surfaces like that easily, as I have several times. Hard-packed ice and snow aren't a problem. But soft, wet, dense snow is.

Here's What Happened

Let me tell you what happened, and then we can discuss lessons learned or what I would do differently if I got a do-over, which in this case, I don't.

January 26, 2023, in the early morning we flew from Springdale, Arkansas, (where we live much of the time and keep our airplane hangared) to Hot Springs, to visit my wife's sister, who has some health challenges. It was a pristine, clear, blue-skies day, and we made the smooth flight in a record forty-five minutes due to a substantial tailwind out of the NW. The snow-covered mountains of the Ozarks and Ouachitas were breathtaking, and flying seemed surreal, which it often does.

Vignettes of Flight and Faith

After our visit, we filled up with fuel and headed north to our mountain-top strip, John Harris Field, or AR05, on the aeronautical charts. We flew lower northbound to mitigate the effects of the NW headwind. At 3500', I slowed the plane and configured it to land to the north. The skies were clear blue, and the north/south runway looked beautiful in the snow. I noted it was 12:10 PM. The winds at 2500 feet down to the 1777-foot landing zone elevation were out of the NW and steady at 10-15 MPH. I held my normal 60 MPH final approach speed steady until it was time to flare. Once we glided near the runway surface, past the windsock at the approach end, and between the pine trees that line the runway, there was practically no wind or drift to correct. Before entering the snow, I held it off in the flare to dissipate as much airspeed as possible.

When I let it settle into the snow, it seemed like our deceleration rate was typical for the landing phase. But it then decelerated faster than I could imagine. The tail came up very quickly, and before I knew it, it was straight up in the air, and then the momentum of the plane carried it on over in a slow tumble onto its back.

I would say from the "fairly normal deceleration" assessment until the tail was up vertical only took 2-3 seconds—unbelievably fast, even when I think about it now as I type. I didn't get the time compression that sometimes accompanies these sudden events. It still seems like a blur. I had my hand on the throttle to add power if needed. If they happen, I'd read that soft snow-related incidents happen at very slow speeds at the end of the landing roll when not much air is going over the tail to hold it down. But nothing I read, thought, or heard about prepared me for this rapid deceleration. It was as if at 20 MPH, some gremlins threw chocks in front of the main wheels.

The only thoughts I had, at the time the tail was about 30° up in the air and moving rapidly, were: "I can't make myself push the power up looking down at the ground at this slow speed, with no real threats around" and, when the prop hit the ground one second later, "This is going to be expensive."

The next thing I know, my wife and I are hanging upside down in our seat belts. We release them and crawl out of the airplane onto the bottom of the pilot's side wing. While she released her belt, I turned the master switch off, the ignition switch off, and the fuel selector off. Then we walked away quickly in shock that it had happened. But we were unharmed and grateful.

To Stop or Not to Stop, That is the Question

Hundreds of experiences work for you when flying in the backcountry from thousands of hours flying fighters and airliners. There are a few things that might work against you.

One such thing is the throttle. For many repetitions and landings, when I pulled the throttle to idle, it wasn't going to be pushed back up. In the backcountry with light aircraft, sometimes you need to do so to get air moving over the control surfaces to control the airplane and prevent mishaps. I have made substantial progress in overcoming this big-muscle memory and demonstrated it at times. But this event happened too fast to react like that.

Further, you spend most of your career thinking snow is slick and the primary threat it presents is getting stopped from the momentum of heavy airplanes landing at high speeds. One never suspects it could be an agent for causing you to stop too quickly.

I will continue to mull this over and think of what I might have done differently and hear from fellow pilots their thoughts. After hearing my story, an F-16 buddy called yesterday and said, "Yeah, but this is different. The snow got hold of you and flipped you over." That isn't a bad summary of what happened.

An older pilot friend with lots of experience told me, "CG (center of gravity) might have had some effect on you. When you fly airplanes like the Maule or a Cherokee Six that carry about anything you put in them and feel about the same when landing, one can get a little lax in thinking about it." That's possible for sure. If I had remotely anticipated anything like this, I would have extra bags or weight in the back to slow or help prevent the tail from coming up. And I might have landed with the power pushed up until it stopped in its tracks—very counterintuitive, though. If I had dreamed it could be a problem, I wouldn't have landed. All of this is hindsight and speculation. But you can't help but try to problem-solve or be a better pilot, even when you're still grieving the loss of something. I wish I had had Don Sheldon to ask about the landing before I attempted it.

Paperwork

I would love to have lived in the heyday of the Alaska bush pilots, my father's generation, just after WWII. If you want to get a feel for what that was like, as much as we can, read *Wager With the Wind* by James Greiner. When four friends flew our two Maules to Alaska in 2017, we landed on downtown Talkeetna's legendary Don Sheldon's grass strip. Back then, friends trying to get you back in the air would address a similar accident as soon as possible, with no reports, insurance companies, or massive paperwork to complete. It was more about adventure, courage, camaraderie, and survival together.

I told the gentleman who called from the Denver office of the NTSB, who was very kind and compassionate, "That's quite a form. I'm seventy. I don't know if I have enough time left to fill that out." I'm just kidding, of course (sort of). I'm not cursing the darkness or calling the NTSB, FAA, or insurance companies bad guys. They are a part of why we have the safest general aviation flying in the world, offering as much freedom to US citizens as we have. And the insurance guy was as kind, sympathetic, and helpful as the NTSB representative.

I'm grateful for the aviation experience, and we'll see where this interruption leads us. It has been a magnificent flight in life. Thanks for listening to my story and to you who have reached out, checking on us, wishing us the best, and hoping we fly again. Godspeed to you on your journey, and His *shalom* be yours in abundance.

What You Don't See...

It's what you don't see that usually gets you! That was the case when I landed my airplane on January 26, in six inches of wet snow on our mountaintop strip. We walked away unscathed, but it didn't end well for the airplane.

I researched snow-depth-landing recommendations on the web and in flying publications. My research indicated that being halfway up on the main wheels or six inches should be fine. The snow depth at the time of the accident was well below halfway up the tires and precisely six inches. I've flown eight years and a thousand hours in this airplane, landing on many types of surfaces, and I couldn't imagine this would be a problem. It's what you don't know or see that gets you!

Evidently there are different densities of wet snow. That was never mentioned in my research. This snow uprooted many trees in the area and broke off many branches. Local farmers reported that they had trouble getting around on their tractors and four-wheelers to feed livestock.

As a result of this mishap, I became friends with a Maule pilot in Alaska who was interested in buying and rebuilding the airplane. I'll record parts of our conversation about landing in wet snow to add to our collective knowledge base, mainly for my flying friends and backcountry pilots. Then, I'll add some spiritual lessons it may teach us.

People Who Know

Question: "What's the deepest wet snow you've landed in? And what size were your tires? How would pilots in Alaska typically answer the question: 'How deep is the deepest wet snow in which one should attempt a landing?'"

Answer: "Six inches of wet snow and 31's [big tundra tires] inflated to 5 psi. If you have tires like 850s [which is what I have], then maybe 4 inches of snow with full back yoke and some RPMs to keep the tail down. I powered up to half throttle after I touched down." He added, "Honestly, I wouldn't recommend any snow—too risky."

My immediate thought was, "Where have you been? Or

where were you when I was researching this? This is precisely the kind of information that could have saved the day—and my airplane! Someone knew it, but I didn't, and it didn't turn up in my research.

Well, "Live and learn," as the old saying goes. Or as a quote attributed to Mark Twain goes: "Good judgment is the result of experience and experience the result of bad judgment." I think the first applies, but not totally the second in this instance. It wasn't bad judgment as much as misinformation or insufficient information after a diligent search that got me into trouble. But the results are the same. It's what you don't know or see that gets you!

The Way It's Always Been

Also, latent pride, or a feeling of invincibility, can get you or be a contributing factor. I mentioned I flew this airplane for eight years, for one thousand hours, and in many challenging conditions. I felt like I knew it very well and trusted its capabilities, as well as my own. Two related memories now flood my mind.

In the middle of my fighter career, I was walking back from lunch to the squadron ready-room with a close fighter pilot friend. He told me, "I'm a major with 1000 hours in the F-4. Statistically, that's when most accidents happen. I need to really watch myself." He was one of the best fighter pilots in the squadron, but a month later, he flew into a mountain, killing himself and his back-seater. Even with a heightened awareness that success can be dangerous, bad things still happen.

During our trip to Alaska in 2017, I asked a mechanic in

Anchorage who filed a nick out of my prop blade about the Maule's reputation in Alaska. He said, "It's a fine airplane, but it's misunderstood because it's a little short-coupled."

I wasn't sure what he meant at the time, but I think I do now. He meant the center of gravity is forward enough that it has a propensity to nose over if stopped too fast. This threat is exacerbated by its flying characteristics being very much the same with any load and not betraying this propensity until it happens suddenly from an abrupt stop.

This issue is demonstrated by what my Alaska friend told me next: "The nose of my airplane is lighter, too. I have a carbon fiber cowl (16# lighter), and my engine is 60# lighter than yours, and I only have a two-blade prop, whereas you have a three-blade prop." He was saying, "Your nose is heavier than mine; therefore, it is even more likely to flip over if stopped abruptly." So, one can get too comfortable and not know the whole story quite as well as he thinks he does.

On a different side of the coin, I have a math, engineering, and physics friend named Sam who researched and pondered my landing-in-snow accident. He's a fighter pilot and an American Airlines pilot. He has flown his C-172 in the backcountry, so he was motivated and interested enough to spend considerable hours with algorithms, diagrams, and a calculator. The layman's summary he relayed to me was: "Dense snow compacted quickly in front of your tires until it became like concrete blocks. I don't think it mattered what technique you might have used. It's like sliding into second base—when you hit the base, you will stop." The final truth is probably tucked between those two points of view, with the overall lesson being: "On unknown snowy condition days, leave the airplane in the hangar."

The Maule MX-7 is a wonderful, trustworthy airplane in almost every environment, but a little tricky in this one—deep, wet snow, which is seldom encountered and to be avoided. It's what you don't know or see that gets you!

Spiritual Lessons?

Could this apply to the church in America and the West? Things have gone along pretty well for a long time. Could there be a sudden stop? One that changes everything? It's what you don't know or see that gets you! Read about the church in Nazi Germany in the 1930s. Read Eric Metaxas' book, *Bonhoeffer*, and his short, strong book, *Letter to the American Chruch*.

Do you think this could apply to our country and culture? Things have gone well for a long time, and even with some major upheavals, we've always been able to right the ship. Surely, these chaotic times will be no different, right? It's what you don't know or see that gets you! Read the history of Israel and Judah around 722 BC and 586 BC. Or read the major and minor prophets sent to them in those times—Isaiah through Malachi.

It behooves all of us, especially Christians and the church, to pay attention to what's happening and carefully navigate our times. We need to return to the fear of the Lord and obedience as quickly as possible. We need to pray for His help and His grace to do this: "Noah found grace in the eyes of the LORD" (Genesis 6:8).

We must put away our idols, seeing them for the life and future-robbing activities and objects they are. Spend time with Him in solitude, silence, reading the Bible, and prayer. He will help you see clearly and to know what to do. This is in effect the message of my last book, *Puzzling 2020.*

If we don't, I feel we're in for a sudden stop, an upside-down upset, and a damaged church, country, and culture, with no clear way to regain what we've lost.

> *"Those who cling to worthless idols forfeit
> the grace that could be theirs."*
> (Jonah 2:8, NIV)

> *"Those who forsake the law praise the wicked,
> But those who keep the law strive with them.
> Evil men do not understand justice, But those
> who seek the Lord understand all things."*
> (Proverbs 28:4-5)

OshKosh B'Gosh

After the crash, I took several months off and then purchased another airplane, a Cessna-182 with oversized tires and an STOL wing modification for flying in the backcountry. I intend to fly it as long as I'm healthy and the Spirit leads. Since retiring early from the airline in 2011, I've had the joy and privilege of flying my own plane into Oshkosh five times. Each time was a satisfying adventure, and it was as much about relationships, friendship, and enjoying the world God has graced us with as it was about airplanes and flight.

When I tell my friends I just returned from Oshkosh, most of them ask, "What's that?" A few will blurt out the slogan, "OshKosh B'Gosh," which is the name brand of a famous line of children's clothing, known especially for its marquee striped overalls, based in Oshkosh, Wisconsin, since 1895. But most pilots will recognize it as the host city of the world's largest airshow and aircraft display every summer since its inception in Milwaukee in 1953.

I just returned from the 2024 edition last week. It was great, as usual! The 2024 numbers aren't in yet, but last year's 70th anniversary saw 677,000 aircraft enthusiasts attend the week-long show. They got to look at 10,000+ aircraft, a fleet that makes the Wittman Regional Airport in Oshkosh the world's busiest airport during the event. Pilots conducted an average of 148 takeoffs or landings per hour, with up to three airplanes landing on big colored dots painted on three runways at the same time, then turning off into the grass, taxiing to parking spaces guided by an army of well-orchestrated volunteers. Amazing!

It's like a huge city springing up out of the ground almost overnight at the regional airport of Oshkosh, a city of about 70,000 located on the western shore of Lake Winnebago. People are there to gawk at airplanes and talk about airplanes—the oldest flying to the latest, greatest, newest technology. Military, civilian, home-built, factory-built, aerobatic—you name it, and it's there.

One of the main reasons I went this year, besides my love of aviation and the camaraderie of flying friends from NWA and FSM (Fort Smith, AR), was to share the experience with two young aviators. Shepherd is an engineering college student who won an AOPA scholarship in high school, paying for him to get his pilot's license. When I first met him at church, he was interested in becoming a missionary pilot. I told him that although I was a retired military and airline pilot, I didn't know much about that, but I would help him in any way I could. I immediately thought of Oshkosh and remembered that all the mission aviation organizations are represented there each year.

The second young aviator, Samuel, is the son of one of my best fighter pilot friends. He's seventeen, a senior in high school, has already soloed, and is working toward getting his private pilot's license before beginning an engineering program the year after next in Missouri. He wants to be an airline pilot. Excellent! I thought, and his dad agreed, sponsoring his way up to the event with Shepherd and me.

Shepherd spent several hours talking to mission organizations and pilots serving around the globe in some beautiful, challenging places to fly—providing airlift, humanitarian, medical, language translation, and spiritual ministry to groups in great need of such.

I went around with Shepherd some of the time and learned there was a great deal I didn't know about mission aviation. I knew the two largest organizations, MAF and JAARS, were there. Still, more than a dozen similar support organizations were there, forming a big, beautiful community of aviators and worldwide support personnel—many needing pilots, especially now, as there is a global shortage of pilots. Moody Bible Translators has an aviation school in Spokane, Washington. MMS Aviation in Ohio trains mechanics and pilots for the mission field. So does the Texas Air Corps in Bullard, Texas. Samaritan's Purse was there, and Samaritan Aviation (a separate organization) serving the remote villages of Papua New Guinea. And that's not half of them. Christ's kingdom is more extensive than you think and is growing constantly, just loving and serving people without fanfare.

This was an exciting development to experience and learn about, and hopefully to facilitate young aviators' finding the path forward in their flying dreams and aspirations.

The main takeaway is: "Don't stop adventuring in life, whether it is flight or whatever your interests and passions are—certainly do not stop adventuring spiritually to know God and the power of His resurrection for living and enjoying life, as well as blessing and knowing others."

****

"If I take the wings of the dawn,
If I dwell in the remotest part of the sea,
Even there Your hand will lead me,
And Your right hand will lay hold of me."
(Psalm 139:9-10)

"Seek the Lord while He may be found;
Call upon Him while He is near."
(Isaiah 55:6)

"And if you seek Him, He will let you find Him;
but if you forsake Him, He will forsake you."
(2 Chronicles 15:2b)

"You will seek Me and find Me when you search
for Me with all your heart."
(Jeremiah 29:13)

CHAPTER SIXTEEN
The Unfinished Story

*"Even youths grow tired and weary,
and young men stumble and fall;
but those who hope in the Lord
will renew their strength.
They will soar on wings like eagles;
they will run and not grow weary,
they will walk and not be faint."*
(Isaiah 40:30-31)

The Master of Your Fate

It's 6:45 AM, and I am up to walk and pray with Elizabeth. I am also thinking about finishing this book. Sometimes it's good to write the summary or the last chapter at the beginning or middle of the process. Then you know what you're moving or walking toward.

"I am the master of my fate and the captain of my soul" is now coming to me. I used to dislike this phrase from the poem *Invictus*, and I still do. I consider it the watchword of secular humanism and a statement of ungrateful, prideful rebellion against God. But this morning, I'm coming to see that it's true.

It's true because God gave you choice as a gift when He gave you your soul. He planned it that way so that you would be empowered like that. What a gift! Choose wisely, and prosper. Or choose to go your way, captain your soul, and determine your fate. Either way, God is the life force that gives you being, and He's gracious to you, giving many gifts besides. That's Who He is: "For He Himself is kind to ungrateful and evil men" (Luke 6:35b).

Like the needle on a compass, your soul feels drawn from birth to the magnetic north or its creator, God. There seems to be an awareness, but the soul can't find its way. The programming starts. Parents, nature, friends, experiences good and bad, spiritual impressions, and what your mind, heart, and will decide to do with all of it. That's who you become. That's who you are. Complex but simple. Thousands of inputs, decisions, and memories are pasted into a complex whole that happens quite naturally, like a stream flowing through a river valley. You become who you are. And you are who you become. Your soul decides, and your soul is you.

If this is true, how does one care for one's soul? How do you choose the best inputs and reject the harmful ones? How do you repair damage already done or remove viruses and malware, to use programming language? How do you start the restoration process and see it completed?

These are the elements, the art, and the heart of soul care. We choose daily, but frequently by careless default, what inputs we allow into our souls, and by doing so, we direct our souls on how to treat (accept or reject) future data that comes to our attention. Joshua told the ancient Israelites at a point of success in their journey, and a time of chapter change, that they had to "choose this day whom you will serve" going forward—the gods of the land they had come to possess, or the God who had led them out of slavery and given them success. He meant the day he was addressing them, but it's also a daily decision for your Earth journey. It's wired into us—the Creator's plan. It's a gift. It's a choice. Your choices say a lot about you, to you, and to the Father of us all (Ephesians 3).

Keep out the wrong data, corrupt files, and malware. Choose healthy, robust, and clean data or inputs. Program your soul to do this at all times going forward. As the soul gets healthier, and it will with this tack, it will automatically almost know what to do. The "almost" is important. The inability to make one-time decisions that last forever is built into our soul's firmware.

Remember the stream analogy? We move along in an orderly, if sometimes chaotic, fashion. The soul must constantly choose daily what information it lets in and how to deal with it. It can be programmed to act autonomously like an autopilot, and in fact, it will program itself to do so based on your instructions or decisions, good or bad. It's never a one-time event. It happens in real time, over time, and requires some attention daily.

The better you program your soul, the better it functions only to take in the good, reject the bad, and deal with all the inputs coming its way. And the more rest you, as your soul's master and maintainer, will experience—and peace.

Care for your soul! Practice life-giving habits, rhythms, and disciplines. Spend time alone, in silence, in nature, with your thoughts, at rest, walking, and with God.

The clatter of the world in this information and technological age of speed is deafening. Try to find a restaurant without several TVs on the walls. Get away from it. Shut it out from time to time. You may even need to shut out some good stuff or better programming, like your favorite podcasts. Walk without your earbuds sometimes, alone with your thoughts and the God of the universe. He's near (Acts 17:27).

As you reclaim silence and solitude, this will become the best part of your life. I wish you His presence, joy, and the pleasure of His company.

Grace — Mystical and Magical

Oh, one other thing: In the practice of soul care, I've scratched the surface of something called "grace." It's a truth about God's character and personality one can experience and know. It's a portal into more grace, light, love, and living. Its discovery by degrees comes with some unexpected power to understand and make grace more experiential and widely known—maybe something like uranium reaching a critical mass.

I imagine it to be something like skydiving. It must be exhilarating to jump from relative safety and experience wind, majestic views, and space disappearing as you go. And it's reassuring, peaceful, and comforting to experience opening shock signaling a serene, slow nylon let-down to terra firma. They say it never gets old. You only experience more of what's happening each time as things slow down for you. That sounds a little bit like grace—jumping into the arms of the Father of life and light. He is faithful and true and likes to give good gifts to His children—those who trust Him with their lives and futures and show it through their habits and actions. It's indicated by your willingness to jump from the ordinary and mundane to an adventure with Him—one that starts and continues with listening and obeying His counsel and real-time impressions. That's the course of my life, and I don't want to stop short of what He has for me or might want to do for me or might want me to do for Him. This is adventure at its highest.

In a previous decade of life, I wrote the book *God Came Near*, which talks about faith and experiences with God. I quoted verses from Proverbs like: "A man plans his way, but the Lord directs his steps." And: "How can a man understand his way when the Lord directs his steps." Also, my life verse: "Trust in the Lord with all your heart and don't lean to your own understanding. In all your ways, acknowledge Him, and He will direct your path." I believed then, and I believe now, that the Bible is completely true, that the Holy Spirit gave it for the good of human beings. Though many attacks have been waged against it in every age, the attackers are gone, and the Word of God endures. I particularly like the verse: "Let God be true and every man a liar." I trust the Word, and I trust the God of the Word to do what He says every time and make it so. This has sustained me throughout my life.

A Story Unfinished

But there came a point when I started to realize that God's plans for me were better than my plans for me. I started to articulate that often and much. I believed it and internalized it. Since those days, and in these days, my faith has become sight. I have the real sense that I haven't seen anything yet! Psalm 23 has become a peaceful and joyful reality with its unfinished story.

I'm writing from my beautiful, simple office, tastefully decorated by my son and wife. Their parts are well thought out, meaningful, and attractive. Maybe I've been distracted a little from that with a pile of books here and there, finding no rest on the crowded bookshelf against the south wall. Now, I stretch my legs and peer at one little grouping of frames on one of the walls.

The first is a framed Bachelor of Theology degree from Lyell College, something I never saw coming. But I'll always be grateful for the introduction to the Hebrew language, learning about our amazing church history, reading many classic books and authors unknown to me, and the beauty of being with a small community of seekers and scholars.

Secondly, there is a pen and ink drawing of the stunning church in Rotenburg, Germany, a gift from my sister from the time we went there with our parents as a gift to them. A few years later, I sat in the shadow of that church at a restaurant after a fantastic meal with four couples, our Fort Smith friends, on a tour of Germany, France, Switzerland, Lichtenstein, Italy, and Austria. The friends left for some last-minute shopping or sightseeing before the shops closed while David and I lingered in the magical atmosphere, waiting to pay our bill. Bill, one of the friends, returned hurriedly, "Dwayne, you've got to head down the street. Rick Steves (my travel guidebook hero) is down there getting ready for the night watchman walk!" I went. We all did, and Rick signed my German book as we ambled along in the magic of a German, walled-village evening. And, yes, the church made a lasting impression on me, too, deepening each time I was privileged to visit, walk the nave, sit, and meditate on the architecture and the worship that occurred there over generations and centuries—hearts ablaze for the God of grace.

Thirdly and lastly, in the grouping, there is a framed black and white photo of a single tree in a pasture with a few cows grazing in the background. The plaque below it states: "He will be like a tree planted by the rivers of water, that brings forth its fruit in its season; and whose leaf does not wither" (Psalm 1:3). Grace.

I think to myself, "That's inspiring. I should look around my office more often." It fills my heart with gratitude and worship for the King. I look at the next wall. A group of three black-framed, back-and-white photos taken near the end of my F-16 flying days. The top middle one is an F-16 in flight on the gunnery range. To the right is one of me sitting in the cockpit. To the left is one of me standing at the fighter's nose, in my g-suit, holding my helmet in one hand and my other around the pitot tube. These photos lived under our bed for years until my son discovered them and said they had to go up on the wall. They remind me to be a warrior for truth and for the people I love. Beneath them, tastefully mounted, again by my son, is my pilot training patch that every class creates and wears on their flight suits while in the year-long training. Ours was the original Army Air Corps patch from WWII. Embroidered on the top is "79-06," our class designator. Under the bottom of the circular patch is an added blazon: "In The Tradition." I've often wondered what percentage of young men who aspire to be a military aviator get to attend and finish flight school. And then fly fighters, no less. I'm not sure it can be known. I know it's rare, and I know I'm blessed. Grace.

On the third wall is another trilogy of framed images. The first is a "Recognition of Service" certificate from American Airlines to Captain Dwayne Bell for twenty-five years of service. Next to it is a facsimile of a page from the Gutenberg Bible. Mainz, Germany, was my home away from home during the last years of my airline career, and it was also home to the inventor of the printing press. Johannes Gutenberg was voted the Man of the Millennium (1000 AD - 2000 AD) in all the hubbub leading up to 2000. His printing press made possible the information explosion we are still experiencing. My page, translated from Latin, begins: "In the beginning was the Word, and the Word was with God, and the Word was God" (John 1:1). From visits to his museum and reading about his life, I discovered this quote about his motivation: "Let us break the seal which binds these holy things; let us give wings to truth that it may fly with the Word, no longer prepared at vast expense, but multitudes everlastingly by a machine which never wearies to every soul which enters life." It was always humbling and exciting to walk the streets he walked, enter the church where he worshiped, and enjoy the vibe of life along the Rhine in one of the most important cities in Germany. Grace.

The next picture on that wall, and the largest, is a painting

The Unfinished Story

of "The Prodigal" by Ron DiCianni. The large canvas is a modern spin on the Bible story ending in Luke 15:20: "So he got up and came to his father. But while he was still a long way off, his father saw him and felt compassion for him, and ran and embraced him and kissed him." The quote at the bottom of the painting is: "As a father has compassion on his children, so the Lord has compassion on those who fear him" (Psalm 103:13 NIV). It's a good reminder that all of us know prodigals, and each of us has been a prodigal. Grace is needed and proffered.

On the fourth wall above the bookcase is a large framed photo I took from the Mount of Olives in 2005 while studying in the Holy Land with Lyell College. It shows the Temple Mount in the foreground, with the mosque of Omar atop it and the Church of the Holy Sepulcher in the far distance behind it. This is the holiest site in Christendom—the site of Jesus' crucifixion and nearby resurrection. Grace was demonstrated, and its power was revealed.

To visit Israel once is the dream of a lifetime. I've been blessed to visit six times, and I'd go back a hundred times more if the Lord led or allowed. There is a strong attraction to...His grace.

Today I'm reminded of grace past, present, and future. It can be experienced and expected every day in every age because God is the same yesterday, today, and forever. I just reflected on God's grace in my past. I experience it daily in the present as I read, write, walk, interact with people, and spend some time alone with my thoughts. Present grace.

I just returned from Malaysia and Borneo (Sabah), where I was on a two-week travel and spiritual adventure with seven others in support of a local church in a Muslim country. This is past grace but recent grace.

I just flew my airplane to Oshkosh, the world's largest aircraft exposition and airshow, with a college student who aspires to be a missionary pilot and a high school student working on his pilot's license. There is a lot about this I never saw coming. This is recent grace.

This fall, we took a family cruise from Venice to Athens to celebrate a special birthday and get the family together. We saw the beauty of the Adriatic Sea and learned of its history from Greek and Roman times to the present. It seems God's grace knows no logical limits or bounds. This verse comes to mind: "For of His fullness we have all received, and grace upon grace" (John 1:16). I'm often reminded of the verse that Charles Duke, the youngest astronaut to walk on the moon, wrote in my Bible at a God and Country service in Fort Smith, Arkansas: "Now to Him who is able to do far more abundantly beyond all that we ask or think, according to the power that works within us" (Ephesians 3:20). Grace.

Over and Out

I have a few more flying adventures in mind. I plan to fly with friends and land at Kitty Hawk, North Carolina, where it all began with the Wright brothers in 1903. I'd also like to read *Undaunted Courage*, which is about Lewis and Clark's epic journey in 1803, and then fly their route with friends from Saint Louis to the Pacific Ocean.

I plan to spend time alone with my thoughts and God daily. I will take long walks in nature with only my thoughts and no phone. This has been my practice for some time.

I will read the world's best-selling, most published book daily for its insights about God and wisdom for living on a higher plain. I will continually remove things and devices from my life that distract me, like cell phone notifications and bad habits. I will be a part of the world but not of it. I will come out of the world system and influences to live free.

I will nurture my relationship with the Father, who loves me and desires to spend time with me. How could I refuse? Why would I refuse? It's not necessarily my utmost for His highest; it's just making an effort with the time He's given me to demonstrate that He is important to me. I value His presence and anything He might say. A watchword of soul care is: "Be still, and know that I am God" (Psalm 46:10a). If you're not still, you won't know.

It's T-I-M-E with God. That's the essence of Soul Care. Spend the time, and He will make himself known to you. Therein lies the fullness of life and joy! Godspeed as you journey to know Him—and Shalom.

****

"Beloved, I pray that in all respects you may prosper and be in good health, just as your soul prospers."
(3 John 2)

"Those who cling to worthless idols forfeit the grace that could be theirs."
(Jonah 2:8 NIV)

"As the deer pants for the water brooks, so my soul pants for You, O God."
(Psalm 42:1)

"This is what the Lord says:
'Stand at the crossroads and look;
ask for the ancient paths,
ask where the good way is, and walk in it,
and you will find rest for your souls.'"
(Jeremiah 6:16)

"Draw near to God and He will draw near to you."
(James 4:8a)

Jesus said: "Come to me, all you who are weary and burdened, and I will give you rest. take my yoke upon you and learn from me, for I am gentle and humble in heart, and you will find rest for your souls."
(Matthew 11:28-29)

"He who dwells in the secret place of the Most High Shall abide under the shadow of the Almighty."
(Psalm 91:1 NKJV)

"Now may the God of peace Himself sanctify you entirely; and may your spirit and soul and body be preserved complete, without blame at the coming of our Lord Jesus Christ."
(1 Thessalonians 5:23)

Quotes for Meditation & Quiet Times

"Think before you speak. Read before you think."
— Fran Lebowitz

"I learned this, at least, by my experiment: that if one advances confidently in the direction of his dreams, and endeavors to live the life which he has imagined, he will meet with a success unexpected in common hours."
— Henry David Thoreau

"Rather than love, than money, than fame, give me truth."
— Henry David Thoreau, *Walden*

"How vain it is to sit down to write when you have not stood up to live."

— Henry David Thoreau

"I find it wholesome to be alone the greater part of the time. To be in company, even with the best, is soon wearisome and dissipating. I love to be alone. I never found the companion that was so companionable as solitude."

— Henry David Thoreau, *Walden*

"Books are the treasured wealth of the world and the fit inheritance of generations and nations."

— Henry David Thoreau, *Walden*

"I went to the woods because I wished to live deliberately…"

— Henry David Thoreau

"Read the best books first, or you may not have a chance to read them at all."

— Henry David Thoreau, *A Week on the Concord and Merrimack Rivers*

"However mean your life is, meet it and live it; do not shun it and call it hard names. It is not so bad as you are. It looks poorest when you are richest. The fault-finder will find faults even in paradise. Love your life, poor as it is. You may perhaps have some pleasant, thrilling, glorious hours, even in a poorhouse. The setting sun is reflected from the windows of the almshouse as brightly as from the rich man's abode; the snow melts before its door as early in the spring. I do not see

but a quiet mind may live as contentedly there, and have as cheering thoughts, as in a palace."
— Henry David Thoreau, *Walden*

"No man has authority to restrain the wind with the wind, or authority over the day of death; and there is no discharge in the time of war, and evil will not deliver those who practice it."
— Solomon, Ecclesiastes 8

"If you want to go fast, go alone. If you want to go far, go with someone."
— African Proverb

"The fear of death follows from the fear of life. A man who lives fully is prepared to die at any time."
— Mark Twain

"The greatest glory in living lies not in never falling, but in rising every time we fall."
—Ralph Waldo Emerson

"When I gave my heart to know wisdom and to see the task which has been done on the earth (even though one should never sleep day or night), and I saw every work of God, I concluded that man cannot discover the work which has been done under the sun. Even though man should seek laboriously, he will not discover; and though the wise man should say, "I know," he cannot discover."
—Solomon, Ecclesiastes 8

"The first and most basic thing we can and must do is to keep God before our minds… to direct and redirect our minds constantly to Him. In the early time of our practicing, we may well be challenged by our burdensome habits of dwelling on things less than God. But these are habits – not the law of gravity – and can be broken. A new grace-filled habit [can be developed]… If God is the great longing of our souls, He will become the polestar of our inward beings"

— Dallas Willard

"Churches only have to ask two questions:
What is your plan for making disciples?
How is that plan going?"

— Dallas Willard

"In solitude and silence you're learning to stop doing, stop producing, stop pleasing people, stop entertaining yourself, stop obsessing—stop doing anything except to simply be your naked self before God and be found by him."

— Dallas Willard

"Suppose our failures occur, not in spite of what we are doing, but precisely because of it."

— Dallas Willard

"Great faith, like great strength in general, is revealed by the ease of its workings. Most of what we think we see as the struggle OF faith is really the struggle to act as IF we had faith when in fact we do not."

— Dallas Willard

"What is thinking? It is the activity of searching out what must be true, or cannot be true, in the light of the given facts or assumptions."

— Dallas Willard

"If we allow everything access to our mind, we are simply asking to be kept in a state of mental turmoil or bondage. For nothing enters the mind without having an effect for good or evil."

— Dallas Willard

"Why doesn't God just force us to do the things he knows to be right? It is because that would lose precisely that which he has intended in our creation: freely chosen character."

— Dallas Willard

"The ultimate freedom we have as human beings is the power to select what we will allow or require our minds to dwell upon."

— Dallas Willard

"History has brought us to the point where the Christian message is thought to be essentially concerned only with how to deal with sin: with wrongdoing or wrong-being and its effects. Life, our actual existence, is not included in what is now presented as the heart of the Christian message, or it is included only marginally."

— Dallas Willard

"The meeting of two personalities is like the contact of two chemical substances: if there is any reaction, both are transformed."
— Carl Gustav Jung

"Everything that irritates us about others can lead us to an understanding of ourselves."
— Carl Gustav Jung

"Your visions will become clear only when you can look into your own heart. Who looks outside, dreams; who looks inside, awakes."
— C.G. Jung

"Until you make the unconscious conscious, it will direct your life and you will call it fate."
— C.G. Jung

"I am not what happened to me, I am what I choose to become."
— Carl Gustav Jung

"You are what you do, not what you say you'll do."
— Carl Gustav Jung

"Every form of addiction is bad, no matter whether the narcotic be alcohol, morphine or idealism."
— Carl Gustav Jung

"The privilege of a lifetime is to become who you truly are."
— Carl Gustav Jung

"In all chaos there is a cosmos, in all disorder a secret order."
— Carl Gustav Jung

"Two things are infinite: the universe and human stupidity; and I'm not sure about the universe."
— Albert Einstein

"There are only two ways to live your life. One is as though nothing is a miracle. The other is as though everything is a miracle."
— Albert Einstein

"I am enough of an artist to draw freely upon my imagination. Imagination is more important than knowledge. Knowledge is limited. Imagination encircles the world."
— Albert Einstein

"The most beautiful experience we can have is the mysterious. It is the fundamental emotion that stands at the cradle of true art and true science."
— Albert Einstein

"Once you can accept the universe as matter expanding into nothing that is something, wearing stripes with plaid comes easy."
— Albert Einstein

"Half finished work generally proves to be labor lost."
— Abraham Lincoln

"I go for all sharing the privileges of the government who assist in bearing its burthens."

— Abraham Lincoln

"Folks are usually about as happy as they make their minds up to be."

— Abraham Lincoln

"America will never be destroyed from the outside. If we falter and lose our freedoms, it will be because we destroyed ourselves."

— Abraham Lincoln

"My concern is not whether God is on our side; my greatest concern is to be on God's side, for God is always right."

— Abraham Lincoln

"Those who deny freedom to others, deserve it not for themselves"

— Abraham Lincoln

"I can see how it might be possible for a man to look down upon the earth and be an atheist, but I cannot conceive how a man could look up into the heavens and say there is no God."

— Abraham Lincoln

"I don't like that man. I must get to know him better."

— Abraham Lincoln

"If I were two-faced, would I be wearing this one?"

— Abraham Lincoln

"Give me six hours to chop down a tree and I will spend the first four sharpening the axe."
— Abraham Lincoln

"You cannot help people permanently by doing for them, what they could and should do for themselves."
— Abraham Lincoln

"You can tell the greatness of a man by what makes him angry"
— Abraham Lincoln

"The better part of one's life consists of his friendships."
— Abraham Lincoln

"I don't know who my grandfather was; I am much more concerned to know what his grandson will be."
— Abraham Lincoln

"We should be too big to take offense and too noble to give it."
— Abraham Lincoln

"We the people are the rightful masters of both Congress and the courts, not to overthrow the Constitution but to overthrow the men who pervert the Constitution."
— Abraham Lincoln

"I believe the Bible is the best gift God has ever given to man. All the good from The Savior of the world is communicated to us through this Book."
— Abraham Lincoln

"Writing, the art of communicating thoughts to the mind through the eye, is the great invention of the world...enabling us to converse with the dead, the absent, and the unborn, at all distances of time and space."

— Abraham Lincoln

"Life is hard but so very beautiful"

— Abraham Lincoln

"You cannot lift the wage earner up by pulling the wage payer down."

— Abraham Lincoln

"And in the end, it's not the years in your life that count. It's the life in your years."

— Abraham Lincoln

"The philosophy of the schoolroom in one generation is the philosophy of government in the next."

— Abraham Lincoln

"I know there is a God, and that He hates injustice and slavery. I see the storm coming, and I know that his hand is in it. If He has a place and work for me - and I think He has - I believe I am ready."

— Abraham Lincoln

"The worst of all deceptions is self-deception."

— Plato

"For a man to conquer himself is the first and noblest of all victories."

— Plato

"We are what we repeatedly do. Excellence, then, is not an act, but a habit."

— Aristotle

"You will never do anything in this world without courage. It is the greatest quality of the mind next to honor."

— Aristotle

"An unexamined life is not worth living."

— Socrates

"The high minded man must care more for the truth than what people think."

— Aristotle

"The golden rule of Sabbath is to cease from what is necessary and to embrace what gives life."

— Mark Buchanan

"All the unhappiness of men arises from one single fact, that they cannot stay quietly in their own room."

— Blaise Pascal

"When we are alone and quiet, we fear that something will be whispered into our ear, [so] we hate the silence and drug ourselves with social life."

— Friedrich Nietzsche

"The practices of solitude and silence are radical because they challenge us on every level of our existence. ...All the forces of evil band together to prevent our knowing God in this way, because it brings to an end the dominion of those powers in our lives."

— Ruth Haley Barton

"There are two things the devil cannot stand: music and silence."

— C. S. Lewis

"We will make the whole universe a noise in the end."

— C. S. Lewis, *The Screwtape Letters*

"What if the quiet that we so fear holds the key to our freedom?"

— John Mark Comer

"It is the paradox of history that each generation is converted by the saint who contradicts it most."

— G. K. Chesterton

"We are silent in the early hours of each day, because God is supposed to have the first word, and we are silent before going to sleep, because to God also belongs the last word."

— Dietrich Bonhoeffer

"The yearning to know what cannot be known, to comprehend the incomprehensible, to touch and taste the unapproachable, arises from the image of God in the nature of man. Deep calleth unto deep, and though polluted and land-locked by the mighty disaster theologians call the Fall, the soul senses its origin and longs to return to its source."

— A.W. Tozer

"The man who would truly know God must give time to Him."

— A.W. Tozer

"What we think about when we are free to think about what we will – that is what we are or will soon become."

— A.W. Tozer

"We can never know who or what we are till we know at least something of what God is."

— A.W. Tozer

"The vague and tenuous hope that God is too kind to punish the ungodly has become a deadly opiate for the consciences of millions."

— A.W. Tozer

"We might be wise to follow the insight of the enraptured heart rather than the more cautious reasoning of the theological mind."

— A.W. Tozer, *The Knowledge of the Holy*

"We need never shout across the spaces to an absent God. He is nearer than our own soul, closer than our most secret thoughts."

— A.W. Tozer, *The Pursuit of God*

"Jesus calls us to his rest, and meekness is His method. The meek man cares not at all who is greater than he, for he has long ago decided that the esteem of the world is not worth the effort."

— A.W. Tozer, *The Pursuit of God*

"To have found God and still to pursue Him is the soul's paradox of love."

— A.W. Tozer, *The Pursuit of God*

"If Satan have half, he will have all; if the Lord have but half, he will have none."

— Matthew Henry

"If the Holy Spirit was withdrawn from the church today, 95 percent of what we do would go on and no one would know the difference. If the Holy Spirit had been withdrawn from the New Testament church, 95 percent of what they did would stop, and everybody would know the difference."

— A.W. Tozer

"What comes into our minds when we think about God is the most important thing about us."

— A.W. Tozer

"The gravest question before the Church is always God Himself, and the most portentous fact about any man is not what he at a given time may say or do, but what he in his deep heart conceives God to be like. We tend by a secret law of the soul to move toward our mental image of God. This is true not only of the individual Christian, but of the company of Christians that composes the Church. Always the most revealing thing about the Church is her idea of God, just as her most significant message is what she says about Him or leaves unsaid, for her silence is often more eloquent than her speech."

— A.W. Tozer

"Music is the shorthand of emotion."

— Leo Tolstoy

"Everyone thinks of changing the world, but no one thinks of changing himself."

— Leo Tolstoy

"It is amazing how complete is the delusion that beauty is goodness."

— Leo Tolstoy

"If, then, I were asked for the most important advice I could give, that which I considered to be the most useful to the men of our century, I should simply say: 'In the name of God, stop a moment, cease your work, look around you.'"

— Leo Tolstoy

"A quiet secluded life in the country, with the possibility of being useful to people to whom it is easy to do good, and who are not accustomed to have it done to them; then work which one hopes may be of some use; then rest, nature, books, music, love for one's neighbor — such is my idea of happiness."

— Leo Tolstoy

God Stays Near

"In the name of God, stop a moment, cease your work, look around you."

— Leo Tolstoy

"Freethinkers are those who are willing to use their minds without prejudice and without fearing to understand things that clash with their own customs, privileges, or beliefs. This state of mind is not common, but it is essential for right thinking…."

— Leo Tolstoy

"Wrong does not cease to be wrong because the majority share in it."

— Leo Tolstoy

"The two most powerful warriors are patience and time."

— Leo Tolstoy

"Anything is better than lies and deceit!"

— Leo Tolstoy

"There is no greatness where there is not simplicity, goodness, and truth."

— Leo Tolstoy

"True life is lived when tiny changes occur."

— Leo Tolstoy

"If you look for perfection, you'll never be content."

— Leo Tolstoy

"An arrogant person considers himself perfect. This is the chief harm of arrogance. It interferes with a person's main task in life - becoming a better person."
— Leo Tolstoy

"He who has a why to live can bear almost any how."
— Friedrich Nietzsche

"If we knew what it was we were doing, it would not be called research, would it?"
— Albert Einstein

"Tell me and I forget. Teach me and I remember. Involve me and I learn."
— Benjamin Franklin

"We must learn to live together as brothers or perish together as fools."
— Martin Luther King, Jr.

"Learning never exhausts the mind."
— Leonardo da Vinci

"It's what you learn after you know it all that counts."
— John Wooden

"Live as if you were to die tomorrow. Learn as if you were to live forever."
— Mahatma Gandhi

"He who learns but does not think, is lost! He who thinks but does not learn is in great danger."

—Confucius

"I am still learning"

— Michelangelo

"If a thing is free to be good it is also free to be bad. And free will is what has made evil possible. Why, then, did God give them free will? Because free will, though it makes evil possible, is also the only thing that makes possible any love or goodness or joy worth having."

— C.S. Lewis

"If in His absolute freedom God has willed to give man limited freedom, who is there to stay His hand or say, 'What doest thou?' Man's will is free because God is sovereign. A God less sovereign could not bestow moral freedom upon His creatures. He would be afraid to do so."

— A.W. Tozer

"Where there is no freedom of choice there can be neither sin nor righteousness, because it is the nature of both that they be voluntary."

— A.W. Tozer

"The human spirit is the lamp of the Lord that sheds light on one's inmost being."

— Proverbs 20:27 NIV

"Whenever you find yourself on the side of the majority, it is time to pause and reflect."

— Mark Twain

"Truth is so obscure in these times, and falsehood so established, that, unless we love the truth, we cannot know it"

— Blaise Pascal

"Bless you prison, bless you for being in my life. For there, lying upon the rotting prison straw, I came to realize that the object of life is not prosperity as we are made to believe, but the maturity of the human soul."

— Aleksandr I. Solzhenitsyn

"The heart has its reasons which reason knows not."

— Blaise Pascal

"You are never too old to set a new goal or to dream a new dream."

— C.S. Lewis

"Not everything that can be counted counts and not everything that counts can be counted."

— Albert Einstein

"Finally, brothers and sisters, whatever is true, whatever is noble, whatever is right, whatever is pure, whatever is lovely, whatever is admirable—if anything is excellent or praiseworthy—think about such things."

— Philippians 4:8 NIV

"To him who is able to keep you from stumbling and to present you before his glorious presence without fault and with great joy—to the only God our Savior be glory, majesty, power and authority, through Jesus Christ our Lord, before all ages, now and forevermore! Amen."

— Jude 24-25 NIV

HISTORY AND MEDITATION—TIMELINE

Having a timeline to place events is helpful, intriguing, and insightful when reading any book, particularly the Bible. So, I have included a simple timeline to help readers remember facts about human history and connect them with significant historical events.

I was a history minor in college and loved it more than my major, mathematics. However, I found history to be a haphazard collection of facts, dates, and details about leaders or influential people—somewhat confusing. Years later, when I started looking at history through the lens of the Bible, it made sense and appeared as a unified whole.

The Bible tells us in many places that God is the same yesterday, today, and forever. Mediating on the stories and history from the Bible demonstrates that fact, increases our faith, and aids the reader in knowing God better—people, too, as they relate to God, His Word, and other people. It becomes satisfying and insightful to see that, as French writer Jean-Baptiste Alphonse Karr says, "The more things change, the more they stay the same." Or, as Solomon wrote, "That which has been is that which will be, and that which has been done is that which will be done. So there is nothing new under the sun" (Ecclesiastes 1:9).

On a recent visit to Greece, I discovered that the Parthenon on the Acropolis in Athens was completed in 438 BC. Thus, it can be placed on the timeline around the same time as the Second Temple, which was completed in Jerusalem in 515 BC, about one thousand years after Moses led the Israelites out of slavery in Egypt.

A timeline also helps us understand the present and future. Winston Churchill said, "The farther back you can look, the farther forward you are likely to see." The Judaeo-Christian faith is the only religion with many prophecies that have come true, with more still to come. Daniel comes to mind, with his dreams and visions foretelling the four kingdoms that would rule over the whole earth in their time: Babylon, Persia, Greece, and Rome.

Recently, as I was reading the book of Esther anew, it occurred to me that three ancient civilizations had Israeli prime ministers—Egypt (Joseph), Babylon (Daniel), and Persia (Daniel and Mordecai). Seeing the hand of God in human history for order and His purposes is fascinating and encouraging. Meditating on this facet of history will add to your wisdom, peace, faith, and the satisfaction of understanding the natural order of things and the God Who controls the destiny of nations and mankind.

> *"Remember the former things, those of long ago; I am God, and there is no other; I am God, and there is none like me. I make known the end from the beginning, from ancient times, what is still to come. I say, 'My purpose will stand, and I will do all that I please.'"*
> (Isaiah 46:9-10 NIV)

Simple Approximate Timeline
(For Your Use and Reference)

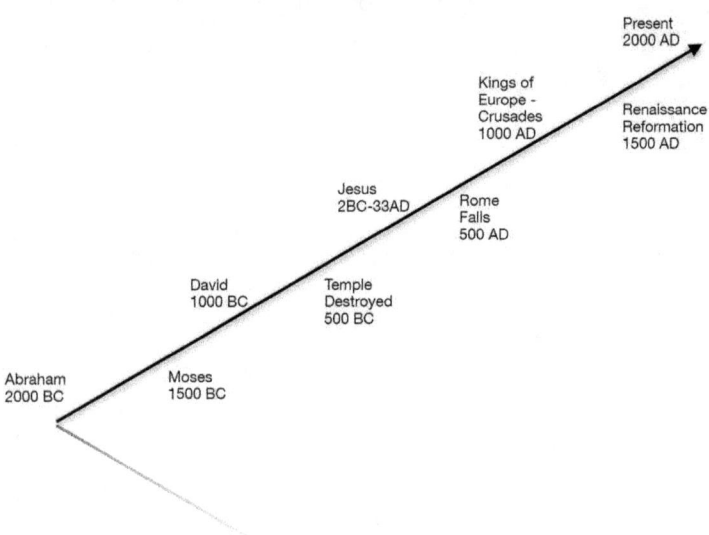